# Bridge of Sorrow,
# Bridge of Hope

# Bridge of Sorrow, Bridge of Hope

## Riva Chirurg

*Edited by Rebecca Camhi Fromer*

*Translated from the Hebrew by*
*Arlene and Jerry Aviram*

JUDAH L. MAGNES MUSEUM
BERKELEY, CALIFORNIA

# Acknowledgments

The publication of the English version of this significant work is the result of efforts of many dedicated people. We are especially grateful to Lee Katz for initiating the project and for her ongoing interest and aid in seeing the project to completion. We thank the Endowment Fund of the Jewish Community Federation for its encouragement and support and express our appreciation to the following donor-advised funds of the Jewish Community Federation Endowment Fund: The Dessauer Trust; The Barry Leonard Katz Memorial Fund; The Hyman and Myrna Mitchner Philanthropic Fund; The Jackie and Uri Berman Philanthropic Fund; The Harvey and Phyllis Koch Philanthropic Fund.

In addition we are thankful to the following individuals for enabling us to publish this work: Lee and Martin Katz; Beth and Roger Helms; Hallie and Richard Normington; Anne Kane; Janet and David Katz; Ellen Sheera and Stan Brosomle; Laurie Ruth and Ahmed Yehia; Paula Citron; Alex Citron; Shirley Citron; Dan, Jill, Harrison, and Austin Cytryn; Eva Markowitz.

We also thank Terry and Jacob Eiduson; Pearl and Morton Gold; Careen and Sam Gourdji; Jean Greenberg; Fran Markus; Grace and Norman Mazin; Florence and Murray Nesenblatt; Lydia and Neil Nesenblatt; Steven Nesenblatt; Jody and David Schwartz; Shirley and Samuel Sheriff; Alison and Todd Sheriff; Lee and Sidney Troster; Barbara, Elliot, and Dina Weiss; Phyllis Abrams and Julius S. Smith.

We are indebted to Rebecca Fromer for her devotion in editing this work, and to Paula Friedman, Leah Heinstein, Nelda Cassuto, Norine Brogan, and Sarah Levin for their assistance in the preparation of this volume.

Most of all, it is the courage and perseverance of Riva Chirurg, the author, that has inspired and guided the English version of this book first published in 1988 in Hebrew in Israel.

—Judah L. Magnes Museum

Published by: The Judah L. Magnes Museum
2911 Russell Street, Berkeley, California 94705

Edited by Rebecca Camhi Fromer.
Cover and text designed by Sarah Levin.
Frontispiece photo of kibbutzniks from the Z.O.A. in the Lodz ghetto.
 Mendel Grossman, photographer.

ISBN: 0-943376-61-0
Library of Congress Catalog Card Number: 93-080667

Printed in the United States of America
10  9  8  7  6  5  4  3  2  1

# Table of Contents

# Preface

I have tried to write a preface many times, but so far I have not been able to express what I want to say. Perhaps now, at last, I will be able to say that which is within me....

I ask myself why I feel that it is so important for me to say something about what I have undergone, for I am not the only one carrying a burden, but it is—and I shall soon explain why. We, who survived the Holocaust, have needed the perspective of time in order to form the events of the past into a shape that can be transmitted to the world around us, a world that was unable to absorb what happened. For us, who could not give utterance to those events any earlier, the time to say what we have to say, to explain what was, what is, and what may be again, has now come.

I do not believe that what happened was a Holocaust that befell the Jews alone. It was a Holocaust that affected the entire world, and it was a tragedy for all humanity. We Jews were slaughtered and murdered, and those in the free world were the murderers and slaughterers—if not actively, then passively—through silence in the face of what they knew to be happening. Not to interfere was collaboration. I do not mean to accuse. No good can come of it. I state a fact that must be dealt with. It happened.

How could what happened *be?* What is a human being, and what can we expect of him? What happened in Europe during the twentieth century is an impossible to ignore indictment of mankind, and I ask myself time and again: "Are we so ignorant of ourselves?"

It is up to those of us who have survived our ordeals to transmit as reliable an account as is possible, so that historians, philosophers, psychologists, and the wise of the world may think about and study the situation of naked humanity when it is stripped down to the infinitesimal segments of the soul. Perhaps if we discover something new about man's behavior, we also will discover how to take suitable measures to prevent the horrors we knew from ever occurring again. I am personally ashamed to be a link in the family of man, but if man is base by nature, perhaps one should not be ashamed. Perhaps one should find the right way to approach him.

What has happened to me has happened. I know, I am convinced, that whoever has not felt the horrors of the Holocaust piercing his own flesh or cannot empathize with those of us who did, not only cannot sense it, but also will find it difficult if not impossible to understand anything of importance as to its dimensions.

In the past what prevented me from telling my story was the fear that I would not be believed—that people untouched by the actual events would say: "It is imagined," or "It is exaggerated." "How is it possible?" I would like to prod the thoughts of those who were not there so that they can identify with those who were brushed by the kiss of death and did not die....Perhaps we removed ourselves a distance of millions of light years from those around us, and it is not their fault that they cannot feel or understand; perhaps, too, it is not our fault that we cannot convey the entirety of what happened. There is no precedent for the events, and there is no terminology through which they may be described. Indeed, there is no proof against many of the guilty—for innumerable witnesses have died. Those who still live, live with death. There is little initiative, because there is little hope of relief and "no way out." There is no cure, because no diagnosis has been made.

Why should the individual who experienced the Holocaust through the pores of his skin fathom the inconceivable more than others? A geological fault lies with the soul of man whose causes and origins must still be bared. The causes need to be found; the dimensions of the disaster need to be measured and understood.

I cannot forget that countless friends as well as the closest members of my family perished along with millions of other European Jews, and it seems to me that perhaps not a little of my strength derives from the desire to both make our story known and to preserve the memory of those who died.

I would like to thank Tehiya Mosel, the mother of my daughter-in-law, Segal. From the time of our first meeting Tehiya became a true friend with whom I shared a common language. Because she asked questions of me, and because she genuinely wanted to know about the fate of the Jews of Europe with whom she identified, she helped me enormously.

I would like to thank Mr. Perlman, the teacher of literature who encouraged me to write my account, and Bosmat Hefetz, who typed the text, delved into its contents, and added to the encouragement I so needed. In addition, I am grateful to Dr. Shmuel Krakowski, Director of Archives at Yad Vashem, for reading the manuscript and providing relevant data, and to both Arye Ben-Menachem and Shoshana Silber-Grossman for permission to use many of the photographs that appear on these pages.

*Riva Chirurg*
*Tel Aviv*

# Ruminations: Summer, 1939

I remember the hot days of August. I remember Fridays and the smell of cooked fish entering my nostrils as mother toiled at the kitchen stove from the early hours of morning; for the kitchen was actually a part of the room where we, the older girls—Gutka, Zosia, and I—lived. I also remember that the door leading from our room to the kitchen area was opposite the window through which we could peek into a spacious yard and at passersby. The yard, which was surrounded by tall buildings, appeared magnificent to me.

Across from the window, on the second floor, lived the Blechsteins: Mrs. Blechstein, a pretty woman who always dressed elegantly; her husband, a handsome, impressive man; and their eleven-year-old son. They had a radio—something special not everyone could afford to buy. I admired them, and I envied their spacious apartment with its modern furniture and fine china stacked behind glassed-in cupboards. Lace curtains fluttered in summer breezes, parquet floors gleamed with the reflection of crystal chandeliers, and I loved to visit. Above all, I was well-received and, because of their hospitality, I went to the Blechsteins every day so that I could hear the news. Tension mounted day by day, hour by hour. I was nineteen and I was active in *Tehiya*, a movement which had a Zionist orientation and had been founded by Yitzhak Greenbaum and Moshe Sneh.

During 1937 and 1938, I went through a difficult period. My beliefs were changing; I felt detached and out of place as my life path darkened. The uncompromising religious education I had received had brought me to an impasse. I felt I had to choose between religion or Communism, but after prolonged deliberation I understood what I wanted to do. I joined the radical Zionist movement, where I met new friends. Among them was Yitzhak Braverman, a graduate of the Lodz Hebrew Gymnasium, whom I called Izio. We read books together, and I remember that Romain Rolland's *1914* was among them. At this time, the factories were closed. We did not work, and each day Izio and I went to Stashitza Park, where we talked and sang and read.

The house in which my family lived stood near the Lodz Central Post Office, at the corner of Przejazd-Kilinskiego. Opposite the gate to the house was the city coal market, at the center of which was a clock. Now, this clock was important to me, because it was the Polish custom to lock the gates to the houses at eleven o'clock at night. A latecomer required special service, and therefore was obligated to pay the gatekeeper for his trouble in reopening the gate. Needless to say Izio and I were careful not to be late, not only because my parents waited for the return of their daughters and because it was not considered proper to return after that hour, but also because I did not have the money. We walked back and forth along the section between the corner of Przejazd-Kilinskiego and the clock. Five minutes to the hour, Izio generally cried: "How early!" The time had come to listen for the footsteps of the gatekeeper. I ran into the yard, and we parted quickly.

Ours was a large family that included my mother and father, a brother, and six sisters. I list them briefly, by way of introduction: my father, Reb Moshe-Eliyahu, a teacher by profession and a scholar; my mother, Feigele, a capable woman who cared for the children and helped with the family income; my brother, Baruch-Leib, who died when he was seventeen, and my sisters…

My eldest sister, Gutka, had large black, kind eyes set in a round face; she was a classic beauty whose curly black hair cascaded to her shoulders, a person who worked hard to help our parents from the time she was very young.

My sister Zosia, the second daughter, was twenty-one when the war broke out; she was a girl with sensuous lips, a delicate face, and straight hair. A clever person, a smart person. Someone who was both orderly and tastefully dressed; someone who worked from an early age to help the family. A girl who would not give up her studies, and made every sacrifice to get an education by working day and night. A modern-minded person who believed it was possible to turn the world around.

I was the third daughter. My sister Esther, whom we called Esta, came after me. She was with us in the ghetto, and with me in the concentration and labor camps. She was always the best student, always at the center of a circle of her friends, and always modest, graceful, and sweet. She believed in man and she believed in society, and from early youth until her brief life came to end in Stutthof, she was a pillar of strength to the family and others in need. On the road from Gerdauen to Stutthof, her impulse had been to break ranks and flee, but she did not do so. She did not have the heart to leave the girls, and so she went to her death with everyone else.

My sister Yehudit was fourteen when the war broke out. She was blonde and green-eyed and thinner than the rest of us. Humorous, full of life and fluttering like a bird, she was nevertheless an excellent student. Recommended to drama school, she passed the entrance examinations with flying colors and financed her studies by giving private lessons. She was a good daughter, a good friend, and a beloved sister.

Little Hanka was the youngest and the smartest; an unusual beauty, loved by everyone. Her large blue eyes were framed by black lashes and brows, and her blonde hair defined a high forehead and round face. At twelve she read voraciously, behaved discreetly, and told no one at home of her membership in the Zionist movement. Mature beyond her age and already writing poetry, she seemed most like my eldest sister, Gutka, and walked with small, measured steps, her body erect, and a smile upon her lips.... Yes, this is how I remember Hanka as she left with Yuditka and my parents for

Kielce...I remember my sisters so well, in fact, that it seems to me they are an inseparable part of me; I live with them even as I live with sorrow, pain, and longing.

♦ ♦ ♦

When I last saw my mother her tormented face was furrowed with care, but even then it did not mar her beauty. Her eyes shone as if an eternal tear had been embedded in them, and it seemed to me that if she could, she would have swallowed those tears along with all sorrow and suffering. The struggle to survive and the death of my brother, Baruch-Leib, had taken their toll.

Baruch-Leib died of typhoid in 1929. The pride we took in him seemed more than justified; he was known as "the crown of the family." He had graduated from the *Mesivta yeshiva* in Warsaw, and was ordained a rabbi at fifteen. In addition to the study of *Torah,* he mastered secular subjects, completing the requirements for both with distinction. When he returned home from Warsaw, he was received like a prince from wonderland. Soon afterward he learned how to weave, and did so well that he became the economic pillar of the household.

One morning after Baruch had fallen ill, my father awakened with a start and ran to the synagogue to pray for him. At the root of my father's anxiety was a dream he had had that very night. As Baruch's fever rose, my father decided to sleep with his son in order to protect him. This time he dreamed that a large black dog came between him and Baruch, and that it touched Baruch. When he related his dream to my mother she refused to understand its meaning, but she was gripped with fear.

The story of my father's strange dream spread among us, and I remember that I experienced it as if it had happened to me. I was obsessed by the black dog. I thought of it by day, and imagined that it touched me at night.

For four weeks Baruch-Leib burned with fever. The disease devoured him, and he died on the 16th of Elul, a Sabbath, at eight in the morning. At the time, my father had gone out to get some medicine, and my mother was resting after having stayed up with him all night. When my father returned, our faces told him that Baruch was dead.

"Heaven and earth are witnesses," he said. "I did everything in my power to save my son...."

On the Sabbath eve before Baruch's death, the large yard of our house, where both Jews and Gentiles lived, filled with *yeshiva* boys in their black visor caps, Sabbath clothes of Atlas-Jupitzes, white socks, and black shoes. They stood vigil that entire night and sang psalms. The Gentile neighbors prayed for Baruch-Leib, too.

A Jewish woman whom we called *die matzeive kritzerin,* or the "carver of tombstones," was particularly depressed. Her two sons had assimilated, and that evening she prayed: "Lord of the Universe, I give you my sons in exchange for Baruch-Leib...," but my mother scolded her: "Do not clear a path for Satan."

It was a long night, as I remember. We girls had been sent off to Grandma Sarele, my mother's mother, who rebelled bitterly. "I do not agree with you, God in Heaven!" she cried. "Baruch-Leib is only seventeen; he has not lived, but I have. Take my soul." "Do not speak like this," said my father, and then he gathered the family around the set table. With a trembling hand he filled a glass of wine for the *Kiddush;* he raised it; and he allowed drop after drop to fall upon the plate. *"Vayichal Elohim,"* broke from his throat, but the words hung in air, empty and unanswered, as if the silence at the table had swallowed them. I prayed as did everyone, for we had been told not to stop so that no space and no crack would remain uncovered. We did not want the Angel of Death to take charge of Baruch-Leib's life.

♦ ♦ ♦

On Friday morning, September 1, 1939, at five minutes past nine, I brought my mother the news that the war had broken out. From a certain point of view, a weight had been lifted from my shoulders—for although I was a Zionist, I was also a Polish patriot. I expected the Polish people to repay the Germans for Hitler's provocations, and I believed Smigly-Rydz, the chief of the Polish General Staff, when he said: "We will not give an inch." Mother straightened her back, put down the knife with which she was preparing the Sabbath meal, and wept. For the third time in my life I saw my mother cry.

My mother had a thousand reasons to weep and she must have cried many times, but I never saw it. I remember her working, laundering, and cleaning; I remember her sewing and altering our clothing. I remember so clearly that on the long nights before a holiday she took down the curtains, and that by the next morning I would see them again, newly-hung, clean, and pressed....

On holiday and Sabbath eves, when my mother finished her work, she lit the candles, took a chair into the yard, set it in front of the house, and sat down. She was like a magnet then, for almost everyone came, brought a chair, and sat nearby. *"Gut Shabbes, Gut Shabbes,"* they said, and in this manner, they blessed one another.

Chayele the seamstress was among those who came, and though she did not wear a wig to signify her piety, my mother thought she was nice in spite of it. Chayele was loved by everyone.

Chayele's husband was Haim-Yosef the tailor, who sat on the porch of his house all week long and made suits until late at night. When it got dark, he lit a kerosene lamp. The light was weak, but Haim-Yosef went on working. Flies and moths flew about; they hummed to the clicking of the sewing machine and the whispering of coals in the iron. He sang as he pulled out the basting, or as he placed the nearly finished garment on the mannequin. Sometimes pulling to the right and sometimes pulling to the left, he coaxed the garment into the desired shape. Only then would he remove it, place it on the ironing board with a moistened cloth over it, give the iron a shake to spark the coals, and begin to iron, remoisten, and repeat the process until the job was done. The steam rose to obscure Haim-Yosef's face, but he always sang.

When Haim-Yosef sat on the drainpipe in the yard, it signalled one of the neighbors, a man named Yosef, the father of five children, to join him. After him came the landlord, a butcher, and after him the landlord's son-in-law and his wife, the fat Rachel, and her little sister. They sat on the stones that lay all about; they told jokes, and from time to time we heard a burst of laughter reverberate into the deepening night.

# The Miracle in the Yard

Our house had a very large yard which we could enter from either the front or from an entrance on a parallel street. The Jews lived close to the front entrance; a Gentile neighbor and the gatekeeper, who allotted himself a small plot of land where he grew vegetables and flowers, lived next to the second entrance. The entire yard seemed like an expanse of glorious grass to me. I lay on the grass, I crawled on it, and I rolled about. Its color and smell intoxicated me and transported me to imaginary worlds. I dreamed my first day-dreams there, and I hoped my father's stories would come true.... It was there that I asked for the Messiah to come speedily, and there that I saw Joseph, the *Tzaddik,* being sold or at the height of his powers in Egypt. It was there that I saw the "Other" when he got down from his mule and walked to his former teacher. I sculpted the figure of Jesus, the Christian, there, and I explained to the Gentile neighbor's son, Mietek: "See, even according to the Christian version, Jesus was a man, and not just any man, but a Jew!"

Once, at twilight, I sat on a stone beneath the window of our room. I sat and waited. The sky turned red, and suddenly a small cloud appeared. Very slowly it swelled and hung over my head. The cloud had become massive. Lightning cut through the blackness and thunder rumbled. I heard the sound of a *shofar.* The thunder subsided, the *shofar* was silent, and the fear of the black cloud passed. Silence descended from heaven, and not a leaf moved. The yellow flowers amid the grass lost their color and the lawn was no longer green. With nothing around me moving, I now was gripped by the fear of a profound silence. The massive cloud opened, and I saw a figure rise. Step after step it approached me until I could see its face. It was that of a man with a long beard; long, thick, silvery hair; and thick gray brows over heavy-lidded eyes—a man with a radiant face bright as the sun, whose huge size was concealed by a shimmering white cloak. A man who carried a *Torah* scroll in his upraised hands, and was completely surrounded by a cloud. I lifted my head and leaned against the brick wall so that I would not fall. I blinked again and again. It was dark, and space emptied. He, the Messiah, had disappeared and was no more. A chill wind wrapped around me. I shivered and neither saw nor felt a thing, and then I had the sensation that my head was being stroked. Mother's gentle hand had awakened me. I fell into her arms and heard her heartbeat; I felt her warmth. She put me to bed—but I could not sleep at all that night because I expected to see again that which I had seen. How futile my wish was, however. The Messiah was gone, and He did not return.

# From Kielce to Lodz

There was a trend in the Poland of those days to promote integration between Jewish and Christian youth. I was in grade school at the time and attended a Polish government school. Some classes were composed entirely of Jewish girls, but others were "mixed," with both Jewish and Christian girls attending. I was in such a mixed class. We were three Jewish girls in a class of about thirty-five.

Once, at the end of the school year, a performance was planned with a choir, a dance group and gymnastics, a play and other events. I was chosen to be in the choir and, like all the other students, I was expected to attend rehearsals for the gymnastics part of the program. I thus had to be present at rehearsals both for gymnastics and for the choir. Classes were held on Saturdays, from which I was released, but all the rehearsals were compulsory.

Saturday morning, in accordance with custom, my father went to the synagogue. Without saying a word to my mother I went to an obligatory rehearsal, which I remember was with piano accompaniment. Immediately afterward I returned home and entered the room where my father sat, an open book of *Gemara* before him. His eyes seemed pained and sorrowful to me, and their normal luster was gone. He looked and looked at me, and then he asked: "Where were you?" "At school," I answered. "What did you do?" "Nothing! I did like this and this." I showed him the movements I had been taught in gymnastics. "Didn't you know that you shouldn't go?" "No, I didn't." Without another word, he lowered his eyes toward the *Gemara*. I stood; I waited; and nothing happened. I left dejected and ashamed, and felt my father's eyes on me. When I looked at him through the window, however, he still was bent over the *Gemara*. His face was pale as the gleaming black pupils of his eyes flitted across the page like ripe black cherries.

My father was a man who cared, and people liked him. On Sabbath eve, the Sabbath, and holidays he was the last one to leave the synagogue. He was concerned lest a single Jew be left without a place to stay or a meal to eat. If anyone had been overlooked and had not been invited, he brought him home. Sometimes two guests arrived; sometimes three; sometimes even more. Among these men in rags I searched in vain for the prophet Elijah, the reincarnation of my brother, or the Messiah.

One Sabbath my father came home from the synagogue at noon, and with him were three Jews dressed in rags. Mother helplessly asked him: "Tell me, Moshele, was there no one else in the synagogue?" "Believe me, Feigele," replied my father, "if the Communists believed in God, I would become one. All the fat bellies went home, not caring that three Jews would not eat on *Shabbat*. Tell me Feigele, what would you have done?"

Once something unusual happened, and my father reacted in an equally unusual way. Since all the neighbors' children played in the yard, it was natural that they sometimes fought and sometimes came to blows. This one time, my eldest sister had a fight with Yosef's daughter. It was my mother's practice to say: "I do not interfere in the quarrels among children. They will fight and cry one time, and play and laugh another," and thus Gutka knew she could not come home to complain. When she left the yard, she simply returned home and sulked. Mother was occupied, everyone else was busy, and father was bent over a page of the *Gemara*. It was summer, and the door was wide open. Suddenly Yosef entered, approached my father, and slapped him on the cheek. Before we had a chance to absorb what had happened, he turned about and left. Father paled and did not stir. The children in the yard, who had seen Yosef come into the house, pressed their noses against the windowpane in father's room; they had seen everything. Wasting no time after Yosef left, they peeled themselves away from the window-pane and rushed to spread the news.

Not knowing why this happened, a tumult arose in Reb Moshe-Eliyahu's house—a noisy, explosive neighbors' meeting. Everyone had a suggestion to make, and each was different. Almost everyone urged my father to lodge a complaint against Yosef at court, but father was restrained. The marks of Yosef's fingertips still could be seen on his cheek and yet he was busy, calming down the angry neighbors who acted as if they were the injured party. "I will not go to court!" my father cried. "I will not lodge a complaint! The moment I file suit against Yosef he becomes my equal, but I do not wish to relate to him at all. His act is his punishment, and I am certain he is already sorry for what he did."

My father was a very knowledgeable teacher, who taught at the *yeshiva*. The students he tutored at the synagogue in the mornings received their lessons free of charge, but he educated many kinds of students. He was both a scholar and a *Hasid,* a "believer," but he suffered shame on account of his economic situation. Our lives improved briefly when we girls were grown enough to work, but the outbreak of war disrupted all possibilities of stability. When my mother's parents became impoverished and decided to move from Kielce to Lodz, my parents followed them. My grandfather built a small factory for finishing knit socks and installed modern equip-ment in it, more or less successfully. Since we lived near one an-other, my grandfather and father met in the *shtibel,* as before. Soon, their reputation spread. They clarified points of law, made many friends, and this was our life until the fateful day when everything changed irrevocably.

After the German invasion of Poland, the government did not have time to call up its soldiers and an atmosphere of indignation prevailed throughout the city. The young, who were not mobilized, were forced to remain idle. On the second day of the war, German artillery could be heard in Lodz. We had no shelters; none at all.

We and our neighbors simply sat at the gate of the building, surrounded by thick walls. It was an opportunity to know one another, and under these circumstances, we met Mirka and Ruth Perla, with whom we continued to be close during the entire time that we were in the Lodz ghetto.

# Fleeing the Germans

The thunder of artillery shattered the air. Shells landed somewhere farther away, and the entrance to the building became a shelter. We learned how to put on our gas masks; we developed study circles in the building, and met at Mrs. Goldner's. The neighbors got to know one another, and we became friends.

Mirka and Ruth Perla, who had come to Lodz from Zdunska Wola, found work and lived on the third floor with Aunt Perla, a teacher by profession. This Aunt Perla frightened me, even though I was already nineteen. Half of her face was marred by an ugly scar; while one eye stared icily, the other twinkled. The ugliness alone repelled me, for there was not a shred of evil in her.

It was difficult for me to believe that the Germans were so near, but the booming of the artillery reinforced the rumors we had heard that they were indeed approaching. Within a few days, on September 6, 1939, the Germans entered the city. The Germans were everywhere!

The Jews of Lodz were helpless before the military might of the Germans. They were unprepared both mentally and physically— and yet they were the principal "enemy" of this military monster. In the midst of chaos, we were gripped by fear. What were we to do? Run? And where to? How does one escape fear? Fright wells up from within, and no logic can provide the answer to the unknown. We had no time to think as we were bombarded by all sorts of rumors. Someone said: "We must escape to Warsaw!" We assumed that our capital would not surrender, and it seemed there was no other choice. If the men remained, the Germans would murder them: the Jewish intelligentsia would be dealt a lethal blow. Many ran; they parted with friends and relatives, sometimes without knowing where they were going.

My father and grandfather stayed at home. They said: "There is no escape. As long as we can sleep in our beds, we will remain." The city had been drained of its men. Here and there one perhaps could see an old man walking about, and that was all.

The flight from Lodz to Warsaw proved to be a successful killing field for the Germans. The *Messerschmidts* flew above the heads of the weary and frightened unarmed civilians and stragglers; they flew low and they fired, but miraculously not everyone was killed. Meanwhile a desperate battle raged in Warsaw, and many of the Jews who fled there joined the fight to save the city. After four weeks, the fighting came to a stop. German planes discontinued their flights, and soldiers wandered the streets; some on foot, some on motorcycles, and some in other vehicles. The motorcycle noise was frightening. A fast-moving car terrified, jeep-like vehicles with machine guns mounted on them sowed dread, and the soldiers who did not roam marched and sang as if they were a satanic horde. The Germans had arrived.

Order followed order and decree followed decree. We heard of the ghetto; we heard of deportation; we heard of hunger.

# The Gatekeeper
## at Kilinskiego Street

Before the outbreak of war, whenever I returned home after eleven at night, I had to ring the bell for the gatekeeper. Sometimes I waited a long time before I heard the sound of his slippers dragging along the paved tiles. Having arrived at the gate, he would peep through the *Judosz eye*—the Poles called the peephole "the eye of Judas Iscariot"—pull back the bolt halfway, and open the gate. I would then place in his hand a 20 groszy coin, which was a real bonus for him. He tipped his hat, thanked me politely, wished me a good evening, and this is how he behaved. He seemed to be a moderate and quiet man, and we liked him. One can never know where evil will strike next, however, for when the Germans came, he collaborated with them in every way.

Changes took place from one moment to the other from morning to night and night to morning....During the first days of September 1939, the Germans posted notices in the streets instructing the residents to continue their normal activities. The teachers organized themselves accordingly. School began a little late, but the teachers came to work and the children came to learn. At times, teachers and students did not show up because they had been seized "for work." They disappeared for unspecified periods of time, and many never returned. For this reason, the pupils and teachers were very wary of going to class.

A livelihood was hard to come by, and children often came to school hungry. Among the school principals, however, there were some with initiative; these managed to obtain food for their charges and enticed their students to overcome their fright, encouraging them to come to school by a roundabout means.

On a beautiful morning at the end of September or the beginning of October, the Germans decreed that every Jew who went out on the street had to wear a 20 cm. wide armband on the right arm. Hanka protested and burst into tears. "I will not wear the armband, I am afraid, afraid. Even from a distance they will know I am a Jew."

Hanka's fearfulness gripped us all, and it showed up in a trembling such as we had never known. We were in terror and uncertain as to our fate. The future was dark, and that alone was clear. I did not tell Hanka that she had to overcome her dread, because I did not see how it was possible to do so. How could she walk without being seen? How could she cover the considerable distance to school in safety? The first area she had to pass was the yard where the gatekeeper lived. How could she do that without being detected? Hanka knew only too well that he listened to every sound and watched every movement in the house; that he took note of anyone who entered or left. At last, worn out and only too aware of the ominous implications of defiance, Hanka and everyone in the household wore the armband; we accepted the decree.

In those days my mother got up early, and at the crack of dawn she left the house to stand in line for coal. All but my father had a job to do on one of the endless queues for bread, oil, flour, coal, and other necessities. Father could not stand in any line because the Germans and *Volksdeutsche* plucked out each bearded Jew, as if he were a raisin in a pudding. They ridiculed him, spat upon and toyed with him.

One day my father came home so pale and frightened that at first I did not recognize him. Everything about him revealed that he had been attacked. His hat sat backward on his head; his eyes darted in terror; and half his beard had been shorn. The left side of his face was bare, and the right side was as it had been. Father's pride in his beard had been ripped apart, and he broke down. He had become a mass of deep suffering, and looked as if he had been martyred. I can still hear the peals of laughter of the criminals who took pleasure in wounding his soul. Among them was the "polite" gatekeeper, the one who had kissed the ladies' hands for 20 groszy before the war....Father fell on his bed without removing his coat, and lay there for many hours. The next morning he rose to go to the synagogue. He tied a bandage about his face to affect a toothache, but he was now a changed man.

One morning we heard the shout: "All Jews out!" I curled into myself, trying to be as small as possible, so that I would not be seen. I looked for a hiding place to conceal myself....Father stood in front of me, shaking helplessly. His half-bearded, half-shaved face was pale, and the heavy fold over his left eye was more prominent than ever. I saw that he also looked for a place to hide; that he too felt hunted...

The apartment in which we lived had been divided in two, and the front of the building was occupied by Germans. My mother, noting that the door separating each side of the apartment formed into a sort of small niche, got an idea. She placed father in the niche and moved a cupboard over into that area. To our relief, father was now safely hidden behind the cupboard.

The Germans were not long in coming. They looked for my father, but they could not find him. The gatekeeper, who had seen my father enter the house, however, would not give up the search. He entered with an armed German soldier, and both of them looked in and under the beds, in cupboards, and everywhere. The soldier poked at blankets with the barrel of his rifle, while the gatekeeper lay on the floor and looked under the table. Finally, they gave up; they had not found him.

My poor father remained in the niche for a long time. We listened very carefully to what was happening outside—and when we were convinced there was no danger, we ushered him out of his hiding place. He came back into the room and, as he sat there without saying a word, he seemed like an abandoned child or a beaten dog.

After many misfortunes my father and grandfather went into hiding in the cellar. The Days of Awe arrived. There they conducted their "normal" lives. They ate the food we brought them and they slept, prayed, and went to the toilet there. They only opened the door at night without so much as lighting a single candle, out of fear that the gatekeeper might see them. They ventilated the cellar and they breathed in the fresh air; after that they again closed the door and went to sleep.

They prayed continually and in utter concentration in that cellar; they wrapped themselves in their prayer shawls, and bent in supplication. Faith and hope alone illuminated their faces. And in this way *Rosh Hashana, Yom Kippur,* and *Succot* passed.

My heart ached for them. "God of Israel," cried my soul. "Can you imagine the air they have to endure? Have you ever strained to hear the thudding sounds of approaching German boots or the echo of their receding steps? Do you know how much my father and grandfather praise your name in that cellar without being able to distinguish day from night? Have you seen the eyes of these two Jews as they open the door to receive food like animals in captivity?"

# A Memorable Queue

Every day I stood in the queue for bread, but I did not always get it. One day I waited many hours, and managed to be among the first in line. At that time no one suspected me of being Jewish because we were not yet wearing armbands. No one bothered me and I simply stood quietly, wrapped within myself, waiting for my turn. When the window of the shop opened, it was as if an electric current flowed through the waiting people. They surged forward and stood on their toes or ran to the front to see what was happening. Suddenly, as if he had sprouted from the earth, a German soldier in a splendid uniform appeared. He positioned himself, legs spread apart, with a whip in his right hand. Lashing through the air, with an echo answering each stroke, he screamed: "All Jews out!" The whip cut through the air, and a frightening whistle was heard before it cracked across a Jew's body.

I left the queue of my own accord and went up to the German. "How do you want us to behave? What are we to do? This is a queue for bread; it is the minimum a human being needs…." A thundering laughter erupted from the German like lava from a volcano, and the *Volksdeutsche* joined him. The death's head insignia on the German's hat laughed; the shiny buttons on his uniform laughed; his belly laughed; and the whip that sliced through the air laughed…

I suddenly stopped hearing; I stopped seeing; I stopped thinking. I had not been beaten that morning, but my spirit had been crushed. Darkness flooded over me. I was filled with insult and sorrow, and I did not have any bread.

# The First Winter

✿ ✿ ✿

The winter, harsher than ever, battered on sad doors. Snow fell, and layer upon layer slowly piled upon earlier snows. Outside it was the frost that hurt; inside it was the cold. The windowpanes were covered with impressions of leaves, trees, heads of birds and animals; more than that could not be seen, and I sat for hours looking at the designs created by the frost. We older girls still worked in the factory, my mother saw to the household needs, and my father and grandfather remained in the dark, dank cellar. The younger girls, Yuditka and Hanka, stopped studying. The schools were closed, it was cold, and we were hungry. There was no help from anywhere; we were abandoned; we were lonely.

After a series of painful deliberations, my parents and grandparents decided to return to their home town of Kielce. There, my parents thought, in a place where people knew them, it perhaps would be easier to overcome difficulties. They decided to take the younger girls, Yuditka and Hanka, with them. We—Gutka, Zosia, Esta and I—were to remain to take care of the apartment and to continue working. It was understood that we would maintain close contact with one another.

A cart was hired for which a huge sum had to be paid. The few possessions they took along with them included father's books—holy books, some of which were bound in leather. Big and heavy were the books of the *Gemara,* that I used to air out on the lawn of our yard each Passover; the pages rustled then, and heralded the coming of spring.

The loaded cart waited outside and everything was ready. My

mother and father had to lie on top of the pile of books in order to balance it. Before climbing up, however, they took leave of us, and this was a special parting. We stood in a row according to age as if it were the eve of *Yom Kippur.* Father went from daughter to daughter, placed his hands on the head of each, and blessed her. Mother accompanied him, and nothing was said. It was the silence that spoke. Before leaving the house, my father stopped at the threshold and asked for Zosia. He handed her my mother's prayer book, *Korban Mincha,* and said to her: *"Fargess nisht ver du bist,"* "Do not forget who you are."

I watched them recede into the distance. Mother looked back at us several times, and I had the strangest feeling that while her body moved forward, her legs lagged. Her hands were close to her sides, and she skidded on the ice beneath her as if her body was that of a wax doll. Father hunched within himself and walked behind her. They climbed onto the cart, all of them: Yuditka, Hanka, my mother, and my father. The cart moved and the frozen snow squeaked under the wheels.

From afar I saw my mother hug Hanka; then I saw Yuditka move nearer to Hanka. Father sat behind them, and put his hands into his coatsleeves. The cart moved farther away. The snow fell in silent whiteness and gradually covered my father's hat and my mother's wig. Soon all four were wrapped in white. The girls waved, and the cart grew smaller and smaller.

# The Bloody Day

❀ ❀ ❀

That Wednesday was like the other days: full of fear, hunger, and terror. The order to evacuate the city and move at Baluty had been issued several weeks before, but the Jews did not hurry. They deceived themselves. Perhaps the "anger" would pass, and they could stay in their apartments with all their possessions. Perhaps…but it was not to be.

The Germans employed every convincing method to influence the Jews to comply with their orders. They taught them a lesson of unmistakable intent, and it took the form of a pogrom on Piotrakovska Street. Jewish homes were invaded and Jews were murdered, beaten, or robbed. The Jews who had until then remained left their apartments, taking with them whatever they could. Some loaded everything on carts hitched to horses and others hitched themselves to the carts; in utter misery they dragged their possessions through the streets of Lodz in the direction of Baluty, the ghetto. The migration had begun.

Day after day at dawn, the dispossessed left on the road to Baluty. Large carts, small carts; some with big loads, some with smaller ones. The Jews tried desperately to balance the piles of goods on the cart—one more blanket and another pot, another piece of clothing and one more chair. Items of furniture served as a railing around the carts, and children of all ages, wrapped in coats and sweaters, sat on the heaps. Next to such a wagon walked the head of the family—his uplifted arm supporting the goods as if it was an extension of the rope securing everything in place, including the children. Characteristically, the head of the family led the cart and the wife followed it from the rear. She watched and protected the precious cargo from coming undone.

Each day hundreds of people walked to Baluty—a neighborhood in the north of Lodz inhabited by a quiet, working population. The Jews were being displaced, and the Poles and the minorities living there were forced to leave their apartments in order to move into the city. By the time the Jews arrived, the neighborhood showed signs of neglect and overcrowding. Some sixty percent of the Jews who lived in Lodz had come to Baluty to be received by their compatriots.

The transition was hardly easy or harmonious. The Poles of Baluty were not pleased to leave their homes for the Jews, and in some cases they demanded an entry fee. In theory these were to have been exchanges, but in practice it was quite evident that the "exchange" was not at all fair. Few Poles lived in Baluty, while many Jews lived in Lodz and this fact alone created incentives for exploitation. On the whole, therefore, the transition was easier for those who had money; they simply bought or rented the apartments from the Poles. For those with little or no funds, however, it was very hard indeed—and because there were many such cases, chaos ensued.

For the time being, we four sisters stubbornly remained in our apartment at 89 Kilinskiego Street.

# Leaving the City

We struggled against all that befell us long before we entered the ghetto. We overcame the cold, we rose early, and we washed with cold water. We tried to be cheerful, and at times we even burst into laughter so that hunger itself was forgotten. We played "catch" with a ball, and we sang; and in all that we did, Mirka and Ruth Perla joined us. We had become a small collective, a family that ate its meals together.

What I have just described did not last, because after the events of bloody Wednesday, my sisters and I alone remained in the entire building....We spent the first day of the week at home, and on the morning of the second day, we decided to cook lunch and wash clothes. I began to do the laundry and was bent over the washboard, when I was startled by the shout: "All Jews out!" I knew the sound of that command, but I could not get used to it. I lost the ability to think as the words sank in, and I ran; I ran and I heard: *"Schnell! Schnell!"* Suddenly I found myself outside. Gutka, Zosia, and Esta were with me as well.

A dark procession made its way on the mud-covered road, and we advanced slowly. Wagon wheels splashed slush onto those who made their way on foot, pushing or pulling their wagons. We had neither money nor possessions. Before and behind us, we saw a migration of miserable skeletons drained of all spirit.

On reaching Baluty we heard that public halls had been set aside for the homeless. My sisters and I were very tired, but we went to one of them. We found old people, women, and children sleeping on the floor. The night passed, and morning came. We rushed out to see where we were. We had stayed at the gymnasium of the Baluty school.

All sorts of rumors reached us, but we did not know which to believe. One claimed that the needy were receiving help at the Jewish Community Center, and another reported that apartments were being distributed. We went to the center, stood in line, and the unbelievable happened. That very day my sisters and I found a small room in a run-down wooden hut. We had a roof over our heads! We got blankets, pillows and sheets, and a table and chairs from good people: our former neighbors from the city and Aunt Perla. Very slowly, the little room became a home I came to love.

We had no work to do in the ghetto. The black market flourished, prices skyrocketed, and we had no money. I began looking for a job by knocking on doors. Finally, at one door, I was welcomed. A family lived there: a husband and wife with a twelve-year-old daughter and the husband's mother. I had come to the home of Dr. Urbach. The elder woman grasped the situation, looked at me again and again, and asked: "What do you want to do? What sort of work do you want?" "It is not important," I replied. "Any work will do. I must make a living." I was invited in and introduced to the woman's daughter-in-law, who hesitated and said: "All right. Come tomorrow, and we will see."

The twelve-year-old remarked that it was a shame that I had to do housework, but the mother scolded: "Quiet Stefchiu! Do not mix into things that are none of your business."

The above happened in April, 1940....

I worked for Dr. Michal Urbach, and faithfully discharged my duties. We grew to love one another, and in the course of time we became friends. Meanwhile, in "my home," the girls were still unemployed. I was the sole support of the hut at 33 Wrzesnienska.

# In the Ghetto: 1940

Before the Germans sealed off the ghetto, and from the first days of its establishment, the Jews began to organize themselves. Class status disappeared and differences eroded between the religious and the secular. Simply stated, local leaders appeared whose main concern was mutual aid. The holidays were celebrated together—whether it was *Pesach* or *Chag Habikurim,* the feast of the first fruit —and we yearned for the spiritual life despite the fact that this was nearly impossible to achieve.

Because the evening curfew began at six, a special life-style developed in the ghetto. After dark, fences between yards were removed stealthily. Anything made of wood—cabinets, tables, chairs, stairway railings, stairs leading to basements, doors of abandoned apartments, window frames, and even floorboards—was burned by us in order to fire the stoves, heat the houses, and provide warm food.

We gathered every night at someone else's house. Evenings of readings, study, singing, and listening to records were organized. We had an old-fashioned phonograph that we had not turned over to the Germans—strictly forbidden on pain of death—which we cranked in order to play. These evenings became famous and young people, among them poets, came from the entire neighborhood in order to attend. There were even girls in our midst who knew "The Step," a popular dance of the period. Our discussions sometimes ended at dawn—and in the homes where friends gathered to play cards, they met until late into the night.

The youth, still full of hope, wrote satires and told jokes. Political movements were organized despite the fact that many leaders had been murdered and only a few had managed to escape. In Lodz, as in most places, the leaders fled and the intelligentsia, whom the Nazis wanted to eradicate, dispersed in every direction. We were quite brave, actually. Political parties of any and every kind had been banned altogether.

On entering the Lodz ghetto, reorganization began; *Agudat Yisrael, Mizrachi,* the Zionist movement in all varieties, the Bundists and the Communists all reconstituted themselves. One thing alone united everyone: each had to function underground. It was forbidden to "live," and we resisted that notion in every way possible. Gatherings were forbidden, exchanging opinions was forbidden, listening to the radio was forbidden, publishing a newspaper was forbidden, and in short, everything we did was forbidden and could have cost us our lives at any time.

One of our answers to these prohibitions was the establishment of public kitchens according to a party key, in order to assist the needy. Later on public kitchens were organized by the head of *Judenrat*, M.Ch.R., Mordechai Chaim Rumkowski, whom we also called the "Old Man." The prime objective of all the parties was to prevent the starvation and death of their members.

The Lodz ghetto was among the first in Poland to be sealed off, and when that was done, contact with the world beyond its walls became impossible. At the start of the war, the Joint Distribution Committee succeeded in penetrating most of the areas in which there were Jews, but the Lodz ghetto was an exception of sorts. The Joint was able to reach us in the beginning, but its help went through the Germans' screening process and M.Ch. Rumkowski's organization. As a result, the ghetto's population received nothing, and mutual aid in the first days of the ghetto's existence was based on our own initiatives and resources alone. Political organizations helped their own members first, and the most crucial service they could render was to find work for them. This too was carried out in accord with a party key.

...Before the ghetto was sealed off there was a mass exodus of the intelligentsia which led to panic, and confusion took over the Jewish street. Some did not make it far from Lodz, but some reached Warsaw; some got as far as the Soviet Union, and others made it to Palestine. Mira Hammermesh, my sister Esta's friend, asked Esta to join her, but Esta refused. She could not leave us. Mira reached Palestine, but Esther perished at Stutthof.

When the ghetto was sealed off on May 1, 1940, our situation worsened. People fell ill and died of hunger—but this was true from the very beginning, when hunger struck down entire families. The overcrowding precipitated depression and disease, and it was not simple to move into a house where others already lived. It was a terrible, nerve-wracking, maddening situation to be forced to live intimately with strangers.

There were extreme pessimists and sworn optimists in the ghetto....The Germans had promised autonomy: they had promised not to grab the Jews for forced labor, and the Jews repressed the horror. They believed the Germans told the truth. This German "truth" was "brought in" by the Jews themselves when they entered, and they held on to this notion in the belief that they would surmount everything and survive. The will to live was stronger than any other impulse. Those who went through the first wave without collapsing began to reorganize. Even though they were fearful and tense about the future, pained and sorrowful over the past, they went on.

The observant Jews gathered together during the holidays and prayed. They expressed an intensity, an enthusiasm and excitement that was not hard to understand. The men stood at the entrance of the prayer house wrapped in *tallitoth,* wearing the *girtel* on their *yopitzes,* as if the war did not exist. One could see the yearning and hope for redemption written all over their faces, but those faces also expressed a degree of relief....The Germans were not to be seen in the streets....The religious women lit candles and tried to create a holiday atmosphere in their homes despite the hunger and suffering. One could say they adjusted to the new situation with stunning speed.

Faith had entered our souls with our mothers' milk; it was the faith that in spite of everything, we would survive even these conditions. As long as the ghetto existed, many fully believed that the war would end "tomorrow." They wove stories: Germany would surrender soon; salvation would come from Russia, England, the United States. But those who did not believe said: "Let something happen already! Whatever will be, will be."

A wonderful phenomenon began to emerge. People did not want to be alone. They did not want to live alone, and they did not want to be deported alone. Our friend, Wanda Rein, got married before the deportation so that she could be with Motek. A new language was born; new concepts were created: "My sister from the ghetto"; "My brother from the camp"; "My mother from wartime." No, this did not happen by chance. People sought support, and gathered in a common house or a common bed.

One day was like the next and the days became weeks, the weeks became months, and the months became years. People were resigned to the harsh and the unbearable, wanting to believe that this is how they would live until the war ended. They tried not to notice the pervasive deterioration. They prayed and hoped that things would not get worse. The strength to rebel diminished until it reached zero. People were hungry and ill; they lacked the will to fight because of physical exhaustion. Everything "good" within them eroded, but after every "deportation," the Germans spread "good rumors" about those who had been "selected," and optimism reigned again.

# Ghetto *"Kibbutzim"* and *"Kibbutzniks"*

The youth movements in the ghetto began organizing in 1940—one might say spontaneously. The initial objectives were mutual assistance and the joy of being together.

Dr. Poznansky was in charge of the Agrarian Department in an area called Marysin. He welcomed the youth movement groups and set them to agricultural work. M.Ch. Rumkowski "jumped on the bandwagon," and officially sanctioned the training farms in the ghetto. They were subsidized by the ghetto "treasury"; that is, the elder of the Jews, or M.Ch.R.

Marysin housed a broad spectrum of youth. All its members—more than a thousand—were organized in a body called the *Hachsharot Noar,* or Youth Training Farms. The left *Poale-Zion* and the *Bund* joined the *hachsharot* after some time, but they were not the first. The aims of these *kibbutzim,* or collectives, were "educational only"; nevertheless, one has to keep in mind that every member of a *hachshara* received an additional food ration. This meant that his ration card could remain at home, where those he loved could take advantage of it in order to live. The girls of *Agudat Yisrael* and the *Bund* also engaged in agricultural work, and every group received a plot of land to work on in Marysin. Our motto was: "All for one and one for all, according to his ability."

Each group had its individual character. There were meetings, committees were elected, chairmen and secretaries were selected, and political and ideological discussions took place. Substantial differences of opinion were expressed, as well as simple agreements and disagreements. Above all, morale was high; there was faith in the future, and belief in the potential of these groups to become the Zionist nuclei which would continue to thrive after the war.

I belonged to a group called O.S.A., *Organizacja Syjonustyczna Agrokultura,* or the Zionist Agricultural Organization. Lectures and lessons were given; we had an internal newspaper; and we discussed both everyday matters or ideology. We studied the geography of Palestine, general history, the history of the Jewish people, and the Hebrew language. We held roll calls and gave orders in Hebrew; we had parties and drank and sang…The food was mainly spiritual…. Birthdays and memorial days of leaders of the Zionist movement were celebrated, blue and white flags were raised, and we saluted the flag and changed the guard. When news of Jabotinsky's death reached us, we held a memorial service; the news, which traveled by word of mouth, enveloped us in grief.

The *kibbutzim* were dispersed in February, 1941. They had existed for a memorable year in which our morale was high as we combined our industry with comraderie. Still, we faced both personal and social crises….

♦ ♦ ♦

I had worked for Dr. Urbach for about two months when I decided to join my friends in the *kibbutz* at Marysin. It was good to be with them, but I did not forget that my sisters were hungry for bread and suffered many deprivations.

The housework in the *kibbutz* was carried out in shifts. Every week a different group stayed in the house to clean it and to prepare meals for those who worked in the field. Members rose early, and the residential area was emptied. We went to work like farmers, and carried our work implements on our shoulders; some had shovels, and some had rakes.

I remained with my friend, Tobcia Topyol, with whom I became inseparable. Tobcia was assigned to the kitchen and I was assigned to the toilets. These toilets were not white porcelain bowls and they could not be polished; they were situated in wooden huts at some distance from the residential quarters, and they consisted of boards which sat over huge pits. The floor to these toilets was made of hard-packed earth, and the doors were made of flimsy boards which could be shut only with the aid of a steel hook....I scrubbed the seats and the doors until they looked as if they just had been planed. Everything was clean and smooth; the color of fresh wood shone in the toilets, and I was very proud of my work.

One day I returned to the quarters where Tobcia and I stayed; I straightened them out and cleaned them. On that occasion, the two of us decided to prepare an especially attractive, tasty meal, but we really wondered how we could do it. We only had groats, and what could one do with that? They could be cooked in salt water, and this we did. What now? How would this meal differ? We finally decided to make the groats look like some sort of *cholent.* We had nice tableware, which the others had brought from their homes, and we set the tables and decorated them with various greens that we had picked from the yard. We cut the scallions we grew on the sill of the kitchen window, and placed the groats on trays or large plates. Since we had brown sugar, we spread a little on the groats. We "drew" the letters OSA onto the brown sugar by using the onions. As far as color was concerned, Tobcia and I were satisfied. The trays looked nice, the house was clean, the meal was attractive, and we were elated. As for the taste? We could not be sure.

When the others returned, they were amazed. They hurried to wash and sit at the table, for its appearance stimulated their appetites. Their reactions, however, were swift and only too sad. First there was veiled criticism, and then there was open criticism—and not just any kind of criticism, either. One said: "This is sweet?" Another said: "Neighbor, what did you put in the groats?" Etka asked: "This is salty" and Moishele announced: "This is the first time in my life that I have eaten onions with sugar." Some coughed and cleared their throats, and others spat out the "delicacy." And if all this did not suffice to insult us, the group began to chant "OSA!

OSA!" For Tovcha and me the ridicule and uproar was an insult and a great sorrow. And from that day on, I kept a low profile. I did not want to be reminded of the OSA episode....While I stayed at the training farm I worked in the fields and was not hungry. My sisters at the Wrzesnienska Street address were, and this was a constant worry to me....

A member of *Techiya,* Shlomo Redlich, the "radio listener" who was caught by the KRIPO in 1944, used to visit our little room, as did Baruch Praszker; he, too, was a *Techiya* member, and he had returned from internment in Radogoscz. With him were Pinchas Gershovsky, my future husband's uncle; my future brother-in-law, Yehuda Videbsky; Mark Feder; and others. They had been imprisoned, but they had not committed any crime. At the time, M.Ch.R. was already functioning as chairman of the Jewish community, and he took care of all those who returned from Radogoscz.

In those days our friend Moshe Veisand returned to us; he had escaped from German internment, and one evening he appeared among us still frightened and agitated. His lovely girlfriend, Frimka Eiger, greeted him. What a reunion, and what excitement. They hugged, kissed, and cried, and Moshe overflowed with stories....He was among the rare few who had managed the feat of reentering the ghetto....Rafael Zelwer, the living soul of the group—a thin, pale fellow with a long face, continually writing articles, editing the group's internal newspaper or maintaining the group's diary, was also with us....I was amazed at his spirituality and perseverance, and, not surprisingly, everyone loved and admired him....Little Bronka Zaks, whose beauty and grace was like that of an expression in the Song of Songs, was there too.

I wish it were possible to mention all my friends, both living and dead. Unfortunately, I can only name a few: Rochele Beim, who sent us a warning from Auschwitz, which we disregarded; Arye Ben-Menachem Printz, a good friend; Zvi Bergman, who was lovely and active; and finally, Etka Fried, a dominant personality who persisted in expressing her views with rare humor and who attracted

Wojtek, Peretz, Alter, Yisrael Lizarovitch, Shlomek Waldman, Haimek Kuznietzki, Yisrael Kliski, Peretz Zipperstein, Shmulik Ginat, and Gutke Dafna, the youngest of the girls....

Baruch Praszker received an important post and had free access to Old Man Rumkowski, upon whom he had a great influence. The party members decided to urge him to find some sort of work for me so that I could help my sisters. One fine Sunday M.Ch.R. was expected to visit the training farms and a roll call of all the groups took place on the parade grounds, where all the members of the various *kibbutzim* waited for him. The carriage drew near, and M.Ch.R. emerged from it. His white hair billowed in the wind, and his eyes darted. He stepped down from the carriage, stood on the stage we had prepared for him, and delivered a speech. This time it was a Zionist speech. He spoke of the Jews and of the youth working the land, and he undertook to support "this wonderful project," the training farms. He predicted that the youth would emerge from the training farms and go directly to Palestine. Who knows? Perhaps on that occasion he actually believed what he said.

Prior to the talk, Baruch Praszker took the opportunity to present me to Rumkowski. The Old Man immediately arranged for me to have a pad and pencil so that I could take down his speech. I was to function as his secretary, but at the end of the ceremony, he appeared to be disappointed in me. The next day I was out of favor. He did not take me with him in his carriage and, on the contrary, left Marysin without clarifying whether or not I had a job. I was taken to his summer home where I remained alone and under guard, and I did not know if I was allowed to return to my friends. Rumkowski had a maid who did the cleaning, a gardener who took care of the garden, and a housekeeper who saw to the food for everyone in the house, I among them.

My friends came to visit, but their attitude toward me had changed; they spoke to me with deference, and it was difficult for me to tolerate this situation. A week passed, then another, and still the Old Man did not come. My fear grew with every passing day and finally, I called for Baruch. He came at once and offered me some support. "Do not be afraid," he said. "You will not remain here. I will see to that."

One day as I sat reading a book in the garden, I heard hoofbeats. I did not even manage to put down the book before M.Ch.R. ordered: "Assemble all the members!" Once more a thousand young men and women gathered, the flower of the Jewish youth of Lodz. The president stood up on the stage, and this time he had a different script for us to absorb: "I have packed my Zionism in a suitcase," he said. "All Jews are the same to me. Only one thing distinguishes you. You are young, and able to work. If you work, no evil shall befall you…," and so on, on and on….He appeared omnipotent and conducted himself like royalty. With him came the "mighty" of the ghetto, a host of bodyguards, and his sister-in-law Helena, who stood at his side like a princess straight out of the royal court. Rumkowski ended his speech and without pausing, he turned to me. "What do you know? What did you study? You will manage the children's summer camp. Go tomorrow to Wrzesnienska Street to organize the place."

It had been a long time since I had visited my little home. I knew that Zosia was ill with dysentery, and I knew that Anjula and Helena Tenenbaum had moved in with us. I knew that they had no work, and that they had nothing to eat. I knew that we had no money for a doctor for Zosia, and I felt helpless. I did not have anyone to turn to, but I did not despair. I went to Dr. Urbach to tell him that my sister needed him, and I did not have to repeat myself. He called on Zosia and provided me with unbelievable treasures: in addition to medicine, I received rice and coffee. These two items made a marvelous difference. Zosia recovered, and I began my work with the children in the summer camp.

# The Staff in
# Summer Camp

❁ ❁ ❁

At the beginning of the summer of 1940, about 800 children attended the camp at Wrzesnienska Street. A team of people who had grown close to one another in the course of their work provided the children with shelter, love, and devotion.

In connection with the camp experience, I remember Sarenka Feldman Silberstein, who could calm the children and bring them to almost absolute attention. I remember Lola and Eva Zederbaum, two lovely sisters, whose work went far beyond what was required and who devoted their energies to singing and dancing with the children. And I remember the great educator Yechiel Abramson, who had been the principal of the school on Samogova Street and was a warmhearted man of exemplary character. Yechiel sang to the children and comforted them, particularly when they had difficulty in falling asleep, and at times I suspected that they stayed awake deliberately in order to hear him. They sat and held hands, moving in unison like a sunlit wheat field swaying in the wind as he sang *Di zun fargeyt in flammen,* The sun sets in flames.

Mrs. Wanner, who was the principal of the school at 6 Samogova, was also there; she later became the director of the summer camp with some one thousand children under her care. This woman was a source of inspiration to me in difficult times. When I did not know what to do, she spoke to me and encouraged me. She never stopped, and she never gave up. When the summer camps closed, she redirected her energies and saw to the education of the youth at the rug plant. This noble soul, who stood guard like

*Rumkowski proceeds to orate after appointing Riva his secretary. Marysin, 1940.*
MENDEL GROSSMAN, PHOTOGRAPHER.*

*Riva with the leaders of the various organizations to have cropped up after the establishment of the ghetto. Marysin, early 1940.* MENDEL GROSSMAN, PHOTOGRAPHER.

*Mendel Grossman, perhaps sensing the disaster to befall the Jews of the ghetto, went about portraying life and events with a hidden camera. By the time of the liquidation of the ghetto, he had amassed thousands of candid portrayals depicting both the morale of the Jews and the deteriorating conditions. Some of these photos survived the war and are in archives in Israel; others were, of course, lost or destroyed. Apart from Grossman, both Rumkowski and the Germans photographed the life of the Jews in Lodz.

*Chaim Widowski. Heroic, ardent Zionist who forfeited his life rather than risk betraying his comrades. As part of the Underground, he monitored the BBC for news and was wanted by the Gestapo.*

*Arek Jacobson and those inspired to resist the Germans in the ghetto meet and train in vain. Their dream of open rebellion remains thwarted due to a lack of arms. Marysin. Typical scene up to the liquidation of the ghetto.* MENDEL GROSSMAN, PHOTOGRAPHER.

*Riva's brother-in-law, Yisrael Brauer; Mendel Grossman's sister, Ruska; and friends. Marysin, 1940-41.* MENDEL GROSSMAN, PHOTOGRAPHER.

*A few of the girls in kibbutz Marysin. Ruska, Mendel's sister, is in the center. 1940-41.*
MENDEL GROSSMAN, PHOTOGRAPHER.

*Clandestine acts of defiance. Many rules are broken as the youth meet, break curfew regulations, sing, etc. The accordion in plain view, for example, should have been turned in to the Germans.* MENDEL GROSSMAN, PHOTOGRAPHER.

*Riva's sister Esta.*

*Riva's sister Gutka and Yisrael Brauer on their wedding day. 1942.*

MENDEL GROSSMAN, PHOTOGRAPHER.

*Right to left: Anjula Tenenbaum, Helunia, and a friend.*

*Photo used as a postcard sent from the ghetto to the U.S. with the following cryptic message: "We are all right, but Baruch Leib is better off than we are." Left to right: Gutka, Esta, Riva, and Zosia.*

a soldier in the hardest of times, kept a diary in the ghetto. She was deported to Auschwitz in 1944, but we met again in Israel.

Eliyahu Tabakesblatt, director of the education department in the ghetto, generally visited our camp at about four in the afternoon, when the parents came to pick up their children. When problems arose he assisted quietly, and it always seemed to me that the suffering of two thousand years had found a lodging place in his quiet eyes. Fortunately I had the privilege of meeting him again in Israel.

Among the kindergarten teachers who taught Hebrew songs to the children I especially recall Hela Peltz, an energetic woman devoted to the children with all her heart. At the close of summer camp, she too saw to the children's education on that factory roof.

During this period I had violent dreams. I was afraid to remain alone in my room, and night after night one of the girls came to stay with me. I was truly frightened, but I did not know why. Rachel Wanner encouraged me: "Do not be afraid, Riva. Nothing will happen to you."

The summer camps were closed in early winter, 1941. Public places, such as the building on 6 Samogova, were intended to be used for people who arrived from Germany, Austria, Czechoslovakia, and Luxembourg. I was again unemployed.

# The Office of
# the Public Kitchens

The Old Man established a committee of ten members; among them were Szczeslivy, Henryk Naftali, Shlomo Kaufman, Eliezer Neumann, Zygmond Reingold, and Baruch Freshker at its head.

I remember well the days when Engineer Gutman labored and ran about, hastening the building of the kitchens. Indeed, 55 public kitchens were established rapidly; one kitchen next to each factory. A huge apparatus was established in order to operate them, and work opportunities opened. Party representatives were on the alert again and every party, from the Communists to the Revisionists, tried to place its representatives. Work in the kitchens was desirable, and even the potato peelers enjoyed an extra ration of soup; this of course meant the prolongation of life. The managers and their teams had rights and if not "rights," they had "possibilities." The people in the kitchens did not go hungry; their families could eat at home and avert starvation.

When the committee disbanded, Shlomo Kaufman remained; he had been appointed manager of the head office of all the kitchens, an organization that employed more than three thousand people. To Shlomo Kaufman's credit, he was a decent man. He was aware of his position and he took advantage of it to benefit everyone, but no one man could relieve the totality of the hunger rampant in the ghetto. There simply was not enough food. Because of him, I was able to prevent the deportations of my friends, organize mutual aid in the Kitchens' Office for the clerks, and engage in public work. All this was made possible when Shlomo released me from my obligations in the kitchens.

My little office was a beehive of public activity, and from there we distributed coupons for potato peels to those who waited in line. Chaim Widowski came to the office every morning to convey the news he had heard on the radio. As a matter of fact, all the senior officials gathered in my room to listen to the news, and among them was Shlomo Kaufman.

In those days I rose early to distribute the potato peel coupons. At six in the morning, however, people already were waiting in line in queues so long that I could not see where they ended. No matter how early I came to the office, others had arrived earlier. Even when I came at four, I found people standing there in darkness and in frost, the frozen snow squeaking under their feet. On a clear night, the long line looked like a huge serpentine shadow. Steam rose from the nostrils of the waiting mass; frozen and wrapped in rags, they crowded and pushed closer to one another in an effort to stay warm. Whoever came early enough and obtained a coupon for 2 kg. of potato peels per day for two weeks, delayed dying. These people recovered for a brief period of time. The swelling in their legs disappeared, and they were able to resume their work at the factory: once more they could receive soup and food rations, and entire families returned "to the living."

Unfortunately, the collapse of a single member of a family could lead to the collapse of the entire family. Family members who shared their food with the weak and ailing, grew too weak themselves. They fell like leaves from trees in autumn. They fell because they starved to death. They died in their beds, on the way home, and on their way to work. Death waited for us in every crevice of the ghetto.

# Anjula and the House on Limanowskiego Street

We changed quarters and now had a living room and kitchen. Throughout all of 1941, we stayed there. The house in which we lived was surrounded by a huge garden in which apple, plum, and cherry trees grew. Our friends came to visit us often and were not deterred by the curfew. With each hardship the joy of life increased, and in those days my family did not suffer killing hunger. All the girls had jobs, and what this meant was that each received an additional portion of soup every day. Zosia worked as a kitchen manager and received a room in Marysin, close to her workplace; Helunia worked in the statistics office; and Gutka worked in the underwear factory. Esta and Anjula, both fourteen, were schoolgirls. We still looked quite well, and we still wore our own clothes. In brief, we were all right.

There was a special atmosphere in our house because of a special presence. Anjula—who rose at five and brought wood, lit the stove and heated water—managed to spread her protective wings over everyone. Without a word escaping her lips, her activity was decisive and total, energetic and perfect—and yet, every flutter of sadness touched her soul. Once as I lay on the couch, not well and feeling nauseated, Anjula saw my condition. She sat down on the floor beside me, rested her head on the couch, and sang lullabies to me. I heard her singing, and drifted off into a strange slumber.

One evening Anjula wanted to empty the garbage, but when she hesitated I understood that she was afraid. I offered to accompany her, and we went out. The garden was encased in darkness.

With one hand she clasped me; with the other she held the pail. The garden was in full bloom. We walked in shadows and on paths lit by a full moon. Suddenly she cried: "Rivosh, I am afraid of the moon." "What are you afraid of? Everything is lit up, and you can see the moon as well," I said, but she was not consoled. "I can see it, but it can see me, too. I feel as if it is touching me." Soon, however, she relaxed. "I am not afraid any more; when I am with you, I lose even the fear of the moon." She held me, burying herself in my arms, and added: "Rivosh, can you smell it? Breathe it, Rivosh. It is the fragrance of the blossoms; if we are lucky, we will eat the fruit in summer…"

Anjula visited her mother's grave every day on the way back from school and, although Anjula was a part of us, it sometimes seemed to me that she did not belong to depressing reality. One night she awakened, weeping bitterly. It was difficult to calm her, but after pleading with her she said: "I dreamed that I was dead. I dreamed that lightning struck and killed me, that I was buried, and that my grave was next to my mother's. Yes, I will die in April." The next day, we did not speak about her dream.

♦ ♦ ♦

Mail service was still available to us and we received letters from our parents, Yuditka, and Hanka. At home, we maintained a kosher kitchen for the sake of our parents. Since this was a period in which horsemeat was distributed in order to deflect the oppressive hunger, we dutifully exchanged the horsemeat for bread.

One day we received a letter from my father, who responded to our questions: "In order to save your lives, I permit the eating of horsemeat. Anything that can save a person's life, is permitted." Yuditka wrote: "You relate to Hanka as if she were a little girl. I want you to know, my sisters, that Hanka has grown up. She is working and earning, and her support of our parents is no small matter. As for me: a registration for a nursing course was an-nounced for those over eighteen with matriculation certificates who were able to pay a fee of 200 zloty prior to acceptance. Even though I was not yet eighteen, and did not have a matriculation certificate or the money, I was accepted. I am very pleased on account of this, because I will be able to work in the hospital. I hope that the situation will change, and we will be able to see each other soon." Hanka wrote: "I can say about myself that I am grown up. I know my obligations. I help our parents, like Yuditka. I am really grown up, believe me!" The last to write was mother: "My father was ill with typhoid. An epidemic is raging throughout the city. He is seventy-five years old. Thank God he was able to overcome it, and has now recovered his strength."

◆ ◆ ◆

A torrential rain poured down on us yesterday afternoon and continued through the night, but the morning of June 27, 1941 was beautiful. I opened the window so as to air the bedding. The sill was still wet and I went to get a rag in order to dry it, but I was interrupted by a pounding on the front door. I recognized Zosia's touch, but thought it strange that she was up so early. When she entered I saw that she was pale and frightened, but in a moment she burst into tears. "What happened!" I cried. "Zoshiu, what happened?"

"Anjula is dead," she answered. "Anjula is at the morgue. She is gone!" We ran to the hospital on Lagiewnicka Street as if seized by madness, and they let us in. Anjula was lying on the floor of a darkened room, covered with a white sheet.

I lifted the sheet. Anjula lay on her back; her face was pale, her eyes closed, and she appeared very tired. She seemed serene, and just as she looked when she slept. I examined her body, but all I saw was a small, purplish-violet stain above her left breast. This is where death had struck her heart in the storm of yesterday afternoon...Zosia had gotten Anjula a permit to go out into the field in order to pick flowers for her friend Esther Ruthenberg, who was in the hospital. Anjula went; she had managed to gather the wildflowers, and when she was found, she held a bouquet in her hand. Two policemen, who happened to be in the field at the same time, hid in a nearby shack and only were injured.

In one stroke, death had wiped out the legend that was Anjula. How were we to go on, and how were we to tell Helunia? Our laughter left us and our singing was silenced. Anjula was buried in the Lodz cemetery, next to her mother, and we visited these graves often, each of us separately.

# The House at
# 30 Franciszkanska

A year passed, and we were joined by other girls who were alone —either because their parents had died of hunger in the ghetto or because they had been deported. Lonya Lipschitz, Zosia's friend, was accepted by agreement of the girls' "council." Bela Koplowitz, Esta's friend, was orphaned and she too became a part of our household.

After Anjula's death seven of us remained in a crowded room, but we were successful in finding another place at 30 Franciszkanska Street. Although we again had one room and a kitchen, it was near where we worked. We did not have to face the daily crossing of the bridge built by the Germans to connect the two halves of the ghetto, and there was a free room under the roof of the house. We accommodated Lonya, Heniek Lipinsky's girlfriend, in the loft and once more we became a large family.

Our friends streamed into the house, and it became a spiritual refuge. Our situation was relatively stable, and everyone worked or helped us to overcome the tragedy of Anjula's death by lightning. No one paid attention to the curfew, and our friends reached us by roundabout ways. Some brought their poems to be read, and oftentimes we shut the windows and turned on the phonograph. This was strictly forbidden, but we listened to the records our friends brought, and dared to be young. Someone always stood guard on these occasions, and we were able to forget our hunger.

The girls from *Agudat Yisrael* visited us, and among them was Minia Shalentzka. It tore my heart to see this tall girl, a true believer, hungry; hungry and laughing, her partially-open eyes giving her an oriental cast. We were in Stutthof when I last saw Minia. The walls were filled with a familiar graffiti: *Here Minia Shalentzka helps.*

Zlatka Borenstein and her husband, Alter Shnur, the renown poet, also visited us. After his children were taken from him, he left a number of his poems with me for safekeeping. I took them to Auschwitz, hiding them on my body along with photos of my parents. The one-armed poetess, Andzha Sandik, also left her poems with me before she was deported. Fela Weiner, Fela Kalmowitz, Marysia Frohman, Manya Filar, Irka Wojdyslawska, Bluma Flambaum, and Lucina Perla came, as did Helina Liss, now working at the Weizmann Institute of Science, and Rozicka Kirschbaum, a doctor at the Beilinson Hospital.

Here and there, tuberculosis sneaked up on our friends, and we lost a few. Others were caught in the "shipments," or selections for death....Dr. Yokish-Greenberg always, always responded to every call we made, and never said: "I cannot help you." She was "the doctor" for all the boys and girls who visited us. Dr. Izio Ser never refused, and the same was true of Dr. Shiker, who always laughed on arrival: "Well, which of the girls needs me?" None ever asked for a fee.

When Marysia Frohman became ill with tuberculosis, her eyes shone like chunks of crystal. Her chalk-white hands grasped the arms of the chair; her lips were red and dry. She had difficulty speaking and sat in the armchair, waiting quietly for Dr. Yokish. After checking her, the doctor grew silent. Marysia was silent as well. Dr. Yokish filled out a prescription, and tried to be light-hearted as she urged Marysia to speak. When she did not succeed, she patted her on the back and said: "It will be all right; it will be all right."

When I walked the doctor to the door, she asked: "Riva, do you know what T.B. is?" She then went on to explain: "Marysia's condition is what is called *Rozpadowka,* a form of tuberculosis which destroys every part of the body. She will simply burn up from the fever. This is open tuberculosis; it is dangerous, and I want all the girls in the house to know that it is an infectious disease, attacking without mercy. One simply breathes in the germs, and falls ill. If you want to spare the girls, move Marysia to the hospital." My only response to the doctor was that we would discuss the matter at home. This we did. Our decision was that Marysia would stay. We could not reject or abandon her.

Marysia breathed her last in her home and in her bed, where she was warmly cared for. She died surrounded by the friends who loved her, and we saw to it that she had a Jewish burial. Lucy Perla died of meningitis and "open" tuberculosis, and I remember her as she had lain on the floor. By then, she was so flat that it appeared as if she already had begun to sink into the earth. None of us cried any more. These were daily occurrences now, and the only question we asked was: "Who is next?"

# The Meanings in Silence

What is the specific gravity of time when an infinite amount of change occurs in each second? What is the value of a moment in which an individual is taken and deported into the unknown? What is the value of the second in which all hope is lost? How can we transmit what happened to us to the people who lived in the free world? How can we explain hunger, cold, and disease? The manner in which disease waits to claim another beautiful being? Does not the expression, "I am dying of hunger" seem banal? How are we to explain the fear of the persecuted when he learns his name appears on a "selection" list? How are we to explain the meaning of *Sperre?*

How can words describe the life of Gila Filar, for example? Gila Filar, who in her thirties, was old before her time? Once I met her in the street, pushing a cart of excrement and taking the place of a horse. I asked her why she did not come to us, but she bowed her head and continued to push the cart. What I remember most, however, was how her black eyes stared at me as if they were solidified lava. Something within warned me that if I touched her innermost being those eyes of hers would ignite, explode, and destroy the universe. Did I exaggerate? Would she simply burst into tears? No, she would not cry, and I do not exaggerate. Gila had become a shadow in rags; she could not see me, and I doubt if she heard me.

The wheels squeaked beneath the barrel filled with excrement, but I wondered if she noticed the stench and if there was some way to reach her. Has she any love for anyone, or is she merely filled with hate? As if coming out of a trance, Gila gave me a knowing glance and said: "I live on Zgierska Street."

The next day I telephoned the office to say that I would not be in. Kaufman, as usual, agreed to my absence. I went to Zgierska Street to look for Gila, and found her at the end of a very long street. She was clean and dressed, and received me with great hospitality. Her face was drawn, but quite alert, when she offered me a glass of water. I sat down and Gila faced me, but it was hard to begin. I asked, "Where is your husband?" "He is a policeman, working," she replied. "Do you have children?" "I have a two-and-a-half-year-old daughter. She is asleep now."

…The conversation continued calmly. Gila did not ask for help, and I did not know what to do. We parted. After some days, however, she appeared at our house. We greeted one another, and then Gila explained: "My husband was deported from the ghetto to a concentration camp. I cannot work; I am sick. I have moved, and I am now living with my cousin. I simply want you to know where we can be found."

Gila stayed a little longer and hardly added another word. I did not know what to say to her and we parted, but this time we embraced, and Gila promised to come again with Buba. I thought this was a good sign, and time passed. We heard nothing however, and I decided to go to her.

I reached a broken-down yard on Brzezinska Street. All the fences had been torn down, and the filth was everywhere. The snow had turned into a blackish-grey slush, and in it could be seen foot tracks leading to the stairway. My feet sank in snow. I reached the stairwell. The stairs were wet, dirty, squeaky, and serpentine. They began right at the entrance and were hard to climb. There were no windows and no lights in the hall—so that the higher I climbed, the darker it got. When I finally came to my destination, I saw that a sliver of light had escaped into the hall from a narrow slot under the door.

I knocked, but no one answered. I tried the door, which was

unlocked, and I entered into a small room. In it were three beds, a table, and a narrow, protruding wall closet. A kerosene lamp stood on the table; its flame flickered, alternately bringing the play of light and shadow into the room. The walls were covered with hoarfrost, and the light from the wick fell on the frost on the walls. Sometimes it produced a rainbow in which the table, the beds, and at times, the motion of a leg or an arm of someone lying in bed was reflected.

A man whose age I could not determine lay in one bed; Gila lay in another, and curled against her feet was the child, Buba. Gila obviously had a high fever; her face was pale and her eyes were darker, larger, shinier than when I had seen them last. The fever brought out her beauty. Her head was slightly tilted, and her eyes—two deep pits—were fixed on the girl. Buba was asleep. Beads of perspiration dotted her forehead, and black curls spilled onto the pillow to form a halo. Her cheeks were red and her brows black, as if the hand of an angel had drawn them, and the long lashes fluttered from time to time, as if she were trying hard to keep her eyes shut. Her mouth was open; her breathing quiet.

"Who is taking care of you?" "My cousin." "And where is your uncle?" "There, in that bed." "Was the doctor here?" "No."

That was enough for me. I stood up, lit the stove, heated some water, and brought it to those lying in bed. As silence fell on the room a strange feeling gripped me, and it was as if my tongue had clung to the roof of my mouth. Buba Dina was still asleep. I could do nothing more, and so I stood up, said good-bye, and left.

Only when I was out-of-doors did I realize that apart from the hoarfrost and the flickering of the kerosene lamp, and apart from the burning in Gila's eyes and the eerie silence, a peculiar odor completely permeated the room. It was an unfamiliar odor, but it reminded me of the morgue and the time I had gone to see Anjula. I find it difficult to express what I felt, but it seemed to me that this was the smell of death. It accompanied me on the way back home, and in fact I brought it into the house. That entire day I kept visualizing the sad picture of what I had witnessed. An irrepressible odor, an odor that spoke, penetrated, strangled, depressed, and paralyzed my soul, clung to me too. The next morning, when I returned, Dr. Yokish-Greenberg was there, examining Gila.

When the examination was over, the doctor said: "Mrs. Sachnowska, you cannot remain at home. You must go to the hospital." "If I go, what will become of Buba?" Gila asked. The doctor turned to me: "Riva, we will take care of her. What do you think?" Having spoken, she said good-bye warmly, as always, and went on her way. Many patients awaited her.

Once more silence descended on the room. Gila was stunned and unable to decide what was best, but Buba was happy and reached out to me. "I want to get dressed, Auntie!" she cried. With small, quick and energetic steps she threw herself first to her mother and then to me, as if she had always known me.

The door opened. A young man, tall, thin, and pale, entered. He did not greet anyone, but rather placed a pot on the table. He approached the niche that was supposed to function as a kitchen, removed three plates, and distributed three equal portions: one to his father, one to Gila, and one to Buba. When he completed this chore, he left with the empty pot in hand and disappeared as quickly as he had come. And still, the silence persisted.

Everyone began to eat. At last, the silence had been broken by the clicking of spoons and the smacking of lips....Once more, I sensed the strange odor....Buba hurried and finished her soup first; she did not lose a moment and approached her mother, shouting and crying and stamping her little feet: "I want soup! I am hungry!" Gila did not hesitate, saying: "Take. Eat. Do not cry." She turned to me: "It is like this every day." The predatory animal in Buba was evident as she licked her spoon and then her plate.

I looked at Gila and said: "Let me open the window and air out the room," but Gila panicked and spoke up vigorously: "No. No, not that!" She became very agitated, collapsed on the bed, and nearly fainted, but after a few minutes she regained her strength.

I felt in my heart that I had hurt her innermost being and once more, we were separated by the weight of silence. At long last, Gila said: "Riva, give me a piece of paper and a pencil." I gave them to her. She wrote down a few words and handed them to me. Gila had written: "There is a corpse in the closet, my uncle's daughter. They are hiding the body so as not to lose the ration coupons. Maybe you can do something."

With Gila's consent I took Buba with me, but before going home, I ran to see Dr. Yokish-Greenberg in order to tell her about the corpse. Between us we found a solution, and we gave the corpse a Jewish burial. Buba remained with us, and Gila was hospitalized. She was taken from there to the extermination camp, along with the other patients.

Our friends came to see our Buba, and she became the focus of our lives. We played with her; we took care of her; and everything changed because of her. Our allotment of bread we exchanged for cheese, and the rationed carrots were not to be touched. They were for Buba, just as the sugar was, and we faithfully reserved these for her.

One night we held an evening of music and readings. Buba was asleep and someone played the violin. Suddenly Buba got up and said: "Birds." And, indeed, because Buba was like a bird, from then on our evenings were called the "bird evenings."

We were now eight in the house on Franciszkanska Street: Gutka, Zosia, and Esta, my sisters, and Lonya, Bela, Helunia, Buba, and I.

# The Lodz Ghetto:
# 1941-1942

❁ ❁ ❁

Anxiety flourished; hunger and disease thinned our ranks. Adults, the young, and infants succumbed. "Fleck-typhus," or typhoid, dysentery, meningitis, tuberculosis: we suffered them all. Vital medicines could not be had at any price. As in all other situations, it was possible to get help for the sick, but deeds of the lowest kind did occur. In some cases patients were injected with water so that the medicine prescribed for them could be sold for bread or soup.

The cold was unbearable and to make matters worse, due to the inexperience of those managing the ghetto, the potatoes supplied by the Germans to the Jews froze and were inedible. As the hunger grew, renewed demonstrations mounted—especially before Rumkowski's house at 36 Lagiewnicka Street. The cry went out for the distribution of food or the opportunity to work in the kitchens, but the demonstrations were suppressed quickly by the police. On one of those days of desperation I witnessed a tragedy. An elderly woman happened to be near a truck loaded with kohlrabi when a mass of hungry people fell on it. The woman was thrown under its wheels and crushed to death.

Death in the ghetto was ever present. In the spring of 1942, there was a change for the better, but it did not last long. The order had been given to increase the bread ration for workers, and the public kitchens distributed bread and sausage instead of soup. When winter came, it was harsh; the snow piled up to great heights, froze into ice, and was difficult to remove from the sidewalks. Many slipped and fell, breaking arms and legs. Meanwhile, the frozen ground made it impossible to dig graves; those who died did not receive a proper burial for days or even weeks.

Because our household on Franciszkanska Street included individuals of almost all political persuasions, it sometimes seemed as if the wolf and the lamb shared the same lair. Each of us, however, had to maintain the rules we adopted. Among them were:

1. It is forbidden to accept gifts in any shape or form;

2. It is forbidden to ride in the carriage of our friend, Baruch Praszker, or that of anyone else; and

3. It is forbidden to use our connections with the people who visit or receive help, or to accept any benefits from them.

I do not remember all the regulations, but I do remember that we observed them faithfully.

During this period I worked in the office of the main kitchen. There it was possible for me to ask Shlomo Kaufman to help those who were close to me, but never once did I ask for myself. My pride did not allow it, and I was bound by our code at home. Thus, even when I organized the distribution of coupons for potato peels to friends, I found it difficult to take anything for myself. As luck would have it, Leah Wroclawsky-Shapira, author of the book *My Midnight Prayer*, worked with Zosia in the kitchen. On her own initiative she "organized" potato peels for us at the house, and said: "If I survive, I will write about what goes on in the house of the Citrin sisters. No one will believe the truth, but I will write of it just the same."

Gelerstein, a very dear person, worked in the office of the kitchen as an "inspector-general." One day, he happened to come by our house while we were having our lunch of kohlrabi soup. "Is this your meal, Riva?" he asked. When I replied: "Yes," Gelerstein's only comment was: "It is not right for you to be hungry." I did not react. What could I say? The following day, when I was not at home, a messenger arrived with a food package.

"What is this?" asked Esta. "I am not allowed to accept packages. Please take it back." The next day he returned, entered the house and, without saying anything, placed a parcel on the electric meter in the corridor.

The truth is that I could not rest in the ghetto. I worked together with Chaim Widowski and had no inhibitions whatsoever, even when my life was in danger. I received lists from the Zionist movement of those who had been taken to prison prior to deportation. As part of my duties, however, it was my responsibility to oversee the kitchen in the prison. I therefore took advantage of the weaknesses in the system to place certain individuals strategically. They were accepted as workers, and were safe from deportation. At times I removed people at the very last moment. I actually took them off the truck that was about to go out of the gate to the waiting train.

Once, when I was in the prison at Czarnieckiego at two o'clock in the morning, I was noticed by the police commander who said: "If I see you here once more I will put you on a truck and you will go with the first transport." The police commander, Rosenblatt, knew very well what I was up to at that hour. I nevertheless continued to go there and be on watch. I tried to save as many as possible from the transports, but I avoided him. I was afraid. I was also very much afraid of Mordechai Chaim Rumkowski. His wife worked in the kitchen's office, and when the Old Man came to visit, I ran to Abugow. Etka sat there too, and both would laugh. "Again he came?"

# The Sparks of Life

The winter of 1942 was cold and wet, and moisture penetrated the house through every crack in the walls, floor, and ceiling. Our clothes became moldy, and we had no way to heat the house....

Esta suffered from sores on her entire body; Helunia still had not overcome Anjula's death; and Gutka had her tonsils removed by Dr. Mazur and suffered from rheumatism. Every morning she awakened in pain. She had difficulty in speaking and in moving her hands and legs. She dressed herself with an effort, sometimes wiping away tears.

In the midst of these gloomy days, we received a letter from our parents in Kielce. About themselves they wrote nothing special. They did not complain. They did not provide any details. Father wrote for everyone. He asked about us, and he asked that we keep him informed. Among other things, he wrote: "I have no strength to wait any more. I would like to have the privilege of hearing that my daughters have married. Do not worry, my daughters, about our separation. I no longer question your choices. If you have men whom you would like to marry, I and your mother, as well as Yuditka and Hanka would like to hear the good news. We will rejoice with you. I hope to hear from you soon...."

Father's letter was naturally the topic of the day. Gutka said: "Father no longer insists that he be religious," while Esta said: "And he doesn't ask any questions." I added that they depend on and trust us, but Zosia's assessment was that they are simply desperate.

"Look at the first sentence of the letter!" she cried. "I have no strength to wait."

Between us we agreed that Gutka and Yisrael should read the letter together and decide what they wanted to do. On that very day they determined to get married, and we dispatched a reply; Gutka and Yisrael wanted to wait for our parents' blessing before setting the engagement and wedding days. We were all satisfied that Yisrael Brauer was a fine person, that he was industrious—even then he worked in the cooperative in Marysin, which was a good job by ghetto standards—and that, above all, he passionately loved my little Gutka.

At the appointed time we invited Shlomo Kaufman and his wife Frimka, who lived in our yard on Franciszkanska Street, Yisrael's father and sister Fella, and the residents of the house—the sisters and the girls and Buba—to the engagement party. The event was festive, even if we did not have anything to serve our guests. We said: "*L'Chaim*," "To life," with chicory coffee, and set the wedding date.

We notified the family in Kielce, and invited all those friends of my parents who yet remained in the ghetto to come to the wedding. Rozka Grossman made a wedding dress for Gutka out of a maroon wool fabric decorated with "gold" buttons. It was a modest dress, but Gutka looked beautiful in it. Everything that Rozka—whom we called Shoshana—made was not only beautiful, but also of such high craftsmanship that it bordered on art.

The wedding day arrived and the guests began to gather. It was a nice gathering, but there was no food. We had received the normal ration all couples received for their wedding celebration, but this was a very small supplement. I had tried, without success, to remedy the situation.

I was afraid to turn to Rumkowski, and I did not ask his wife for anything either. It was rumored that she had no authority to do anything, and I did not want to embarrass or sadden her. For the first time, however, I decided to go to the meat department to ask for an extra ration, but the manager refused to help me.

Gutka stood next to Yisrael as silent tears streamed from her eyes. Yisrael took the ring from his pocket and said: *"Harei at mekudeshet li,"* and broke the glass in remembrance of the destruction of the Temple. Cries of *"Mazal Tov, Mazal Tov,"* and *"Besha'a Tova"* assailed them. Perhaps they drank wine under the *chuppah:* I no longer remember.

The guests sat at the tables we had prepared, but it was disappointing. There had been an expectation of a filling meal, but there was none. We had done our best and had failed. Suddenly, someone knocked on the door. I opened it, and there stood the manager of the meat department, Mr. Rosenson.

Mr. Rosenson greeted me and handed me a parcel that contained a great many sausages—good, assorted sausages of the best quality. These we divided and placed on the tables. They made a great impression—and to this day, I do not remember any other food. Our guests were famished and they devoured the sausages so that they could have seconds. When sated, they sang, laughed, and joked; they forgot the bride and groom. Rosenson was the center of attention, and everyone wanted to be seen speaking to him.

Gutka and Yisrael had been married according to Jewish law and had been given a room in which to live, as was the custom. It was not far from where we were on Franciszkanska Street, and they were now on the second floor of the house at 23 Brzezinska.

We wrote to our parents and told them about Gutka's wedding, but we heard nothing from them. We wrote again and again, but there was no answer at all. Later on, we found out that the Germans had deported the Jews of the Kielce ghetto to Treblinka and Majdanek.

♦ ♦ ♦

A ray of light entered the gray life of the ghetto. Youngsters who had studied before the war continued to do so, and even managed to complete their high school studies. My sister Esta was among those who received their diplomas.

The graduation ceremonies took place in January, 1942, and were held at the "House of Culture" in the presence of the teachers, principals, and prominent persons of the ghetto. Among the latter were the heads of the Education Department: Rumkowski, Rosenblatt, the Police Minister, and Aharon Yakubovich. These were great moments...

I remember my Esta and how she prepared herself for the event, radiant with happiness and full of hope, as if nothing unusual had happened in the ghetto. I remember her transition from childhood and her entry into the maze of adult life...

Many speeches were made that day expounding plans, paying homage to M.Ch.R., and thanking him for being instrumental in establishing this glorious enterprise. Indeed, there seemed to be no limit to the praise he received. Rumkowski, the last to speak, became emotional as he directed his words only to the youth, and it was quite evident that he was proud of his achievement. He handed out eighty-five certificates, and "arranged" for graduates to work in the woodworking plant that manufactured furniture for the Germans. This was thought to be quite advantageous because the workers received an allocation of sawdust in order to heat their homes.

# Political Party Activities

Every party believed that its way was the "right way," but the situation in the ghetto did not permit expanding political argument. Due to circumstances, most differences were pushed aside.

A roof organization called "The Executive" was established in the Zionist movement. I was not a member, but due to my activities I frequently participated in its meetings. I knew everyone: Shlomo Uberbauw, Chaim Widowski, Moshe Karo, Elimelech Shiffer and his wife, Leon Greenfield, Yisrael Tabakesblatt, Haim Eliyahu Tobias, Bernard Freund, Eliezer Baum, Mr. Blatt, and Baruch Praszker. At times, these meetings were very stormy. As part of my duties, I became acquainted with other leaders and worked with both Mark Feder and Emanuel Wolinsky.

The Bundists, along with the other parties in the ghetto, continued to adhere to the principles they espoused prior to the war. They believed that redemption would come with the end of the war in a liberated Poland. Their leader, Moshe Lederman, managed one of the kitchens, and although our paths and beliefs differed, that which united us took precedence over everything else. Lederman routinely participated in the mutual aid meetings of the public kitchens and sometimes brought his friend Golda Yakubovich along with him to our office. Once there, he referred to the notes he had made which listed the names of those who required help. Golda and Moshe went to Shlomo Kaufman in order to get certificates for extra soup rations for the needy, and they came to me to get coupons for potato peels or an item on hand in the mutual aid store we had set up for the sick in the Kitchens' Office.

Yosef Flash was a Bund member, a colleague at work, and a close friend. The Bundists turned either to him or me with their problems. Mrs. Anna Feifel was the Communist representative, who acted as the secretary to both Shlomo Kaufman and Mrs. Perses Weinberger-Rumkowski. She was as solid as a rock, and protected the members of the Communist movement who worked in the kitchens or in the office. Yechiel Hirschhorn, called *der royter Chiel,* or "Yechiel, the Red," visited her as did Ziula Paznowska. At times I met them quite by chance, exchanged views, and continued on my way, but the activity in the Kitchens' Office reflected the overall activity in the ghetto. Each of us did what we could with our "possibilities," and it now seems extraordinary to me that except for the uprising of the hungry workers during the early days of the ghetto in 1940—which was suppressed with lightning speed with the assistance of the German police—no "unusual activities" took place.

The Bundists and the Communists developed patterns similar to those of the other parties. Everyone conducted gatherings; everyone maintained a mutual aid activity; and everyone showed concern for the education of the youth. These activities were extremely important. They reinforced the members' morale, and they imbued them with the strength to go on in the face of grim reality. Individuals lifted their thoughts past the mundane and moved on to another, higher plane. Above all was the wish to continue living; the wish to see the defeat of the Germans; to live to see a new world that was free and could boast a just social order.

The secular organizations "dug in" with the principles they believed in before the war, and the religious organizations continued to believe in the Messiah and mysticism. The evil that befell the Jews was seen as a prelude to redemption and, in the days of the Marysin training farms, the Zionist youth looked upon these pious Jews as the nucleus of those who one day were to be settled in Palestine.

Everyone—absolutely everyone—believed, arranged celebrations, and sang songs of hope. They sang when they were hungry, and they sang when they were miserable. They were exhausted and broken, and yet they sang. I did not meet a single person in the ghetto—not among the young and not among the old—who believed in the annihilation of the Jews. Even while we spoke about "extermination," or of "rumors" about Auschwitz, Kolo, and other places, we did not believe them. Our awareness was dulled, just as our other senses were dulled. We heard. We were told. We knew, but we did not accept and we did not want to believe. We, in fact, refused to believe. In 1942, we already had evidence which clearly demonstrated the truth of the rumors of extermination; we knew about the gas chambers and mass graves, but we rationalized that what we "knew" was either exaggerated or rhetorical. I accept the reality now, but even so I sometimes doubt. Is it possible that I was inside this system? Am I alive? Do I understand? Do I remember?

On the eve of Yom Kippur, 1943, our Zionist friends gathered at twilight for Kol Nidrei in the house at 30 Franciszkanska. Suddenly, in the awesome atmosphere of the Kol Nidrei prayer, Rumkowski appeared in the company of Baruch Praszker. M.Ch.R. had asked Praszker where we were praying, and simply came to join us. Upon his arrival, however, the atmosphere changed. Although we prayed, we lost our connection with God. Some were in awe of the white mane of the Old Man, some tried to approach him in order to be seen with him, and some actually managed to exchange words.

At the end of the prayers most people dispersed, but a few, including the members of my household, remained. On that occasion, M.Ch.R. was calm and silent. Suddenly, however, he turned to speak to me: *"Zog mir, men vet mir areinlozen noch der milchome noch Eretz Yisrael,"* "Tell me, will they allow me to enter Israel after the war?" I replied as follows: *"Ven es vendet zich in mir, volt ich eich nisht areingelozen,"* "If it was up to me, I would not permit you to enter." At that moment, I was not afraid of him.

After reflection, M.Ch.R. said: *"Nu meila, zol men mir nisht areinlozen, zol shoin zein noch der milchome. Ich bin bereit zu shtehen far a mishpat! Vi derleb ich shoin! Zwei mol shtarbt men nisht!"* "Well, so what if they don't let me in? May the war be over! I am ready to stand for judgment. I should only live to see it soon. One does not die twice."

It seemed to me, and so I want to believe, that this was an evening in which M.Ch.R. searched his soul together with all of *Bnei-Yisrael,* and that he was aware that he was in a maelstrom from which there was no escape. At any rate, it took a great deal of *chutzpa* or "nerve" to speak to him as I did, for I too was among those who were afraid of him.

...We have spoken of the strong, the active, and the affiliated, but it remains to be said that those who could not contend with the sad reality of our existence, despaired and fell. Others fell for quite different reasons. One friend, a well-known and admired youth leader in the ghetto, went of his own free will to an extermination camp after his parents were sent there. He followed them, believing he could help them.

...If not believing that masses were being murdered was a sin, then we sinned. The party leaders sinned, the religious sinned, the optimists sinned. Everybody sinned.

# The Lodz Ghetto
and the Transports

Evil winds buffeted the ghetto and carried waves of humanity to
and fro. As early as September, 1941, a transport arrived from
Wloclawek with about nine hundred women and children. Almost
immediately following this first transport, another arrived from the
suburbs of Wloclawek. Again, only women and babies spilled out
of the trains. On their backs they wore yellow triangles identifying
them as Jews, whereas we in the Lodz ghetto had to wear a yellow
Star of David.

Each transport to reach the ghetto had to go through an important artery, the Public Kitchens' Office. Kaufman received orders to
prepare for their arrival and to provide them with hot soup. The
Housing Ministry saw to it that they were lodged in houses scattered throughout Marysin, and in the initial period they received
free food. The women had no belongings of any kind; their husbands had been sent to an unknown place; and the stories they told
were depressing.

The ghetto organization for the refugees was very efficient, and
all the institutions worked as rapidly as they possibly could to
absorb them. Before long—and largely due to the consideration
given them—these uprooted Jews became an inseparable part of the
ghetto population.

At the same time that these transports arrived from Wloclawek,
strange activities were taking place in a particular area at the end of
Brzezinska Street. Ditches similar to fortifications were dug, high

tension electricity poles were erected around the ditches, and barbed-wire fences were strung up. Rumors, all sorts of rumors, went the rounds of the ghetto.

Barracks were built within the camp that was thus demarcated, and it was absolutely forbidden for anyone other than the workers to enter. The Germans meticulously examined those who came and went, and everything seemed shrouded in secrecy. It did not take long and then, one day, about five thousand men, women, and children arrived by a roundabout route and on a side track that led from Radogoszcz. The rumor spread that these were Gypsies.

Shlomo Kaufman received orders to organize a public kitchen for them. He and his staff were assisted by the kitchen in Marysin under Feinmesser's direction, and together they supplied hot soup to the newcomers; their camp representatives received it at noon, together with other food products. Clearly, what we had here was a ghetto within a ghetto; a ghetto isolated from the Jews, who were themselves isolated.

The Kitchens' Office supplied the Gypsy camp for a brief period only; after that the connection was broken, evidently on orders from the Germans. In 1944, the camp was liquidated swiftly. German murderers shot everyone, but someone always survives; there is always a survivor, and this time it was an eight-year-old girl who had hidden. The Germans' orders had been executed, with one exception.

Upon the child's discovery, a soldier asked his superior what he was to do, but the superior wanted to know if she was smart. "Yes, very," said the soldier. "If so, another bullet," came the answer, and that was the end of the Gypsy camp. From that point on, the food went to the ghetto management, and it was "as if" five thousand Gypsies had never existed.

At the end of 1941, Kaufman was summoned to Baluty Square by Rumkowski. We awaited his return anxiously, for we knew that whenever Rumkowski summoned him, something was about to happen. When Kaufman returned, we followed him; we knew our manager well and could tell if he was "pleased," or if new problems—of which there was never a shortage—had arisen.

This time, Rumkowski notified Kaufman to prepare to receive refugees from Germany, Czechoslovakia, Luxembourg, and Austria. Assisting him were Elias Tabakesblatt and Moshe Karo from the Education Department. They were to empty the school building at 6 Samogova for the refugees. When the transport from the west arrived, I was there with others on behalf of the Kitchens' Office. We served bread and coffee and distributed a bowl and a cup to each person. By this time it was quite late, and everyone was exhausted.

Although the people who arrived were of all ages, they were mostly elderly. In general they looked well and were well-dressed. I recall seeing a woman who sat in a corner, next to her man, and that both wore fur-trimmed winter coats. The man obviously was concerned about the woman next to him. He removed a thermos from his bag, uncapped the cup, and poured coffee for her. The steam rose from the thermos and fogged his glasses. He did not drink; he merely licked his lips and waited patiently for her to finish. He later recapped the thermos, and returned it to its place next to the suitcase.

The air was oppressive; the room was packed. Some sat cross-legged on the floor; others leaned against their belongings and fell silent. A few smoked cigarettes. When the distribution took place, people took what was given, ate, drank, and returned to their things. The night before they had homes and beds; now they were refugees. They lay where they were, and fell asleep.

Early the next morning I returned. It was a clear winter day; the sun shone, and the snow, having melted, slithered its way into the building. When I entered, however, I found scarcely a soul. I went into the yard. The refugees were there, talking loudly. They did not seem to be tired or miserable after their ordeal. They waited in line for their turn at the water faucet so that they could wash. Half-naked and even naked, they stood under the cold water tap. They washed and scrubbed themselves vigorously, and dried themselves with towels that came from home. The men who had washed and dressed, hung hand mirrors either on the fence or on the branch of a tree in order to shave; women stood or sat as they put on their make-up.

Breakfast arrived. The kitchen staff distributed coffee, bread, jam, and little triangles of yellow cheese. Again, the refugees stood in line to receive their food. Bit by bit, they began to exchange words with the "locals." It seemed to me that they accepted their plight, but we soon learned that this was not so. These people deteriorated sharply and suffered greatly from conditions in the ghetto.

The drastic change in surroundings, the welfare, social and spiritual aspects, broke the newcomers. The change was too extreme, their mentality too different from that of the ghetto residents. The radical shift required of them entailed a willingness to adapt, an absolute transformation in thinking and behavior patterns, but they seemed unequal to the task. They began "stripping." They sold their clothing for any amount of extra food. They sold their watches and their most precious personal belongings; and when everything was gone, they were overcome by despair.

Very few of those who had come in on this transport went to work; they simply refused to consider themselves part of ghetto life. We did our best for them. We opened a special office to help those who came from the west or from Wloclawek and its environs. This office, headed by Henryk Naftalin, tried to resolve their problems. We also created a home for the elderly.

For a certain time the mail service still functioned in the ghetto. The refugees had contact with families and friends from their countries of origin, they received money from their bank accounts or from their families, and they used it to improve their lot. When these resources were cut off, they ceased coping. Life went on in the shadow of death.

From time to time I visited Dr. Oscar Rosenfeld. Once on a rainy day in October, 1942, I entered his room at One Daborska

Street. The room was both dark and cold, and he paced the floor dressed in a warm overcoat. It was obvious to me that he had lost a great deal of weight. The coat sagged about his shoulders as if he were a scarecrow, his back was bent, and his bones protruded. He wore a wool hat topped by a tassel, and a pair of plaid flannel slippers. On occasion he rubbed his hands and said: "I will sell everything, just so as not to be hungry. I have cooked potatoes, but they did not satisfy my hunger. I will buy more, I will cook them, and I will eat them." He went on and on, and mentioned the name of "Hanushi."

Dr. Rosenfeld was sent to a convalescent home, and when he returned after a week's stay, he looked better and was in higher spirits. When I visited again, he told me how good it had been for him to meet the Jews of Vienna, Prague, Frankfurt, Hamburg, and Berlin, and he wondered how the Old Man had managed to bring everyone together socially.

The doctor was invited to every festive event sponsored by the Zionist groups within the ghetto. We knew that he was a writer, and we treated him with great respect. He met with Leizerovich, the painter, Dr. Oskar Singer, and members of the Zionist Executive, and he was assisted by Baruch Praszker, in whose home he always was welcome.

Dr. Rosenfeld was a man of many facets. He worked together with Theodore Herzl in Vienna and he served as the representative of the Zionist movement in Paris and London, Yugoslavia, and Bulgaria. He wrote for Yiddish and German newspapers, and he was a newspaper editor. Between 1938 and 1939, he wrote for the "Jewish Chronicle" in London, completed *The Fourth Gallery*, a novel, wrote "Mendel Ruhig," a Jewish story, and *Days and Nights*, an anthology. He dealt with the theater and literature, was a playwright and director, and translated the works of Mendele Mocher Sfarim, Shalom Aleichem, Linick, Frishman, Numberg, Bashevis Singer, and others. In some of his endeavors he also worked with Jabotinsky, Dizengoff, and Bialik.

Apart from the above, Dr. Rosenfeld kept a diary in which he mentioned many of those with whom he came into the ghetto. Of these, some died of hunger, some committed suicide, and some were transported from the ghetto to the crematoria. Not one person remained alive and like so many others, he too disappeared.

I think about the people who came from the west and how we were brought together by chance. Twenty thousand Jews....Twenty thousand people wrenched from their roots, their work, their language, their customs....No, I do not believe they could have been absorbed. Even those who were sensible and wanted to integrate or tried to find work, failed to establish a relationship with the rest of the ghetto population. Their strength did not suffice. They fell like flies. They simply fell. Lying or standing, leaving the house or entering, in the streets and on the bridges, they fell.

At about the same time that the refugees came from the west, another transport, whose deportees were mainly skilled tailors and shoemakers, arrived. They succeeded in bringing along with them a little of their property and a little food, which was taken from them on arrival by the ghetto office. These individuals adjusted very quickly. They found themselves all sorts of work, and they became an integral part of ghetto life.

*Starving child.*
MENDEL GROSSMAN, PHOTOGRAPHER.

*Starving child—Yankusz, or Jacob, Mendel Grossman's nephew.*
MENDEL GROSSMAN, PHOTOGRAPHER.

*Feiga, sister to both Mendel and Ruska and mother to Yankusz, at the Gas Kitchen Abteilung, where food was brought to either be cooked or heated in the evenings after work. Both Feiga and Yankusz were in hiding with Riva from September 1-14, 1942.*
MENDEL GROSSMAN, PHOTOGRAPHER.

*A queue for soup.* MENDEL GROSSMAN PHOTOGRAPHER.

*Human-drawn cart laden with bread.* MENDEL GROSSMAN, PHOTOGRAPHER.

*The arduous task of seeing to a "decent" burial.*

*The yolk of servitude.* MENDEL GROSSMAN, PHOTOGRAPHER.

*Tank full of excrement hauled by humans in servitude. Note seated woman, lower left; and queue, upper left.* MENDEL GROSSMAN, PHOTOGRAPHER.

*Hauling excrement to and fro. Note shacks and woman climbing stairs.*
MENDEL GROSSMAN, PHOTOGRAPHER.

*Above and below: hauling excrement.* MENDEL GROSSMAN, PHOTOGRAPHER.

*The bridge dividing the ghetto in half, from which many Jews leaped to their death in utter despair.* MENDEL GROSSMAN, PHOTOGRAPHER.

# The Mounting Crises

✻ ✻ ✻

In January, 1942, there were persistent and disturbing rumors of impending deportations and the liquidation of the ghetto. These rumors spread following the establishment of a medical committee by the deportation apparatus, which was supposed to examine virtually the entire population of the ghetto. The rumors were denied by M.Ch.R. at every opportunity. Here and there "celebrations" were held in honor of the new year, and M.Ch.R. utilized every opportunity to survey the past years, mention the efficiency of the workers, or convey information that new work orders had been received from the German authorities. Nevertheless, he conceded that the Germans demanded twenty thousand individuals for deportation, and acknowledged that he was able to limit that number to half, or ten thousand persons. "I have complete confidence in the implementation committee," he said of the deportations, "although they too can err." In this same talk, he also said: "Here in the ghetto, is a commune. One is responsible for all, and all are responsible for each."

Rumkowski spoke like a prophet who believes in his God-given mission to the Jews. He warned, he preached, he promised. He laid down the path to be followed. He swore on his word of honor that nothing evil or dangerous hid behind the committees and the general lists. He condemned the originators and sowers of rumors, and he fervently swore that no evil would befall decent working people. The result of this famous speech was that the people of the ghetto grew calmer.

Hunger was rife, the cold was unbearable, and people died. The price of food on the black market soared. A chase began for quantity at the expense of quality: vegetables and potatoes in place of sugar, meat, and margarine. The administration which consisted of a small number of the privileged, including the doctors, enjoyed extra rations. They were sated, "fixed up," and well-dressed; they stood face to face with those who were starved, ragged, and slated for deportation.

M.Ch.R.'s promises were not kept. Two weeks into January, the deportation committee sent out the first notices for the Jews to report to various locations in the ghetto. The first to receive these notices were the so-called "unwanted elements"; that is, those who were imprisoned for offenses like stealing potatoes, kohlrabi, carrots or a spool of thread, or for stripping a fence for firewood. They had three days to settle their affairs, and they were "given the privilege" of selling their furniture. If the furniture was of "special value," an assessor could be called in to evaluate the goods so that they could receive "fair value." If need be, the workers in the carpentry shops helped to collect the furniture. All these and other matters had to be seen to within the specified time. Each day, seven hundred Jews had to leave the ghetto. They could carry 12.5 kg. with them, and they were told their money would be exchanged for German marks prior to departure. What hypocrisy, and what satanic fraud!

The cold was fierce, the hunger gnawing. Disease and despair were oppressive, and the Germans worked on all levels. At that time there was a general distribution of rations, but those who went on the transports received an extra half loaf of bread, sausage, and jam. Some therefore "went voluntarily" in order to get the food supplement, but others went into hiding. Ten thousand Jews from the west were deported—many of whom went willingly, claiming conditions elsewhere could not be worse.

To go into hiding meant to be without rights. To be without rights meant to have no food coupons, no work, and no means of staying warm. It meant having nothing, and yet there were many who managed. Even though they were stripped of their rights, they were supported by their families and friends. Some even managed to survive, and they now live in Israel.

The deportations stopped for a while, and then resumed.

The year 1942 was one of nerve-wracking and total impoverishment; and it was the year that Bibov, the German chief in charge of ghetto "management," liquidated the periphery of the Lodz ghetto. It was the period during which displaced persons arrived from adjoining towns, broken and exhausted. They had no homes, no livelihood, and no property to speak of; it had all been taken away. Dear ones had been torn from them and sent to places unknown; heads of families disappeared as did their women and children; and utter misery prevailed.

Neither alive nor dead; hungry, impoverished, diseased, isolated, sad, in mourning and in an utterly wretched state, the Jews of Ghetto Lodz were about to withstand another calamity: the *Sperre,* or general lockup.

# The *Sperre*

Our power to resist decreased. Winter passed; summer came. Typhoid and tuberculosis spread; hospitals overflowed.

On September 1, 1942, the Germans surrounded three hospitals, removed the patients, and threw them onto trucks in a brutal manner. They sealed off approaches to these hospitals, scattered the passersby, and did their work without interference. The Jews had been removed from their beds, operating tables, and lavatories.

At first no one understood what had happened, but they soon caught on and began to help those who still could walk. Patients were dressed in white smocks and made to appear as if they worked there, and in this way they were saved from deportation and certain death. The Germans, aware that many patients had escaped and were in hiding, demanded that the Jewish police hand over the "fugitives." And indeed, there were some who were caught and imprisoned at Czarnieckiego.

On that day we plunged into despair. We did not know what to expect as rumors circulated about the liquidation of the ghetto. The following day, the Germans demanded an additional twenty thousand Jews for the transports in addition to the children and the infirm.

It is impossible to describe the panic that ensued. The old wanted to look young; they wanted to work. The ill wanted to look well, and the children wanted to look older than ten years of age—but no one knew *what he must be* in order to survive.

The deportation committee worked day and night, and all the departments compiled lists. Those holding key positions within the various parties acted as if possessed, and tried to save their constituents without exception. It was not easy to choose the Jews for deportation, despite the fact that the departments prepared lists throughout 1942. Behind each worker there was a "protector." Meanwhile, the Germans promised to exempt the children and sick relatives of the privileged. As a result, the quotas demanded by the Germans were difficult to deliver.

On September 4, 1942, the Jews were summoned to a meeting at the fire brigade square. Among those who spoke were Attorney Stasiek Yakobson, David Warshawsky, and the Old Man, M.Ch.R.

Rumkowski asked, demanded, and begged the Jews to deliver the children to the Germans; he informed us that the Germans had promised that those who remained in the ghetto would continue to work. I did not see Rumkowski on that occasion, but a great deal was said about it later. It was a historic speech, and to our heartfelt sorrow, the Old Man took it upon himself to conduct the *action* with the aid of the Jewish police. The children who were exempt were kept at 37 Lagiewnicka, while the children meant to go on the transports were next door, at 36 Lagiewnicka. The two buildings were separated by only one number, but that number made the difference between life and death.

On September 5, the Sabbath, an order was issued expressly forbidding anyone to go out into the streets until further notice. We panicked like madmen. Some who had not gotten their food rations were afraid that they would starve to death; these disregarded the order and ran to distribution points. Others were restless; unable to stay at home, they wandered the streets aimlessly. Still others went to friends for advice. The two bridges connecting each half of the ghetto were filled with swarms of people, and from below, the bridges looked as if they were twin peaks enshrouded in a black cloud. By curfew time everyone returned to his home; the "action" had begun. The Jewish police initiated it by taking the elderly out of the old-folks' homes, and by removing the children from the orphanages.

In the building next to ours at 30 Franciszkanska Street there was an orphanage for infants. It was forbidden to draw the curtains or peer out of the windows, but I did this. I saw how the Germans threw babies out of windows, directly into the waiting truck. If the nurse managed to catch a child, the fall was "soft." The children cried and screamed, but all we could do was watch and weep.

The familiar shout: "All Jews out!" was heard throughout our yard. *Selection.* We passed in front of a man in the Gestapo. Some were waved to the right, and some to the left. The sick and weak and the children went to the left. At this time, Buba was with Gutka and Yisrael at their place....We girls had painted our cheeks before going into the yard. We were directed to the right, and all of us returned.

This form of "selection" marked the beginning of a new tactic for deportation. The Germans worked with vigor, and some Jews helped....A procession of all the Jews in the Ghetto Lodz was made to walk past Bibov and his aides. They conducted house-to-house selections, and signaled their intentions by firing a shot in the yard. There was no longer any criterion by which we could determine who would go and who would stay. Once a person went because his face was pale; another time because it was ruddy. Once because he had a beard, and once because his nose was crooked; once because of beauty, and once because of ugliness. The fate of a Jew depended on the flick of a finger. In some instances, when all of the residents of a given building were taken, we were told that they remained quite calm.

There were many victims during the implementation of these raids for deportation. The Germans shot people without hesitation, and not only those who resisted. It was enough for an individual to err in understanding an order....People died in their houses before coming down into the yard—some of fear and some of hunger. And then, there were those who committed suicide. There were those who went mad.

The action lasted eight days and came to an end on September 12; quiet reigned in the streets, silence in the yards, and destruction in the homes. We began to lick our wounds, but at every turn the disaster that had befallen us was revealed.

Zlatka Bornstein came to us and wept: "They took my two children. What can be done? Isser is a big boy; he can work." Yes, indeed. Isser was all of two-and-a-half years of age.

Until the *Sperre,* I did not know that a person could see children thrown out of windows and not go blind. I did not know that it was possible to hear the weeping of mothers whose children were forever lost and not go deaf. I did not know that it was possible to comfort and embrace the parents of the children who had been taken from them and not turn to stone. Even they themselves did not turn to stone—meaning that everything is possible.

…And the arm of the Nazis was still uplifted….Our girlfriends came to say that their parents had been taken. Brothers cried for their sisters. There were the "volunteers" who had decided to follow their families…

That September 12, 1942, Bibov signed a proclamation stating that the action had been completed, and that all those who remained were to report for work. That same day, the Old Man issued a notice in which he again promised better nutrition and improved conditions. He demanded the surrender of the food coupons of those who had left the ghetto, and he shut and sealed their houses to "preserve them from destruction and looting" until their return.

# Between the *Sperre* and the Liquidation

Many months passed before things calmed down. People went back to work, continued to be hungry, and death thinned out the population. Summer ended; winter returned. It was not an especially harsh winter, but within the ghetto we were consumed by epidemics, among them typhoid. At our house Gutka was the first to fall ill, and after her, Helunia. The healthy cared for the sick in shifts around the clock. In that way, we could continue to work. Our friends fell ill, too.

I supplied what was needed for the sick, and confess that I asked for help in high places. For the first time I asked my boss, and he responded with pleasure; I asked Mrs. Prezes, and she did not refuse me; I asked Yitzhak Ross for calcium injections; and I asked Zilberstein, the tailor, who helped many people. I obtained sugar, rice, tea, and even a lemon. (The lemon came from Zilberstein.) I divided what I got into three parts: one for Gutka, one for Helunia, and one for Henia—Sara Stern's sister, who was also ill.

One day Sara Stern came to tell me that Henia was dangerously anemic and needed blood. We went to the hospital together and I donated a unit of blood. The next day Gutka's doctor reported that she had to have a transfusion, and I donated a unit for her as well. For the time being, Gutka, Helunia, and Henia recovered.

# Three Sketches

## Sketch One: Mark Feder

Mark Feder was a man of few words, but he always made sense. Periodically, I encouraged him to share his views with me about happenings in the ghetto. He was a member of the Left *Poale-Tzion* and although he did not work, he "came to work" every day. He did not do anything, it seemed, but this did not bother him. Mark entered the office I shared with Flash, stood by the oven, warmed his hands, left for an hour or two, and then returned—and all this was with the knowledge of our manager, Kaufman. For years, this is how he passed "his working days." From time to time, he smoked a cigarette between nicotine-stained fingertips.

After the great curfew, Mark stood by the oven even though it was warm at the time. He chewed on his yellowed nails as I asked: "What do you think of the Old Man's speech? What right did he have to ask mothers to give up their children?" A torrent came out of my mouth. I felt that perhaps I had embarrassed him and that I had made him uncomfortable, but he "owed me an answer," and this time silence would not do.

"Miss Citrinovna," he said. "We are isolated. We are hermetically sealed into the ghetto. We have no contact with the outside world. Our only weapon is time. The year is nineteen forty-two. The war has raged for three years, but this is not a war over a region; it is a war between mighty forces. Whoever wins, will rule the world. If our enemies win, it will be the end of the entire civilized world—and, of course, our end as well. I believe that the world of light will win, and within it—I hope—our existence will be assured.

"We must fight with all possible means. Unfortunately, all we have is time. Sooner or later, the war will come to an end. I do not know whether or not I would do what M.Ch.R. has done, but I have no right to criticize him. It would be difficult for me to step into his shoes. My shoes are too narrow for me; they bother me when I stand here, in the Kitchens' Office, to make sure that my relatives, friends, and comrades do not show up on the lists for the transports to God knows where.

"I do not always accomplish my objective, even though I am on guard faithfully. I do not know the people who are being deported according to the lists. I suppose I would not be able to remain silent if somewhere on the list there appeared the beautiful black eyes of a girl I recognized, if the face of my friend's son appeared. He is a prodigy; he should be protected—so we think now. This distorts, because everything distorts. We are all important and we are all impotent; we are all in the same boat. The storm has thrown us into the sea. We must avoid the sharks. We must swim in the direction which appears to be the shortest distance to the shore."

## Sketch Two: Comrade Wolynsky

Comrade Wolynsky was tall and stooped over. He wore spectacles with double and triple lenses, and he had a way of examining every nook and cranny. It was his job to manage a kitchen at the Metal Division, and we office workers only saw him when he needed something for that kitchen or its workers. Still, he attended every meeting we held to deal with matters concerning internal aid for the office.

Wolynsky, like Feder, was a member of *Poale-Tzion*. He did not hesitate to ask for aid coupons or injections in order to help the needy in his kitchen, and he himself distributed whatever he was able to obtain. He was a sworn pessimist, and he did not believe in anything that could make things easier for him. Once he revealed to me that he knew what was being done to the Jews outside the ghetto. "Sooner or later, the Germans will finish us off; meanwhile I cannot be hungry. I cannot. I also cannot die." While he said these things, his straight, thin hair stood up on end like the mane of a wild horse. He then picked up the coupons for potato peels I had given him for his workers, and left.

## Sketch Three: The Lembergs

The Nazis liquidated the Jewish settlements in the vicinity, but they conducted selections first and sent the stronger persons to the ghetto. They came from Pabjanice, Zgierz, Ozorkow, and Zdunska Wola. Among them was the family of Berzek Dov Lemberg: his sister Renia, and his mother, Frieda.

Despite my strong desire to describe how they looked when they arrived or when they were absorbed into ghetto life, I only can visualize them hovering over the valley of the spirits. Still, deep within my heart there remains that marvelous feeling I once had for them. They were like figures in a fairy tale to me, and I am convinced others thought so as well. They inspired respect, and I recall entering their home with reverence.

The Lembergs arrived without the head of the family, Dr. Yaakov Lemberg, who had served as the elder of the Jews in the ghetto of Zdunska Wola. When the Germans demanded that he supply them with ten hostages to be hanged in a public execution to be held in the marketplace, Dr. Lemberg offered himself and his family as the first four victims to die. From that time on, no trace of him has been found. All we know is that he never reached Lodz.

Mrs. Lemberg was an aristocratic woman who bore everything that befell her with dignity. I can testify to the fact that I never saw her sad, and that the joy of life never left her. Renia devoured books, and was an engrossing conversationalist, but it is difficult to see her apart from Dov Berzek, even as it is difficult to see him apart from his friends. To this day, I think of Berzek as being alive. I cannot do otherwise. When he arrived, he immediately joined the youth movement. From the start, he behaved as if he always had been an integral part of the group. He became the movement's representative, its leader, and its spokesman. He was a weaver of dreams who believed in a better tomorrow, and he had a boundless imagination. He knew how to give unstintingly of himself and he had an easy temperament, bursting with love. His presence dispelled sorrow. I recall that he sang Hasidic and love songs, and the folk songs of many peoples; that he danced a dizzying hora, and that he loved both folk and ballroom dances. He was a gentleman, a brother, and a friend.

After the war, reality separated Berzek from many of our friends. We saw him as if from afar. He smiled a mysterious smile that implied so much, but he did not say anything; his lips were sealed. We knew that he was swimming in a large ocean toward some destination; we knew that he was acting modestly and in silence. We were certain that he was on some sort of a mission, and that he fully intended to achieve his goal.

…We did not know about Dov Berzek's role in bringing Chaim Widowski's body to Israel, but I learned some of the details of Berzek's activities when he delivered the eulogy for our comrade.…

Berzek had appeared among us like good tidings, and disappeared like a spark into infinity.

# The Seder at
# 30 Franciszkanska

All the furniture had been removed from the room, and it suddenly seemed very large. Friends brought benches from the nearby school, and the youngsters prepared the decorations. Small blue and white flags were attached to string and stretched across the room. The lampshade was decorated with flags and the walls with Stars of David.

Mrs. Berman, a *Hatechiya* member, prepared delicacies from potato peels, and Arek Yakobson prepared the program for the evening. Leizer Neuman read from the *Haggadah,* and Grabowski sang *Vio, Vio, Susati.* People recently arrived from the outlying districts were invited, among them the Lembergs, Fishman from Ozorkow, and all those who were active in the Zionist movement and were homeless.

Chaim Widowski flit about like Charlie Chaplin, bringing cheer to the refugees. He told stories, wore white shirts in the manner of the men's *kittel,* and frequently hitched up his trousers, which fell much more often than usual.

Our comrades kept constant watch outside, and patrolled the intersection of Brzezinska-Franciszkanska up to the entrance of the house. Because gatherings were forbidden, all of us were in mortal danger. Nevertheless, the entire Zionist leadership of the Lodz ghetto was there: that is to say, all those who survived the liquidation of the ghetto periphery.

94

The following are among those who were there: Aharon Yakobson's father with his wife, a veteran Zionist, idealist, and member of the *Hatechiya* executive before the war; Comrade Warshawchik, Secretary of *Hatechiya,* the man who carried out all the office work before the war; Elimelech Shiffer and his wife, both of whom were on the executive board; Yisrael Tabakesblatt, a member of the executive, and his wife Manya; Shmuel Lippel, Moshkowitz, and the Leizerowitz family; and Shammai Rosenblum and Grabowsky, both of whom sang and recited. In short, everyone who had been invited came. No one wanted to miss this opportunity, and the house filled completely. The youngsters stood around the tables, in the kitchen, in the hall, and in every corner.

The *Kiddush* delivered by Rav Eliezer Lozer wafted in the air. Silence fell, as if not a soul was there....We drew special meaning and inspiration from the words: "Blessed art Thou, O Lord our God, King of the Universe, who hast chosen us from all peoples, and exalted us above all tongues, and sanctified us by Thy commandments. And thou hast given us this feast of *matzot,* the season of our freedom and holy convocation, as a memorial of the departure from Egypt."

The tables were set "according to tradition." We used beet borscht for wine, *matzot* were on the table, and a *charosset* was made out of potato peels. We had *karpas* in the form of kohlrabi, and other dishes as well—some prepared by the skilled hand of Comrade Berman, and some brought in from the kitchen of the Zionist movement.

The song *Ho Lachma Anya,* "This is the Bread of our Affliction," reverberated in the room. A feeling of freedom, hope, and joy filled our souls and raised our spirits as we sang and read from the *Haggadah.* When Shammai Rosenblum sang *On a sheine zummer nacht,* "On a Beautiful Summer Night," everyone joined in the refrain. All in all, it was a wonderful holiday atmosphere. We dressed up; we visited; and we felt as if we just then had been freed from slavery. What a sight! The room, the drinking of the "wine,"

the *matzot,* the *Haggadah,* the happy faces, the reverberating songs!
Who knows? Perhaps such things kept us alive; perhaps they reinforced us in those difficult times.

Suddenly we heard a knock on the door. I approached and
looked out. A tall figure, whom I recognized at once, stood there. It
was "Pan" Goldstein, one of the Kripo collaborators. I opened the
door, and he entered. Everyone knew the significance of his visit,
but the singing continued as if nothing had happened. Goldstein
asked if he could stay, and permission was granted. He stood at the
side, in the hall, and posted himself as if he were one of the guards.

The ceremony continued. I sang:

*Gey ich azoy zich shon wochen chodoshim*
*Arum in die gassen biz shpet in der nacht*
*Un ich zuch altz a mittel ich zol kennen fargessen*
*As ich vel vie nechten haint vider nisht essen*

*Gey ich azoy zich un kler mir un tracht*
*Gey ich azoy zich un kler mir un tracht*

*Falt mir ein plitzling ich vel hint in gas tzilen*
*Ferhanten hint vos loifen hungerig arum*
*Ferhan hint baputzte mit markes un gleklach*
*Ferhan hint ferdarte vos zehen ois sherklach*

*Gey ich azoy zich un kler mir un tracht*
*Gey ich azoy zich un kler mir un tracht*

*Vi of lehachis dem shotn a shpitzel*
*A hund shteit un griziet a trukenen bein*
*Bald kumm a zweiter, sei nemen zich beisen*
*Vil einer dem zweitem dem bein aroisrissen*

*Gey ich azoy zich un kler mir un tracht*
*Gey ich azoy zich un kler mir un tracht*

I go about for weeks and for months
Circling the streets until late at night
Searching for a way to be able to forget
That today, just like yesterday, I won't eat

I go about thinking and thinking
I go about thinking and thinking

Suddenly I think of counting the dogs in the street
There are those who run about hungry
There are those who wear a collar and a bell
There are those who are starved and look horrible

I go about thinking and thinking
I go about thinking and thinking

Like a satanic trick to make one angry
A dog stands gnawing at a dried-out bone
And here is another, and they bite each other
One trying to wrest the bone from the other

I go about thinking and thinking
I go about thinking and thinking

The guards who had been on duty came indoors and were replaced by other comrades. We opened the door for Elijah the Prophet, and kept it open until the last guest had left at about midnight. We had spent the night as free people; for a moment in time we had forgotten the curfew. We had no problems because of "Pan" Goldstein. He, too, was a party to our "crime." He, too, was present at the *Seder*.

# Zosia, Yehuda, and the Kripo

September, 1943. The mood in the ghetto is dark; we are depressed and in despair. The lists are made up; the deportations continue. We break down. We get ill. We commit suicide. No night passes without a house search. The Jewish police act in accord with the lists; the Deportation Committee, which consists of the "important people" in the ghetto, use methods like those of the Germans.

The laws of nature do not change. In rags and in clogs—and even after pushing an excrement cart by day—the couples manage to meet at night. Love blooms. The young wear the best of the clothes that remain to them. If both work, they generally decide to unite. It is easier. Youth and love are what decide. In spite of everything, many weddings take place, and Zosia and Yehuda are among those who decide to marry.

Yehuda worked in the carpentry shop managed by Rosner, and Zosia worked in the kitchen. *This was truly a dowry of the "rich."* They loved one another, and they were young and beautiful. Yehuda's parents were still strong, they worked and received their daily soup. Yehuda's brother was employed as well.

Rumkowski was the only one who performed marriages in those days; he was the only one permitted to raise the *chuppah,* and the only one to say the blessings. He approved Zosia's request to marry and he set the date for the ceremony. Due to pressing circumstances, Rumkowski scheduled several ceremonies to take place at the same time.

Zosia's and Yehuda's witnesses were Pinchas Gershowsky, the

famous philanthropist of Poland-Lodz before the war, and Chaim Widowski, our dear friend. The *chuppah* took place on September 26, 1943 at the school on Franciszkanska Street, and the newlyweds received two loaves of bread, sugar, oil, and potatoes. Most importantly, they were given separate quarters in which to live at 21 Wolborska Street....There was no need to notify our parents. We had no address for them, but later on we learned that they had been deported and killed in Treblinka....That day we did not have a party; there was nothing to serve.

Zosia and Yehuda made their home a new meeting place for the youth, and there were now two places in which to gather: our place on Franciszkanska Street, and theirs on Wolborska. The youth bolted the shutters and listened to music. Outside their window, an armed German guard made the rounds. Barbed-wire fences which separated the ghetto from the city did not stop them from living their lives in a house right on the border.

When a healthy man was summoned to the Kripo offices, he left them seriously wounded and literally broken. The backbone and ribs were broken; the arms and legs were broken. Fingernails were extracted, and head wounds or skull fractures were inflicted. Sometimes the healthy man became a corpse.

One day, quite by chance, I happened to be at home. It was afternoon when a pale and restless Zosia came to the door. When I asked her what happened, she said: "Yehuda is in the Kripo."

Anyone who spent any time in the ghetto knows the meaning of Kripo; knows the fear and terror of the entry gate to the kingdom of death. If a person had the choice of either going to Kripo or dying, he surely would choose death—but the choice was never given. Kripo simply came and claimed its victim. This time, they came for Yehuda.

I thought ceaselessly about what to do and whom to see, but I did not have any connections or acquaintances among the Jews who worked there in standard jobs. My only recourse was to worry: What do they want of Yehuda? Who denounced him?

Zosia and I decided to go to Yehuda's parents. They were frightened and ready to give whatever they had to save their son. Unfortunately, they had nothing other than a gold fountain pen and, of course, they were ready to give that. Meanwhile, Yehuda was being tortured. We fell silent. We could not say anything to the worried parents.

Waiting at home for us were Chaim Widowski and Shmuel Lippel, with whom we discussed the matter. Chaim said: "One thing is clear. The gold fountain pen should not be mentioned, lest the Germans interpret it to mean that the parents are ready to give the pen because of the beatings. They will think that the Jews generally begin by offering a trifle, but that additional blows will move them to give more." Chaim claimed that if Yehuda had once said that he had nothing, he could not change his story. What is more, it was the truth.

That very evening we decided to consult with Shlomo Uberbaum, a member of the Executive, representative of the Revisionist movement, and our close friend. He heard our story and said: "Let us see. Perhaps we should go to Zilberstein tomorrow. He makes suits for the Germans in Kripo, and he is a very decent fellow. Let us go, and see." We arranged to do so the following evening.

Zilberstein's house was circled by a garden, and in that garden a table and chair had been placed under a tree. It was autumn, and leaves rustled underfoot as Mrs. Zilberstein ushered us into a warm, pleasant home.

The Zilbersteins had guests—people whom I had never met and whose names I did not know—but we were invited to join them at the table. We talked over a cup of real tea and cookies. I was amazed at how lovely it was, but I also was embarrassed. Afterwards, we went out to the garden. Some of the guests sat by the table, but others secluded themselves. Shlomo began: "Mr. Zilberstein, Riva has a matter for you." "Come," said Zilberstein. "Let us sit here, you and I." He directed me to a small bench for two. I felt uncomfortable; I thought of my purpose for being there, and I wondered why he should want to help me. "I know, Mr. Zilberstein," I began, "that you owe me nothing at all. I know that every day and every hour someone asks you to intervene on his behalf; I also know that it is not an easy thing to lobby with your supervisor, but I have no other way. I am speaking about my brother-in-law, who is very close to me. In addition, I promise you that he has nothing to give, and therefore the beatings will not do any good. They can only lead to one result, and I am so afraid." Without promising anything, Zilberstein said: "I heard you." After that, we both stood up and joined the other guests. The next day, Yehuda returned home. He required a week of intensive care in order to be able to function.

After some time, Shlomo asked: "Riva, how did you manage to influence Zilberstein? When I spoke to him, he said: 'This girl did not demand, did not request, did not beg, but when I heard her, I knew I could not refuse her. I felt a kind of obligation...'"

After the war, I saw Zilberstein in Paris. It was difficult to recognize him, and even harder to speak to him. I did not mention his act of charity. My impression was that he was unable to remember anything; that he was lonely and confused.

Zilberstein was one of those who had enough to eat in the ghetto; in spite of it, I look upon him as one of the thirty-six righteous.

# Lolka

I did not spend much time at home. I went to work early in the morning, and after work I visited the sick. I brought with me whatever I could, even though not much was available…We girls took turns visiting the sick, and there were many who needed us.

One day I happened to return home earlier than usual. Standing in the kitchen was a girl of about eleven, thin and small, washing potato peels. "What is your name? What are you doing here and how did you get here?" "I am Lolka; I brought potato peels, and I work with Zosia," she said. "I was here yesterday and saw that you have nothing to eat, so I decided to bring the peels. At least, you have that coming to you…" This little girl is looking for justice, I thought.

Lolka became a part of our family, with one exception. Each night she returned to her widowed mother. In time, however, Lolka decided that we ought to meet her. We discovered a modest, virtuous, and religious woman; a woman short of stature, with a noble face and bright eyes. "I came to thank you," she said. "Why do you want to thank me?" I asked, and Mrs. Wroclawsky answered: "For the warm home you are providing for my daughter." She was very moved. "I believe we will yet see better days than these," she went on. "God certainly will reward you." I saw that she trembled, and that she lacked the strength to utter the words she wished to say. I tried to calm her. *"Ssh,* lady; *ssh,"* I said.

Mrs. Wroclawsky collected herself: "For some time I have wanted to go willingly with my entire family. I do not believe the

Germans will kill us, but whatever happens to the people of Israel will be our fate as well. My daughter Lolka does not want to go. She wants to stay with you. She says that there are no other such people in the world."

I recognized Lolka's style in her mother's words. "Please, madam," I replied. "We have nothing to say. As long as we can stay in the ghetto, we will do so. This is our decision. If we are forced to go, we will go, but we will try to stay together." And indeed, so it was. When the time came, all of us left together.

When we reached Marysin after leaving the cellar with our possessions, we were joined by the Wroclawskys: Lolka's mother; her brother, Joseph; and her sister, Marilka. Tired, sad, and noble, they came to us as if we were their salvation. They came laden with bundles on their backs and in their hands.

Marilka stood out. She was a beautiful blue-eyed girl who moved with agility and grace. She was a girl whose golden hair spilled across her forehead in silken strands; a girl whose knowing laugh made it evident that she grasped things very rapidly. That laughter was a ray of light in a darkness that was blacker than black.

# Chaim Widowski

I have been silent for a long time. I needed the passage of over forty years to be able to write about Chaim, my friend, my guide, and my teacher. The two of us became especially close in the ghetto—Chaim, Shmuel Lippel, and I were always together and never did anything without consulting one another. In the morning, Chaim came to take me to work; in the evening, he came to take me to the Executive meetings and to listen to the radio broadcasts. These broadcasts were heard at 36 Wolborska Street, in the home of Altschuler—our comrade from *Hatechiya*—who was one of those caught during the raids on the "listeners," and was never seen or heard from again.

Before hearing my first broadcast, Chaim prepared me for what was to follow. I do not remember the precise words he used, but the content of what he said is still fresh in my mind: "Do not speak to me during the broadcast. Do not ask questions. Observe total silence. If a single word is missed and not heard, the entire broadcast may not be understood. They broadcast without stopping, and do not repeat anything. At the end of the news, there is no one to whom we can direct our questions. We merely shut off the receiver and remain silent."

The first broadcast I heard took place in January, 1944, and was unforgettable. The sun had set at the end of a frosty, clear winter day, and I accompanied Chaim with indescribable awe. We went up a flight of rickety wooden steps until we reached the attic. The stairs creaked under my feet, and then we entered a place strewn with old junk. From out of this pile of junk and as if by magic, Chaim produced earphones for each of us. He helped me with mine before putting on his own. We listened, and my heart pounded.

The announcer spoke in Polish and reported news about the Allies, but I admit I did not understand everything. When the broadcast was over, we did not speak. Chaim held my hand, turned me toward the tiny attic window, and pointed. The street lights illuminated snow-covered barbed wire fences, and I saw the play of light and shadow within the homes of those who lived outside of the ghetto. Below, the streets were empty with the exception of an armed German guard, who paced to-and-fro in measured strides. He was so near that I heard the sound of his footsteps. Suddenly, Chaim said: *"Mir hoben zei in drerd,"* "They stand so near, but we hear the news from afar under their very noses." I was stunned, but Chaim laughed with his eyes only.

When we were outside, Chaim explained many things to me: the significance of the Montgomery Plan and who Montgomery was; the meaning of the second front in Europe, etc. I confess I did not understand the details. I only understood that he was pleased with what he had heard. It now seems to me that he spoke of the "invasion by the Allies," but I am not quite sure about this.

Chaim behaved as if nothing had happened, and we went straight to my house. We met with Lippel, who was waiting for us, and Chaim reported the news.

Chaim listened to the news twice a day, but around 11:30, he appeared at my workplace. Shlomo Kaufman and the rest of us awaited his arrival impatiently and gathered in my little room to hear what he had to say. Between one sentence and another, Chaim hitched up his pants to keep them from falling. This was so characteristic of him, that some humorously tagged him *Chaim hoyzenzier,* or Chaim, the pants puller.

Chaim was not the only Jew to monitor the radio. Others also knew how to breathe life into even those who seemed to be mere ghosts wrapped in rags. Starved and swollen, the sick who were unable to move were happy to hear that the end of the war was approaching. There were those who died when the faith in redemption, like an invisible hand, closed their eyelids. Such was the activity of the news spreaders, Chaim among them.

D-Day, June 6, 1944,—the Allied invasion of Normandy in northern France—was a day just like any other day in the ghetto. Toward evening, Chaim appeared at Franciszkanska Street for our daily meeting. His face was somber, and it was very clear to us that something extraordinary had happened. (Helunia Tannenbaum, who now lives in the United States, was there at the time.) "They are looking for me," he said. "I have to get out of here as soon as possible." He removed the ring from his finger, took out his wallet, placed its contents—money, documents and personal things—before us, and went on: "Give these to my sister. Promise that you will take care of her."

It was after six and the curfew was in force, but Chaim and I went to Marysin, which bordered on the cemetery, and to Gutka's house. She was alone since her husband worked on the night shift, and I left Chaim with her. Helunia had waited for Lippel as we had asked, and they were both at home when I arrived.

Lippel and I were on duty, and could move about in relative safety during curfew. We therefore returned to Chaim, but on the way we started at shadows and the sound of every falling leaf or the croaking of a frog. We heard our footsteps, breath and pounding hearts. Out of the dark and essentially-silent night, we also heard the sound of galloping horses and the squeaking of carriage wheels turning on their shafts. Someone was looking for us.

A carriage approached and in it were Ribovsky, a Jew who worked for the Kripo; Neumann, of the Sonderkommando, a Jew as well; and our friend, Shlomo Redlich, a radio listener who had been caught by the Germans. Shlomo, a veteran Zionist, brightened upon seeing us, in the belief that his salvation was near. Trusting the Germans to "free him" if he helped them find Chaim dead or alive, he begged and even pressured us to betray Chaim's whereabouts. In that vain hope, he had given the Germans our names and had identified us as those closest to him.

Ribovsky, a moderate, quiet man, asked penetrating questions, but Lippel and I had coordinated our story beforehand: Chaim threatened to commit suicide, we were worried about him, and we had gone out to look for him. When Ribovsky asked where we thought Chaim might be, Lippel and I mentioned several places— among them were the houses of Mitek Lizarovich, who lived at one end of Marysin; and that of our *Techiya* comrade, Moshkovitz, who lived at the other end. Within moments, all of us became a "search party." Ribovsky and his entourage traveled in one direction, and Lippel and I traveled in the other. First, of course, I went to see my sister so that I could warn Chaim; Lippel, meanwhile, remained outside as the lookout.

I found Chaim holding a cup of chicory with saccharin; one shoe was off—so perhaps he had intended to lie down. Chaim immediately put the cup on the table, and we hurried out with Chaim holding on to one shoe. We knew the neighborhood well, and stopped by an abandoned house that was not far. Chaim sat on the doorstep and, between us, we arranged that he was to wait for me or for Lippel. I returned to Lippel, who in the meanwhile had visited one of the addresses we had given to Ribovsky, and once more we heard the sound of the approaching carriage. Ribovsky had arrived and addressed me: "Miss Citrinovna, I heard that your sister lives in Marysin." "Yes," I said. "We want to go there; maybe Chaim is with her." "Certainly," I replied, "but I would like to enter first; I want to tell her that you are a Jew, even if you do not wear the yellow star. She may become frightened."

Ribovsky agreed to my request, and I entered Gutka's house alone. I asked her to be strong, and to answer all questions by saying that Chaim had not been there; I also let her know that Ribovsky was a Jew. After that, I left and returned with him. Gutka proved equal to the task and answered Ribovsky's questions—all the while frightened and shaking like a leaf. "I did not see," "I did not hear,"

"Chaim was not here," she cried. We left, but after several seconds, Ribovsky wanted to speak to her alone. Several minutes later he came back and said: "Your sister has told me that Chaim was here two hours ago." I protested that I knew nothing. "You must do what you think is right," I said. "In that case," replied Ribovsky, "I will ask you to give Chaim a warrant to report to the *Kriminal Polizei* tomorrow morning at nine."

I was not happy with his suggestion, and said so. "I cannot accept this notice. I do not know if I will find him by tomorrow morning, and taking the note entails an obligation. Do you want to place this responsibility on me, Mr. Ribovsky?" Perhaps my response had impressed him, because he looked at his watch and said: "It is two in the morning. Go home." "Mr. Ribovsky, permit me to go in to my sister," I asked. "You can understand that she is frightened." "Yes, why not," he replied. I returned to Gutka, and Lippel again stood guard; Ribovsky might return.

At four that morning I went to Chaim and found him in very bad shape; he trembled on account of the cold, and he had a tie wrapped around his neck. "I gave myself another half-hour to wait for you; after that, I would not have been found alive," he said. Dawn came. The skies were gray. We went back to Gutka's. Chaim was given a large overcoat, the collar of which hid his face, and we started out. In a little while we arrived at a relative of Chaim's, who lived in a yard that connected two houses on two streets: Drewnowska and Podrzeczna.

From that moment at dawn on June 7, 1944, Chaim Widowski went underground. For three days he stayed in a cellar. During that time, Chaim asked for help—unequivocal help. He knew he could not withstand torture, and was afraid of betraying his comrades; he knew that there was no hope of escape, and that his fate had been sealed.

I consulted with Shlomo Oberbaum, a moderate man from the Zionist Executive. He agreed with Chaim, and I went into action. I went to a pharmacy where a man named Kahana, whom I had not met previously, worked. I believed that Kahana would be prepared to help us. When I left the pharmacy I knew that this was not the way. I knew that someone had to be ready to put his life on the line. Meanwhile, Helunia and I took turns bringing food to Chaim, and the tension grew in the ghetto. The search for Chaim intensified, and the Sonderkommando visited our house and the Lippels' quite frequently. Since no one other than Helunia and I knew anything, the "investigators" failed to achieve their goal. It never occurred to them to question Helunia, and I kept out of sight.

On the day before the last day of Chaim's life, the Sonder-kommando came to Shlomek Oberbaum and said that they wanted Chaim dead or alive; otherwise they would arrest the entire Zionist Executive. Shlomek transmitted this message to me. I contacted Dr. Orbach, my friend at 11 Brzezinska, some time after my unsat-isfactory visit with Kahana, and he encouraged me; he agreed with Chaim, and was prepared to help. Dr. Michal Orbach, may his soul rest in peace, contacted one of his patients who worked in the metal department under Chimovitz, and asked him to obtain cyanide. Orbach promised me that the poison killed instantly, without caus-ing suffering, and I asked him to get enough for three: Chaim, Helunia, and me. We were the only persons who knew where Chaim was, and we might need the cyanide too.

Everything happened with lightning speed. Dr. Orbach's con-tact agreed to help, and Helunia went to get the poison. The package was handed to me and we divided it. At nine o'clock the following morning, I awakened Chaim. He came out of the cellar, his face red, his eyes virtually shut, and he said: "You are witness to the fact that I devoted my entire life to my family and my friends. I want you to know that I know I have succeeded—I have succeeded in seeing the beginning of the end for the Nazis. The invasion of Normandy is the beginning of the end of the war." Chaim asked that we not forget him, and that if we could, transfer his remains to *Eretz Yisrael.*

We parted, and I went to work. This was on Friday. Around

eleven that same morning, the rumor that Chaim was no longer alive spread.

We found Chaim in the bathroom in the large yard between Drewnowska and Podrzeczna Streets. In his pockets were letters: letters to his family, his friends, and me. Ribovsky transferred all of them to me. As it so happened, however, Chaim left one letter with the relative in whose house he hid; that letter was later used by the relative as a means of blackmail. For a long time thereafter, this individual extorted from us our allotted bread for the entire household. Fortunately for us Shlomek helped us out of this predicament, and we were finally able to retrieve the letter. It was given to the friends for whom it was intended, and I took all the remaining letters with me to Auschwitz—but, of course, they were lost.

Unlike others who disappeared without a trace, Chaim was given a Jewish burial. Friends, including Dov Berzek, brought his body to *Eretz Yisrael* in accord with his wish, and he was buried in the *Nahlat Yitzhak* cemetery on May 17, 1979. Inscribed on his tombstone are the names of all the radio listeners in the Lodz ghetto, and it now serves as a memorial to the heroes of the ghetto who worked in the underground.

Chaim gave his life in service to his supreme values; in the giving of that life, he saved the lives of his friends. He knew how to remain clear of delusion and false hope. He knew that his end would come one way or another, and he did not believe the Germans who promised that if he came forward, he would come to no harm. He never ceased thinking; not even for a moment.

Chaim's suicide changed things; after three days of unbelievable tension, his friends and the inhabitants of the ghetto were able to relax.

# The Final Deportation

A new deportation notice was issued by the Germans for twenty-five thousand additional Jews, and the noose tightened. Shlomo Kaufman was asked to go to Balucki Rynek—to the "President," Rumkowski. He returned in under an hour, a sad—very sad—man. An urgent meeting was called. Shlomo gave his report and all those who were there paid careful attention. More transports, and again more lists! *We cannot do this. We refuse.* This was our attitude.

Kaufman decided to go back to Rumkowski. When he returned he was white as a sheet, and we were still in our seats. "Comrades," he said, "I want to repeat Rumkowski's words, word for word: 'If you do not submit lists, you will go first—at the head.'" We scarcely had an opportunity to react when the loudspeakers blared: "It is forbidden to be in the streets. Everyone must go into the yard when the order is given." It had happened so swiftly that frenzy gripped everyone, including me.

The order to go to the yard came and we were instructed to sit. We went and we sat. *Selection.* When the selection was over we were permitted to go to the office, but all of us wanted to go home to find out what was happening there. To this day I do not know how I managed to get from the office into the yard, and from there to Devorska Street.

The street was empty. Gripped by anxiety, I ran in the direction of home. From Devorska Street, I crossed the road and reached a yard. Suddenly, a policeman's cap appeared. I threw myself against

the opposite fence without being observed, and succeeded in dart-
ing into the stairwell. It was a good lookout point. The policeman
moved away, and I went out again. I managed to reach another yard
closer to home. Policemen cropped up like mushrooms after rain.
Again, a policeman; this time, an acquaintance who stood over me.
I crawled until I reached another stairwell. It was totally dark. The
policeman came to me where I was and whispered: "Go upstairs.
Hurry!" I went up a flight and then I heard the boots and the
screams so familiar to me: "All Jews out!" A shot was fired in air;
and a question was asked: "Is anyone else in the building?" "No
one, Mr. Officer," replied the Jewish policeman.

What a shame that I do not know the name of my benefactor—
but as I write, I think that pure souls also hid under the caps of the
Jewish police. The accepted view that every policeman collaborated
with the Germans is not a universal truth.

I crawled from stone to board, from threshold to attic, until I
reached home. The curfew was over. The entire family was there,
and it was still twilight. A large pot of potato peels stood on the
stove, and my head began to spin. I was hungry....We ate heartily
and all of us together, but we were silent; we knew the situation.
We had been spared, however the question that hung in air was:
"And what now?" Shmuel Lippel knocked on the door and entered.
Helunia's friend, Novak, came next. That night, for the first time,
all of us discussed the idea of going into hiding.

The Germans demanded another seven thousand Jews.

In the yard of the Kitchens' Office, below and across, was the
department managed by Obogov. Etka Fried and all the workers
there, including Obogov himself, were my friends. Since Obogov
was a Polish patriot and claimed he had contact with the Polish
underground, I tried to find out what could be done. Does Obogov
have weapons? If so, I wanted us to kill Bibov. I argued that it
would not be hard to kill a German. What alternative did we have?

What could we lose? I spoke to Aharon Yakobson and to Dov Lemberg, but there was nothing. We had no weapons and we were utterly helpless.

Obogov alone was not negative. He smiled ambivalently and said, "We will see," "We will do," and so on…

*Two Jewish policeman aid a man too frail to make it to the train that will take him to his death.*

*Unable or unwilling to integrate into the general population in the ghetto, a number of Czechoslovakian and German-Jewish refugees "volunteer" for deportation. They smile and mock those who remain behind and even express the view that nothing "could be worse" than Lodz, but their entire transport was gassed in Chelmno. End of 1941 or beginning of 1942.*

MENDEL GROSSMAN, PHOTOGRAPHER

*Liquidation of the ghetto: The last of the Jews are transported on August 28, 1944.*
MENDEL GROSSMAN, PHOTOGRAPHER

*Reflective, anxious, and weary, the Jews await the "readiness of the train" and the Germans' signal to board the transport that will lead most of them to death in Auschwitz or to other concentration/labor camps.* MENDEL GROSSMAN, PHOTOGRAPHER.

# The Broom Cellar

We knew we could not escape, but we determined to hide. We were not clever enough to have prepared, and we did not have a store of food. Meanwhile our child Buba, now almost five years old, fell ill. For her sake and for the first time, I asked Rumkowski to help me. The Old Man gave me a note which said: "200 grams of sugar." Yisrael, Gutka's husband, worked in a food store in Marysin, and he was able to get us a little food; Etka and Obogov also helped. I got nothing from the kitchen managers and dared not ask anything of anyone else.

We hid in the cellar at 4 Koscielny Square in the house of Heniek Lipinski, a friend of our friend, Lonya Lipschitz—with whom we lived. The cellar was filled completely with long straw brooms suitable for sweeping yards. We built walls out of the brooms and we covered the entrance to the cellar with brooms; in this manner, they acted as insulation. Bibov appealed to the masses, but no one paid attention to him any more.

We, who were in the Zionist movement, received notes from comrades which were hidden in prearranged places in returning railroad cars. In these, it was written that everyone was being taken to Auschwitz. One of the notes we received was from Rachelka Bohm, and is now at the *Kibbutz Lochamei Hagetaot Museum*. Shmuel Lippel's parents kept saying: "They are not killing everyone; they are not burning; they are not strangling; we do not believe it. We want to go. What is happening to everyone will happen to us, too." Meanwhile, total anarchy reigned in the ghetto. The Germans no longer trusted the Jewish police and only asked them to assist with unimportant things. They decided to carry out "resettlement" by themselves, and with their own hands they pulled the Jews out of their hiding places.

Thirty-three of us were down in that cellar. The single opening was covered with brooms throughout the day, and was opened only at night. It was stifling. We could not breathe. Hunger gnawed at us. Thirst burned us. There was barely room to lie down and there were differences of opinion between us, but we were disciplined. The darkness dulled both vision and thought and Buba alone was a bright star, a ray of hope, and a symbol of the future for us. We taught her her full name—Buba Dina Sachanowska—and hung a dog tag on her neck. Young as she was, she understood that she had to be silent; that our hiding place was in a central location, and that we could not risk detection.

No one knew how long we would have to remain in the cellar, and the tension mounted. Some argued that it was impossible to hold out much longer under such conditions. Others were prepared for the worst, and would do anything but leave; they believed that under no circumstances should we go out with the child, and vigorously opposed going willingly. Zosia and her husband, and Gutka and her husband agreed that whatever we do, we must all do together.

Esta, Bella, and I stood fast for as long as we could. We almost had a majority against going willingly to the "resettlement" camp, but in the end, it was fate that decided. Helunia fell ill with jaundice. We barely had any food, and water was difficult to get because the Germans had shut off the main water valves in the yard. Helunia's illness caused real pressure, but Shmuel's parents and their "logical arguments" influenced us, as well.

One day, in the midst of an argument over these matters, we heard German boots overhead. Buba whispered, "Gutush, the Germans," and shut her eyes as if blocking the vision of the boots we had heard. The Germans reached the cellar door, poked about with their rifles, listened, spoke among themselves, and fell silent. We heard them clearly, and we saw their rifle barrels; we held our breath, and we did not move. The darkness was all-consuming and the search seemed to be endless, but an "end to the endlessness" did come. The Germans left, and we remained silent out of fear that perhaps they were near. After dark, my brother-in-law and I left in order to get some water for everyone.

It was a moonlit night. The skies were clear. A tree someone had chopped down was lying on the ground, its shadow doubling it in size. I was terrified as our shadows accompanied us, eerily lengthening and shortening with each step, and I thought of Anjula in the flowering fruit garden. I was overwhelmed with emotion and lost my equilibrium, unaware that we had reached our destination and the life-giving tap. "Riva, what is the matter with you," asked Yisrael. "Look," he said, "someone was here. The earth is wet and the tap is not closed properly."

I heard the dripping and understood that we had to hurry. I washed the containers for our physiological needs, and Yisrael cleaned them as well. We worked in silence. I heard the flow of water: the stream was very, very noisy. We sated ourselves and walked back to the cellar as quickly as we could.

The wick of the kerosene lamp flickered in the dark. The girls placed a little food and a little water in the center of the room, and then we shifted the brooms and opened the window. Fresh air and moon rays entered, and with them a wisp of hope. Everyone ate a little—but Helunia, who had a fever, only asked for water. She said: "I will not get well here. This place will be my end..."

In the morning, Shmuel once more repeated his parents' argument that what will happen to everyone, will happen to us. It was a familiar story, but when we heard it this time we hesitated. Shmuel's parents were elderly, we had no food or medicine, Helunia was ill, and we had to consider Buba.

At that time we thought: "Well, really, how is it possible for the Germans to kill everyone? How could they be burning children?"

When Helunia said: "Nothing evil will befall Buba. Any murderer who looks into her big black eyes will surrender to her," it began to influence us.

*Another night? Another sortie from the cellar? More drinking water? What then?* We had no contact with anyone. We were cut off from the world; we had no idea of what was happening in the ghetto, and we did not know whether or not another Jew remained alive.

That night I did not sleep. Broomstalks pierced my flesh, the cellar was dark and silent, and everyone seemed to be dead. What a responsibility! What was I to decide? I bolted down the shutter of my feelings, and determined not to participate in the decision. By morning, however, a stream of thought ran through me. "They say they are gassing and burning everyone. I am so afraid of the unknown and hidden, the atrocity that may be the truth..."

A shawl of thick fog smothered my soul and stole my peace of mind. I knew so well that I would not be able to escape. I had to decide. No one saw me and no one heard me. Everyone was still, but they were waking up slowly. I got up, and when I hurled the words: "I am going" into the cellar space, I was both broken and exhausted.

There was no argument. Everyone knew all of us were going. We did not speak; we dressed, and left. The streets were empty, and we headed for the house on Franciszkanska Street. There we packed one bundle each. My bundle contained a winter blanket, the poems of Andzhe Sandik and Alter Shnur, Chaim Widowski's letters, photographs of my family and friends, my diary, and a present from Shmuel—a string of beads which he had brought with him from *Eretz Yisrael,* where he had been before the war.

The bundles of the others were similar. Thirty-three people left the broom cellar that day; four survived: Zosia, Helunia, Lolka, and I.

# From the Ghetto
# to the Camp

It was a clear day; the sun shone, the air was fresh. The bright light blinded our eyes as all of us walked together. We wore layer upon layer, and each of us carried a bundle. Stricken and beaten, we walked.

When we left the cellar we knew we would have to contend with hardship, but we did not believe that we would stand face-to-face with death. Those first moments of realization were therefore very difficult for us. We had no contact with or news from anyone, and like so many others we went "willingly," out of despair.

On the way I met Shmuel Rosenstein, who was the editor of *Ghetto Zeitung,* the ghetto newspaper. "*Nu,* Riva, why are you so sad? It's not the end of the world." I pointed to Buba, who wore her best dress and the ribbon Gutka so lovingly had tied in her hair. "What do you want? They will not do anything to her! She will go with you, and you will be able to care for her!" Helunia, who heard these words, cried: "You are right, sir! No one will be able to harm Buba once they look into her beautiful eyes!" Rosenstein went on his way and we went on ours.

*Wandering. Eternal aimless wandering of masses from one place to another...* The unknown loomed before us. The multitudes were crestfallen, starved, and sad; their eyes spoke into the strange silence that surrounded us all. Only the shuffling of feet could be heard— a trudging mass pulling along the old, the young, the women, and the children.

We reached the end of the road—a huge lot in front of the

railroad station in Marysin. It was not fenced in, but whoever entered never returned. The German police were armed with rifles and guarded the area well, but the Jewish policemen were there with truncheons. We were very careful; the Germans beat everyone indiscriminately.

The lot was very crowded, but every family had its own "sitting space." We relieved ourselves of our bundles, placed them on the ground, and sat in a circle. I looked around and saw a mass of mostly white heaps, both large and small; these were the bundles that did double duty as pillows. Women rested their heads on their husbands' chests, and babies lay close to their mothers' breasts. Some were lying down, sleeping the sleep of the just. Perhaps they even dreamed; who knows? At twilight, we were still seated. We were served hot soup and bread for the trip, and so we said in our hearts and to one another: "It is not so terrible; they are giving us soup and bread."

The screeching of the train upon the tracks shook us out of momentary calm and reverie. A familiar shrill cut through the air. The wheels screeched their last, and the train came to a stop.

The sun, wrapped in the grayness of twilight, was ringed in fiery gold—but I do not remember how long I sat there taking in the panorama of people or looking at the horizon. I only remember waking up in the last hours of the night. *Did I do right?* I asked myself. *Should we have stayed in the cellar?* Buba slept. Couples clasped one another. We are together, I thought. And we will help one another. Maybe we will overcome these trials in spite of everything.

I cannot forget anything—and nothing of that day, August 27, 1944, will be forgotten. The things that happened then and on the days that followed, are carved into my flesh; they live in me and they are what I am…

I heard whistles. They hooted and stopped; they stopped and started. The Germans were rearranging the cars, moving some to the front and others to the back. They moved the locomotive while the Jews slept or rested. The process seemed endless, but when the Germans were ready they shouted: "Enter the cars!"

The Germans abused, beat indiscriminately, and pushed us into cattle cars. *"Schnell, schnell; los, los!" "Hurry, hurry."* Families were separated. Cars were crammed. Locks were bolted and secured. The Jewish police helped the deaf and the lame to climb onto the cars, but the Germans beat them with their rifles. In all that confusion and calamity, we girls desperately wanted to stay together...Before entering the car we saw the Old Man. He was given a special car—but perhaps this was not so. Perhaps there were others in it. I did not see, and I did not know. He appeared as he always did. Introspective. His wife, his adopted son, and his brother and sister-in-law were with him.

The Germans gave us a container of drinking water and a bucket for waste. We entered the car. No one was missing. Buba, who was frightened, held on to Gutka and Yisrael. We heard a screeching. The doors of the car were closed. We heard a strong knock. The bolt was shot. Another knock, and we were locked in. There were four small, barred windows in the car, and whoever managed to sit near one of them had fresh air. This caused a flurry of discontent, but finally everyone settled down.

*Afraid, afraid.* The sense of responsibility I had deferred pressed me and weighed heavily in my conscience. Questions as to where we were going and what would become of us tortured me. The others had become calmer; once they were left alone and were not abused, they began to hope. Any situation which continued without change was welcome.

As I sat I looked about me. Rays of light penetrated a barred window at random, and from time to time those rays illuminated one or another face. I do not know how many of us Jews were in the car, but there were many, very many...The silence continued. We were too weary to either speak or listen.

Suddenly a commotion broke out. A woman screamed horribly. Someone had received a resounding slap, which was followed by heart-rending weeping. Within seconds, a woman shoved me energetically: "Take it! Take it!" I had no idea what this was about. "Take it, and keep it for an emergency!" Only then did I see that one of the women was holding on to a container of water with all her might. She handed the container to someone, and it then passed from one person to another, until it reached me. I wondered then, as I wonder to this very day, why was I entrusted with safeguarding the water? I did not know then and I do not know now, but it happened. The responsibility for the precious water in the car was great indeed.

We rode on and on. From time to time the train stopped at a station, but we did not know where we were. Those who fainted were revived with a few drops of water. We ate the bread we had received and drank water measured into a cup. Whenever someone thought I had given him one drop too little, or that someone else had been given a drop too much, there was an immediate outcry.

Night fell. We relieved ourselves in the bucket. Some had stomachaches and groaned; some lay their heads down and fell asleep. Sporadic outbursts of anger and frustration came and went as naturally as the waves of the sea. Some snored; some had nightmares and cried out; some were hysterical. They wept and laughed.

Gutka and Yisrael were lying in one another's arms and Buba was stretched out between them. It seemed as if she dreamed, and once in a while a smile crossed her face. Shmuel Lippel's father wandered among people's arms and legs with a flashlight in hand, apparently looking for friends; his mother lay without lifting her head. She did not speak and she did not sleep; she seemed to have sunken into apathy. Someone had a stomachache, but could not manage to seat himself on the bucket. He splattered everyone around him and soiled himself. His wife helped him to tidy up. Esta's face got soiled. She kept still, but the tears flowed. When she wiped them away, they flowed again.

The night passed and people awakened. The wheels screeched on with a steady, monotonous beat. We rocked within the car, each person silent and deep within thought. There was nothing to say. There was no room for doubt, no room for belief; there was actually no room for anything any more. If we lived, we would see!

A tall man rose and stood by the bars, hoping to see where we were, but he did not manage to reach the window. Shmuel turned to me and said: "Riva, let me lift you; maybe you will see something." He lifted me, and I peered out. We were passing fields and avenues of tall trees on both sides of the tracks. The wheels turned slower and slower. A house. Another house. A town. Sloping red roofs, shutters bolted down. One shutter was open. A girl in her nightdress stood at the window. The mother rushed to the child, covered her mouth with her hand, and gently lowered the finger with which the child pointed at us. She lifted the girl in her arms, bolted the shutter, and the houses disappeared. We rolled on, and the train whistle tooted from time to time.

Once more the wheels turned slower, and we stopped for a few minutes. Then we moved again; we went forward a little and we went back a little. Forward again. And then we came to a stop. We heard a screech. The Germans had taken down the bar, and they had released the bolt. The doors opened ponderously and a wave of light flooded in to blind us.

The orders came at us fast and furiously: "Get down! Get down!" "Everything will be taken from you. If you have gold, jewelry, watches, give them to us! Everything will be taken from you!" "Get down! Leave everything in the car. Your belongings will be brought to you." "Men and women separately!"

*"Zu fünf, zu fünf!"* "In fives; in fives!" "Right, left."

Each of us took only the most personal things: family pictures, letters, diaries, poems, books...

*Whistles.* We were marching in step with the shrill, tremorous whistles cutting through the air and the coarse commands the Germans barked out at us, but we were still together. All the girls and all the women. *Fives! Fives! Fives!* Suddenly Esta grabbed me and said: "Look!" I looked and saw. I could not identify him exactly, but one man from our group was lying on the ground. A giant of a *kapo* stood on his chest with sadistic pleasure.

We were in fives. We walked farther and farther. We walked and walked, and on the way we saw new horrors. We spoke among ourselves and had only one aim: not to separate. To stay together.

Words were whispered from mouth to ear: there is a selection. Old people separately. Children separately. The ill separately. In the distance we saw a flatbed wagon on which were Old Man Rumkowski, his wife and adopted son, and his brother with his wife, Helena. They traveled on and disappeared from sight.

I do not remember the faces of the Germans. I would not be able to identify them. Their faces melded into a single face. They were in full uniform and held whips in their hands; they looked at us, pointed at us, and ordered our strides: "Left! Right!" Beautiful girls—smartly-dressed and seemingly in very good shape—urged us on, too. *"Schnell, schnell; los, los!"* We walked on and on. It was hot, and I removed one article of clothing after another.

Buba walked along with us at our pace and was as frightened as we were. She walked next to Gutka, and the Germans asked: "Whose child is this?" We did not say. According to what Helunia had foreseen, Buba would be safe even in the Germans' hands. Someone would adopt her! Someone would care for her! But over and over again the Germans persisted: "Whose girl is this?" Once more we did not speak; and finally, Lolka's mother took hold of her. They walked together. We had no time to think, and we could not feel. Everything had happened too quickly. With sealed lips and open eyes, with fear and exhaustion, we walked at the pace demanded of us.

As we were being led a German paused in front of Helunia, who looked like a little girl. She gazed into the murderer's eyes and asserted: "I am grown up. I am healthy. I can work." Helunia had succeeded in convincing him, and he let her go on.

On the way we had discarded our coats, suits, and bundles. By the time we got to our destination, it was almost easy to walk.

We crossed a threshold. We entered a hall. The floor was made of wooden slats like those one might find in shower stalls. An order was given: "Remove your clothes!" We removed them. We entered the showers; and we finished showering. A supernatural force moved us. We were like puppets on strings. *"Schnell, los; los, schnell!"*

They were waiting for us and they shaved us of our pubic hair, the hair on our heads, and the hair under our armpits. We went forward. There was no return. *Walk and walk!* They prod us. They chased us. We ran. We ran forward. We ran out of inertia. We did not think and yet the brain recorded everything. We were told to queue. We queued. We got dresses. We dressed. One girl got a long, transparent nightgown; another received a short, sleeveless thing; still another received an item with vertical stripes. Before long we looked for one another, but we had difficulty recognizing our friends and loved ones. When we finally did, we cried out: *Gutka? Zosia? Esta? Helunia? Lonya? Is that you?* We laughed hysterically because we looked like monkeys. Never before had I realized how much hair and clothing affect personality. *Where is Marilka? Where is Lolka? Where is Fella Brauer?* For some reason no one prodded us, and our sanity returned. We began to look for the girls.

"Tzila Nugrishel, is that you," I asked of a girl I met in the barber shop. Yes. It was. Tzila had been a teacher at the seminary in Fabianca, and she recognized me. "Do not be afraid; take your shoes," she warned. All the girls had left without their shoes, but I had mine. We had received clogs and dresses, whether or not they fit, and this was our attire in Auschwitz.

Little loaves of bread suddenly fell on us like hail from heaven. We managed to catch some and so, equipped with bread, "dressed" and "shod," we went out into a large yard surrounded by barracks. From afar, we could see barbed wire fences with electric poles bent inward at the top.

A chubby, well-dressed girl shouted: "Muster-call!" Other girls joined her, one prettier than the next, all of whom were well-dressed. They urged us on as the Germans had; and they spoke to us in the language of the whip: *"Los! Los! Schnell! Schnell! Fives!"* It is impossible to say how long this lasted, but it felt like an eternity.

A truly elegant woman whom I later learned was the *Blockältester,* or Block Commander, introduced the functionaries in the barrack and—with booted legs spread apart—spoke to us: "You are to stand here without moving, until you receive permission to leave. Even if there is a downpour; even if there is hail the size of huge stones, you will not be permitted to move from this place! You will only move from here when given permission..." And, as if on cue, a black cloud appeared in the sky. It was not rain that fell; it was a cloudburst. The *Stubendienst* and the *Blockältester* moved under the overhang of the nearest barrack roof and began a macabre dance. It was the dance of satanic Lilith and her daughters.

We were still together. Wet, shivering from cold, humiliated and depleted, we stood as we had been ordered, but from time to time we hugged one another for warmth. At that sight, the *Blockältester* charged with lightning speed to beat us indiscriminately. At last the rain stopped and the skies cleared a little. Rays of light appeared behind the dispersing cloud, and a rainbow appeared. We saw it, and I remember how good it felt. At home, I had been taught that a rainbow was a sign that there would not be another "flood."

A man in the SS in full gear approached us; he walked in measured strides, a hint of a smile in his eyes and a whip under his arm. As he inspected the "parade," the whip did not rest. We learned at once that to have been standing at the edge of the formation of fives—whether in front or in the rear, whether to the left or right—meant that one was especially subject to abuse, and we dared not move. We knew that we were now in a situation where one person confronted another with an indescribable inequity of power between them. When the SS officer signalled the *Blockältester* that the parade was over, we were moved into the block—a long barrack without windows. It basically was divided in two, however there was a raised platform in the middle and on one of the walls there were three tiers of pallets. The *Blockältester* announced: "The crematorium pipes pass through the middle."

We heard her. I must testify that we heard her and that none of us accepted this explanation. We simply did not believe it—and yet, I knew very well that we do not hear what we do not want to hear. How can I; how can we have been so stupid? How could we not believe, even then, when we had seen all that I have described? We knew we were in a concentration camp, but Poland also had its *Bereza Krautska,* a concentration camp in pre-war Poland. People were indeed tortured; they suffered, but they were not murdered. We therefore did not believe in the murder. The fact was that we were alive.

When the *Blockältester* spoke, the silence was total. She walked under the electric light that hung over the elevated segment of the barrack, and made her pronouncements from there. At last she permitted us to lie down, and the lights were turned off. Esta said: "I will not be able to bear this slavery," and then she fainted. I "buried my head in the sand." I pitied Esta. I pitied the girls. I pitied myself.

# The Second Day
# in Auschwitz

*"Up! Up!"*

We were still sleepy. The voice that had cried: *"Up"* seemed to rise from the bowels of the earth. It was still dark. Three in the morning. We did not rub our eyes. We did not stretch our bodies or straighten our bones. We heard the familiar prodding of yesterday. *"Schnell! Schnell!* Prepare for the lavatories!" screamed the *Blockältester.* The lavatories were outside the barrack, and again we marched in fives. We were allotted "time." When the *Stubendienst* blew her whistle, we squatted over a row of pits; when she blew it again, we had to get up and vacate the place. Inasmuch as our physiological activity was not always so "disciplined," we would then suffer throughout the entire day until the following morning.

Because I was the only one who had retained her own shoes, I guarded them as if they were precious. When I went to sleep, I removed them and put them under my head. The moment I opened my eyes on the morning of the second day in Auschwitz, however, I realized that the shoes were gone. Someone had taken them, but I could not react until after I had returned from the lavatories, for to have done otherwise would have been exceedingly uncomfortable. When I returned from relieving myself, I told the girls that I was not going to give up, and that I almost certainly would find my shoes. "Someone in our barrack stole them," I insisted.

I made use of the quiet in the barrack and walked from pallet to pallet, but the shoes were not to be found. A shout was heard: *"Raus! Raus! Raus! Los, los; schnell, schnell!"* We ran to the door like mice in a stupor, so as not to receive blows from the Jewish "servants." Outside, the light was clear and the air was fresh. We stood in fives. From a distance I saw a girl, one of the prisoners, trying to wear my shoes.

There was no stopping me. Without thinking, I ran toward the girl. I was fearless. The *Stubendienst* ran after me, shouting horribly: "Return to the ranks!" I continued to run, with her right behind me. I stood in front of the girl and said: "These are my shoes, my shoes! You stole them from me last night!" The *Stubendienst* stopped. She did not strike me. She looked at the girl and then at me. She saw that the girl could not put on the shoes, and that they were too small for her. At that, she turned to me and said: "Put on the shoes. If they fit, you will get them. If not, you will not leave here alive!" I got the shoes, and only later on did I realize how muddy the yard had become from the downpour of the night before. I wanted to be treated fairly even in Auschwitz, and it was very fortunate that nothing happened to the girl.

I returned to "my five" very pleased. We stood and waited for the *Appel,* or roll call, which took place several times a day. The SS officer passed among us and stared, sometimes in frightening silence; at other times he went wild and delivered ferocious blows to an unfortunate victim. We stood at the *Appel* that entire morning—which actually began in the early hours before dawn.

We were thirsty. Bella broke down. She ran to the fence where there was a puddle of rainwater, bent, cupped her hands, scooped some water into them, and drank. The *Stubendienst* did not spare her and whipped her without mercy. Bella was silent and did not react, but when the *Stubendienst* delivered a resounding blow to her face, she cried out in anger: "Sadist!" The *Stubendienst*'s response was both swift and fierce. A torrent fell upon Bella, and it did not end until the SS officer arrived. We stood and looked. We saw. We trembled and kept quiet.

*Inspection.* For a change, I received a stroke of the SS officer's whip. Evidently I did not stand still enough for him, and he decided to "calm me down." The *Appel* ended. The "parade" was over, and we were permitted to sit cross-legged. The ground was muddy, but we sat there just the same. Two prisoners arrived with huge cauldrons. We remained seated and unmoving. We were given a bowl of krupnick soup that seemed very tasty to us. I repeat. The soup seemed very tasty to us. We were very hungry, and I cannot describe its taste. I only can say that we had not eaten in a long time. When we had finished, we were ordered to stand once more. Now even though this was the end of August and it is generally warm at that time, we suffered quite a bit from the cold. I do not remember how long we stood, but we finally were allowed to enter the barrack.

The pallets had to be entered from a more or less horizontal position, and the space between the bunks did not allow for sitting. We lay five women to a pallet and three pallets were ours, meaning that we were fifteen girls in all. Thus far we had managed to stay together. We forgot the people we had lost on the way.

"Is Citrinovna here?" The question reverberated throughout the barrack. "Yes," one of us answered. "Riva, go. He means you…" I followed my fellow-prisoner and was ushered into a room at the end of the barrack. A *Kapo*, who wore a peculiar cap, sat in one of the compartments in the room.

"Your name is Citrin?" "Yes," I replied. "I am looking for Niusia Citrin from Lodz." "My name is Riva." The *Kapo* dismissed me and did not want to know anything more, but he added: "Be careful that they do not beat you." "Why should they beat me? They are all Jews!" I thought the *Kapo* chuckled sarcastically, but perhaps it was with sorrow.

I left the *Kapo*'s compartment and walked toward our pallet, innocently using the platform in the middle of the block. The *Stubendienst* appeared, as if from ambush, and fell on me like an animal. She slapped me left and right and kicked me time and again. When I fell she kicked me again, this time with the point of her boot. "Get up, you accursed!" I stood. I wanted to explain to her what had happened, but I could not manage to say a single word. She beat me as before, and I snapped; my patience had come to an end. Like a wild animal, I returned her blows. I did not feel anything any more; I only heard the girls beg: "Riva, stop! Riva, stop!" I do not know how long this went on. Eventually I stopped, and she stopped as well. The *Stubendienst* mounted the platform, as I lay on the floor helpless and almost unconscious. No one dared to approach me until she left, and only then did Zosia and Bella move me.

# The Third Day
# in Auschwitz

*Darkness in the barrack.* The *Blockältester* paced back and forth on the platform and cut the air with the whip in her hand. Her voice, like that of a *dybbuk,* emerged from her throat: *"Ferfluchte Juden,"* filthy Jews, "Get up! Get up, you filthy women. Get out! Everything stinks in here!"

After the usual morning procedure to the lavatories and back, we reported for the *Appel.* Dawn broke. The sun "peeked out of its hiding place," but the atmosphere was gray. "The fives" stood at attention. When the cold affected us we drew nearer, becoming joined in clumps. We got some relief, but we still shivered. *Heaven help us should the* Blockältester *see us hugging!* As the day drew on, we were warmed by the sun. A cold wind blew, but it was refreshing and invigorating. We were without supervision and we jumped, massaged, and hugged one another.

We heard the shout of *"Appel"* as if it had come from the depths of the earth. This time our ordeal passed mercifully, and there were no beatings. The number of the prisoners conformed to the Germans' lists. We received coffee that was supposed to have been hot, and we were told to sit cross-legged. We rested a little; the supervisors were not about, and we saw this as an opportunity to exchange glances. We paid no attention to how quickly we had adjusted to how we looked. This was our first opportunity to talk, and we arrived at several decisions: under no circumstances were we to accept any position in the camp; we were to contact individuals who knew what was happening outside the camp; and we were to try to find out what really went on in Auschwitz. *Was it true that people were being cremated here?* The very fact that we were still alive was proof that the horrible "rumors" could not be true. We thought that the number of natural deaths would be greater here than in the ghetto, and could not believe otherwise despite the fact that we were in Birkenau.

There was another *Appel* and once more we were counted; this time we stood at attention for the entire time it took. A beautiful girl who seemed to be very cultured passed in front of us, and I determined to speak to her. I could not overcome my need to know, and I did not hesitate to say: "Tell me, are children being cremated here? Old people? Anyone at all?" "Do you see the towering smoke? Look at the chimneys! There it is, burning day and night!" She did not stop walking, and added: "You are now facing selection. You will be sent away from here. Go. Go willingly. Any place in the world is better than Auschwitz."

We stood and waited. This time we waited for selection willingly, and in the belief that all of us would get out of here. The word *Achtung* passed over us like wind over water. *Achtung, Achtung!*

The *Blockältester* and the *Stubendienst* ran about, striking, slapping, and screaming: "You there, stand straight! Straighten 'your five.' You accursed, undress! Undress!" We were prepared for this selection, and did as we were told. In two days we somehow had developed a "defense mechanism" for Auschwitz, and I remember how Marilka, who was a bit stooped as she passed before the SS officers, raised her head high and flashed her eyes. She covered her breasts, and did not wait for the Germans to signal. She simply walked over to us without stopping.

Zosia and Helunia had not been "selected," and were separated from us. We then knew beyond a doubt that we had lost them both, and within our hearts we cried: "Zosia and Helunia are no more." Yisrael's sister Fella, Gutka, Lonia, Bella, Lolka, Marilka, and I were now left.

Sorrow. Frustration. Pain. There is no time. No time to think.

*Order! Stand in line!* That very day we received clothing and went on our way in a passenger train.

The trip was long. We did not know where we were going, but we were dressed—some more, some less. We sat on benches, and we could look out of the windows. I remembered well the words of the girl in Birkenau, and I felt that I had gotten out of hell. This is my truth: I felt a degree of relief....Only after we had traveled farther, was I upset by the thought of having lost Zosia and Helunia.

We traveled and traveled and night fell. We lay down and slept. When the train stopped, I opened my eyes. It was morning and we had arrived, but where were we? *"Out of the car!"*

# Stutthof

We had nothing with us and again faced our one concern: to stay together. We spilled out of the railroad car with screams and blows and prodding. Again there were the *Kapos,* and again there were the beautiful, well-dressed girls who treated us with cruelty. The barbed-wire fences and lighting poles were there, too, as were the guards who stood over us with their weapons cocked.

We lined up for the *Appel* in fives, and each of us received a bowl and a spoon. After roll call, we were taken into a giant barrack. A thousand women were crowded into it. The barrack was divided into three sections along its width—something like cells—and *Stuben* were on both sides of the barrack, ten to a side. In the middle, was an open platform on which the Nazis and their helpers walked about during inspection. There was a great deal of light in the barrack since there were no walls separating the cells. A board, about a foot high, sufficed to mark the boundaries between cells. There were twenty windows and twenty cells in all. Fifty women were crowded into each *Stube;* i.e., ten fives.

The moment the soldiers left the barrack, we searched for and found those we knew and with whom we had something in common. Poriya from Zdunska Wola; attorney Hanryk Naftalin's sisters, who were devoted Communists; my sister Esta's friends, whom I cannot remember by name; and Anizh Gutman's two sisters, who were as noble as he. We managed to organize a *Stube* of young girls, most of whom knew one another, and this proved to be a calming factor in our disrupted lives. After we had organized ourselves and sat down, we felt that the greatest danger was over. We were thankful and relaxed, and once more we remembered the girl who said that no place bears a likeness to Auschwitz. The significance of Stutthof camp was still unknown to us.

Life took on the semblance of order. Our *Blockältester,* Katya, was a Czech girl who had come with us from Auschwitz. As usual, she had two assistants—*Stubendienst*—two young, pretty sisters who also had come with us from Auschwitz. These girls shared a room at the end of the barrack.

The *Appel* took place in the early hours of the morning. We went into the yard, stood in fives for hours on end regardless of the weather, and waited for the SS officer who conducted the count. If everything went well, we received coffee. After that we were free, and actually were permitted to do whatever we wanted. Our heads had been shaved, we looked like army recruits, and it was strange to see our girls bald. From time to time we were called to roll call for an additional count. There was roll call in the morning, roll call for coffee, roll call to get soup, and sometimes a roll call for amusement's sake.

During inspections by the SS officers, we sat cross-legged. We did not dare lift our eyes. We saw the approaching boots and above them, green army trousers. The boots were followed by pretty shoes, shapely legs, and the fluttering of fancy skirts to the right and left of the SS. These inspections did not last long, but the preparations for them caused unbelievable stress.

One day as we lay outside, we confessed to one another that we suffered from an annoying discomfort: we scratched and scratched. We removed our clothes and began to search. Soon enough, we found lice embedded in the seams of our clothes. We got busy. We sat and killed them until our thumbnails changed color. When it seemed to us that we had finished, we "got dressed." We adjusted to the situation, and we got used to the dirt and lice; they became an inseparable part of us.

The weather was good. The days were sunny, and only the

nights were cold. We sat together as much as possible. We talked. We made decisions as to what was allowed and what was not. We agreed not to accept any position in the camp, because there was no possibility of facing this test. It was impossible to change the situation or the conditions, but there was room for mutual help within our *Stube*: we could support and encourage those who broke down in body or spirit.

After roll call and at dusk, the *Stubendienst* entered and distributed our daily bread ration, jam, and a triangle of cheese. The women of our *Stube* decided to eat in a particular order. One third of the bread and all the jam was to be eaten on the same evening. The rest of the bread and the cheese was to be saved for the next day. We believed that in this way, we might be able to hold out longer. We had a rare discipline and, unbelievably, we even managed to keep up our spirits. After "supper," we organized a sort of game: someone pretended to "open" a particular "book" on a particular "page" and "read" an excerpt describing this or another character. Based on these clues, we had to try to identify the work. A variant of this game involved the singing of a musical excerpt, which then had to be identified. This was how twilight passed.

We were not aware of the actual time, but we knew by the setting sun and the appearance of the stars when it was late. We had to think about the *Appel* that awaited us before dawn...As it happened, we did not have enough room in our *Stube* for all of us to lie down in. We therefore tried resting our heads on one another so that we became a braided body like that of a Sabbath *challah,* but that did not work. There still was not enough room for everyone. We had no recourse other than to take turns standing, and each night another girl stood in the corner or curled herself up like a snail. When it was my turn to be in the corner, I curled up, fell asleep, and dreamed—but who knows? Perhaps I was in a trance.

On a moonlit night twenty "moons" shone in from twenty windows on the miserable souls living in the barrack. The lights from the outside flickered in the wind and illuminated the faces of the girls lying nearest the wall. That light was silvery and cruel. I was lonely and every sound frightened me; every sound brought me back to depressing reality. The girls lying around me, dressed in rags, appeared like creatures from another world. Sadness and sickness gripped me. I thought of Zosia, Helunia, and Buba. I thought of all those who so recently were taken from us. On such a night, the longing was unbearable. Nothing comforting surfaced, and the cold clarity was pitilessly cruel to me. My blood froze at the least sound that was not the breathing of those around me.

At times the stars reminded me of a song I knew and sang at *Beit Yaakov,* which was composed by Nathan Berliner. I used to love it, and perhaps that alone came back to me to bring me a measure of comfort.

> *Shlof shein feigele, shlof*
> *Cholem fun glick un fun freid*
> *In mairev die zun is shoin weit*
> *Die zun dort pamelech fargeit*
>
> *Toizenter goldene shtern*
> *Boyen a goldene brik*
> *Zei wachen un hiten getreie*
> *Biz kumen die zun wet zurik.*

> Sleep, beautiful little bird, sleep
> Dream of happiness and joy
> The sun far in the west
> Sinks ever so slowly
>
> Thousands of golden stars
> Forming a golden bridge
> Stand loyally on guard
> For the return of the sun.

I taught the song to the girls, and we sang together. The song made a promise of a new day: *tomorrow sun rays will spill into the yard, and we will bask in the warm sand...*

The song transported me to the realm of hope. I no longer saw the legs that looked like dry bones; I no longer saw the hands that were clenched. The moon was no longer cruel...

I do not remember if I slept the first night that the song came back to me, but I do remember that the next morning I felt "healthy." I decided to walk. To walk, if only to the fence, and to see what lay beyond. Could I find a source of news? Could I discover what was happening in the world? I remembered that when we left the ghetto, the Russians were at the gates of Warsaw and the Allies were advancing on all fronts.

# From Stutthof to
# the Labor Camp

*"Appel! Up, up!"* Katya, the *Blockältester,* and the *Stubendienst* Bozhka
and Alzhinka—the two sisters—were just as cruel as they were
beautiful. The sound of their voices, voices that had become hoarse
and harsh from incessant screaming, aroused terror in us all. *Another roll call!* This was not the usual time at all! We did not know
what this could signify, but we knew we wanted to stay
together…We were still standing "in our fives" after receiving and
drinking coffee….What did they want of us?

The overseer arrived. She was dressed in a dazzling army uniform and seemed very "polished" indeed. As she stood in front of
the first row of girls she asked: "Which of you wants to travel to
work?" We could not believe what we had heard, and we had
reservations about this innocent question. Fear and panic gripped
us. Is this a ruse or is it real? What is happening? Why are we now
being asked instead of being told? Why do we suddenly have a
choice? We understood that we had to decide and that we had very
little time. We were on the threshold of a new danger. If we did not
say *yes* or *no* unequivocally we would not be able to alter anything,
and we might have to face separation.

Everything was done with lightning speed. We decided that we
had nothing to lose, and that we would see what fate held in store
for us. As one, we went over to those who "volunteered" for work—
Gutka, Fella, Lonya, Bella, Lolka, Marilka, and I. We were joined
by Poriya of Zdunska Wola, Reizel from the Bund, Mrs. Bernman
from the Zionist movement, and the two Braun sisters whose broth-

ers were with us in *Techiya*. We were twelve girls; another three joined us, "filling-in" the third "five."

"*March, march,*" ordered the overseer—and, as if hypnotized, we marched at her pace. We walked a long time until we reached a wooden hut that was used as a clothing depot. We could not believe our eyes. The *Aufseherin,* or overseer and her assistants, looked for suitable clothes for us. They gave each of us a pair of good shoes that actually fit. We were dressed well! We looked at one another and rediscovered ourselves. Our hair had grown while we were in in Stutthof, and it now crowned our heads like fur hats. For the first time in the camps, our appearance approached a semblance of humanity.

We left Stutthof "five by five," in the standard formation. We reached a railroad track, and came to a passenger train. We were told to embark, and we embarked. We were now on a train that had both benches and tables. We got food and water, and everything indicated a thousand times over that we were indeed going to work.

The train began to move. We sat like ordinary human beings and talked among ourselves without interference. Not one of us was not glued to the windowpane. We left behind us plowed fields and farmers at work. They did not look at us, but rather gazed into the distance. Their aspect said a great deal more than words can express, and it seemed to me that these were the faces of a suffering people. We looked and saw, and I am almost certain that some did cast a glance in our direction. A silent dialogue appeared to be taking place, a dialogue of despair. They were old and tired, and we were young and imprisoned.

The train rolled on. The squeaking of the wheels deafened our ears, and we fell silent. Fear crept in to return us to the real world. Where are we being taken? The sun set slowly and greyness settled within the cars, but the air was fresh. I breathed deeply; I felt helpless and almost desperate in that twilight.

I started to sing a lullaby as I sat by the window with my Gutka next to me and Esta next to her.

*Ay li lu li lu*
*Ay li lu li lu*

*Shlof shoyn mein teier feigele*
*Mach shoyn zu dein kosher eigele*
*Shlof shoyn shlof a zisen shlof*
*Ay li lu li lu li lu...*

Sleep my precious little bird
Close your innocent eyes
Sleep, sleep a sweet sleep.

The girls joined in, the wheels clicked, and the sun's rays disappeared. We traveled, we sang, and we fell asleep. When we got up we were in Gerdauen, near Koenigsberg.

*"Out! Down!"* It seemed as if I had dreamed a dream, but that now reality had returned. We got off the train and stood in fives; we were well-trained. We walked and reached a large area, almost a square, surrounded by barbed wire. Four towers were manned by Germans who had their weapons aimed at us, and this was our greeting.

Our complement of one thousand individuals—nine hundred women and one hundred men—was assigned to three large barracks. The *Lagerführer* was a Wehrmacht officer; and two women in the uniform of the Hitler Youth served as overseers, or *Aufseherinnen*. From the start, it was obvious to us that this was a new place without a "tradition of organization." The German girls prodded us: *"Hurry! Hurry,"* but we concentrated on and succeeded in staying together.

Unlike Auschwitz or Stutthof, the *Lagerführer* here did not lash out at us with his whip. Many prisoners sensed his "weakness" and approached him. They asked to work in the kitchen or in the distribution of food, or they applied for the jobs of *Stubendienst* or *Blockältester*. We, on the other hand, affirmed our resolve to not seek or accept any position. As luck would have it, one overseer behaved decently—like the *Lagerführer*—but the other enjoyed beating us until our blood flowed.

After a rather sloppy "parade" the following morning, we went out to work in the field, an uprooted orchard. Our job was to dig out and remove any roots that may have remained, in order to prepare the area for an airfield. When we returned from the field, however, we discovered that there was no meal, although those in charge had received the supplies with which to feed us. The kitchen staff, manned by Czechoslovakian and Hungarian prisoners, was unskilled and unequal to the task. They had obtained the jobs, but they could not handle them.

Of the nine hundred women who arrived with us from Stutthof, five hundred were from Lodz. Undoubtedly among them were individuals who knew of my work in the ghetto, because the very next day a delegation came to me demanding that I step in. "Riva, you are experienced. We ask you to go into the kitchen. At least, we will have a representative from Lodz." What could I say? It was very flattering, and I was almost filled with pride. No place is more important than the kitchen in a concentration camp, and any one of these women could have applied for the job. Esta, who was a die-hard Communist, said: "I think you are now being rewarded for your devoted work in the ghetto." To hear such words gave me great satisfaction, but I did not accept the premise that I had to work in the kitchen.

More surprises still awaited me. One of them was that the women of Lodz had organized themselves, and had addressed their complaint to the *Lagerführer*. When he came to see me, he merely appointed me the deputy to Mrs. Shwimmer, who managed the kitchen. This was an order, and the girls and I fell silent; under the circumstances, it was impossible to resist.

The first day in the kitchen I had to create something out of nothing—for there were no knives and none of the essential utensils with which to function. I worked feverishly, trying desperately to solve the problems I had inherited, determined that those who worked in the fields would not go hungry. I therefore approached a German guard who supplied me with the necessary implements. It was an exhausting day for me, but when everyone returned to the camp, the soup was ready.

The head of the women's camp was a Czech woman by the name of Olga, who had been in the Lodz ghetto. The head of the men's camp was a fellow by the name of Stoczinsky, and his helper was Heniek Maroko. I knew that Chaim Maroko was a Zionist comrade. We found a common language, and our influence was considerable. Through our efforts, the beating of Jews at the hands of the Jews who had "positions" was put to an end.

During those first days in the kitchen I thought I had control of the situation. I wanted everyone to receive his portion because it was the minimum to sustain life, and I thought that if I remained alert no theft would occur here. Disappointment, however, came quickly...After a hard day's work, I went to the barrack to lie down on the pallet. Camp discipline was not strict and it was possible to move about from place to place, and so one night at about eleven a girl came to me and said: "Riva, I looked through a knothole in one of the boards of the kitchen and saw the cook cut away large pieces of meat. He put them in a pail and hid the pail under the table."

This was bad news. I was unhappy about the theft and disturbed about the kitchen staff. It was clear to me, for instance, that the cook could not do this on his own. I dressed hurriedly, ran to the kitchen, and went straight to the hiding place. I removed the pail with its contents, let the cook know that someone had seen him, and warned him that I would not report him this time on the condition that it never happened again. He promised, and I went back to the barrack.

That night I tossed restlessly and did not sleep at all. What was I to do if such a thing happened again? After all, I knew that our "superiors" were Germans.

I increased my guard over the kitchen. The staff was not pleased—not with me, and not with my devoted work. It was disturbing to them to have me there all the time. One midnight, as I stood by the cauldron, the *Lagerführer* entered. I became frightened, but my fear dissolved as he stood beside me and struck up a conversation. His human side was reinforced when he confessed that he objected to how the Germans treated the Jews, and it helped me to understand his moderate behavior toward us.

Quite by chance the *Lagerführer* asked: "Actually, what are you doing here at this late hour?" When I said: "I wanted to make sure that those who returned from the field got their soup; I am having trouble controlling the situation," I saw that he was concerned. He probed further and asked for suggestions. I said that skilled, reliable people should be assigned to the kitchen—people with ethics. And so it was. At my recommendation he installed Comrade Reizl from the Bund, and members of the Zionist movement who had worked in the public kitchens of the ghetto. Mrs. Shwimmer, a good-natured woman with few values, and the *Lagerführer* continued to rule at the top; they and the cook.

It seemed to me that everything would be all right now, and that not a single crumb would be stolen from those who labored outside the camp—but that is not what happened. I did not succeed. One day Mrs. Shwimmer offered me a bowl filled with meat and fat for my friends. When I refused, the sky "fell in." Those who were opposed to me simply boycotted me. Yes, boycotted me! Moreover, the *Lagerführer* was sent to the front—and in his stead we now had Hans Moses, an SS officer "polished" to the very last of his buttons; a man with a pistol set in its holster and fixed at his hip; a man with white gloves on his hands and a whip under his arm.

One day, *Lagerführer* Moses entered the kitchen very early in the morning. The Czech girls, Mrs. Shwimmer, and the *Lagerältester* knew how to speak German well—and also knew "the drill"; that is to say, they knew how to appear before German superiors. This was the formula: "I humbly report that so and so many people work in the kitchen. Present are so and so many, and so and so many are absent..." I did not know how to salute, and I did not know how to report. The *Lagerführer,* noting my silence, asked: "What do you have to report?" "The head of the camp and the manager have reported; I have nothing more to add," I said. He would not leave me alone and continued: "Are you able to prepare a report?" "No. I do not know the procedure," I replied, and thus ended my unceremonious introduction to *Lagerführer* Hans Moses.

I returned to the barrack rather frightened of our new ruler. I told the girls how the morning went, and let them know how badly I felt at my post. I could not control the situation, and I no longer could help. "I have decided to resign," I stated. The girls agreed with me. That very day I approached the "nice" overseer, and said to her: "Do not ask me why, because I cannot explain, but I want to be released from my job in the kitchen. I want to be with the girls who work in the field. Please present my request to *Lagerführer* Hans Moses." She seemed to understand, and a smile escaped her lips. "I will present your request to the *Lagerführer,*" she said, and true to her word, she asked to have me released. The deed was done.

The following morning, Hans Moses asked to see me in his quarters. I arrived and stood in the entryway, but no one seemed to be there. I looked around, somewhat at a loss, when suddenly I heard: "Come here!" The *Lagerführer* sat behind his desk, which faced the wall. His voice was collected and calm as he asked me to sit in the chair to his left. "Why do you want to leave the kitchen?" "I want to be with my sisters." "You know that the work outside is hard?" "Yes, I know." "And in spite of it you want to leave?" "Yes." At this he lost control: "Stupid duck, go to the field!"

As the *Lagerführer* calmed down, his voice became soft as silk: "Very well, you do not want to work in the kitchen; work here. You will clean my house; you will keep an eye on what is happening in the camp; and you will keep me informed." "No, *Herr Lagerführer,* I cannot." "Are you a Jew?" he asked. "Yes, *Herr Lagerführer,*" I replied. "Maybe you are of mixed race? How is it possible for a Jew to refuse to take an order from a German, or to turn down better conditions?" "I am not of mixed race. My mother is a true Jew, and so am I. My father is a Jew in every bone of his body. He is a *Talmud* scholar. He has a beard and sidelocks." I eventually lost my balance. Forgetting where I was, I burst into tears. Hans Moses repeated: "Stupid duck, go to the field!"

I left, and a weight lifted from my heart. I ran to the barrack as quickly as I could, but no one was there. Everyone was in the field. I was alone for now—but when the girls came back, I shared my news. The following day I went out with my sisters and friends.

And so it was every morning. I partook of the routine. I was in the early morning *Appel;* and I was a figure wrapped in rags, trudging on the road, clapping along in clogs, sinking in the mud—a mud so deep at times that some of us lost our shoes or clogs in it.

Smoke rose from the chimneys of the homes scattered through the area and here and there, the electric lights shone from within the windows of the houses. After a long and weary walk—in bare feet for those who had lost their shoes or clogs—we arrived at a huge field filled with trees that had been felled. We then faced the grueling labor of extricating the gnarled roots from the surface of the earth and below. The prisoners and the guards were not the only ones in the field, however. There were birds there, too; birds who in singing their songs helped us to keep up our spirits. We listened to the them, and we held up. It is as simple as that.

Once it was truly a spring day. The sky was blue, and the rays of the sun caressed us and warmed our bones. The earth softened and yielded. Clods upon clods of earth were lifted and thrown aside, exposing the roots we had to remove. Gutka, who was very musical, paused for a moment to listen to the birds. Suddenly, one of the German guards approached her and said: "You remind me of my wife." A meat sandwich slipped out of his coat sleeve and he went on, continuing to supervise us as if he were a stern taskmaster. From that time on the guard found many reasons to approach Gutka where she worked, and each time he gave her a meat sandwich.

The weather remained balmy for several days, and the mood among the girls was almost good. Although we did not have enough food, the fresh air, physical work, and walking tended to improve our health. At night we were left to ourselves. We spent our evenings singing songs and making up all sorts of games. We knew that the end of the war was near, and we prayed all of us would remain alive.

For three weeks we rose in the early hours of the morning, heard the shout *Appel,* stood in the yard for roll call, and made our way on the road. Generally speaking, the counting in our block passed without incident, but there was one block—the largest of the three—whose prisoners always got up late. As a result, we were subjected to communal punishment. Once the entire camp had to kneel until it was time to go to the field; once we did not get any coffee; once we had to hold our hands in the air—and Moses was not finished yet…

Spirits were high among our girls. With the help of local people, I discovered how to find out what was happening in the world.…When we were in the field, we relieved ourselves at the riverbank while the overseers looked the other way. One day, however, I made a discovery. An unknown hand had left a wrapped sandwich for us within which was a note containing the latest news. From that time on, I went to the bank with devotion. I "drew" from the "source," and every single day we had news from the outside world. Our strength to live often derived from this fact alone.

We knew that the Russians were advancing on all fronts in Eastern Europe. The expectation was unbearable; the desire to attain freedom indescribable. At the same time, we worked at full speed. The food was tolerable. We were able to wash in cold water, and our pallets were clean. We had paper sleeping bags, and they protected us from the cold at night. We scarcely could believe that crepe paper had the capacity to preserve body heat.

A new day; another *Appel.* As always, we stood in our fives. We prisoners were in the yard in front of the barrack, and that, too, was the same. Suddenly, I heard *Lagerführer* Hans Moses call out my name: "Riva Citrin, step out of the ranks!" I presented myself, and stood at attention. "From now on, you will be the *Blockältester* of Block three." "I do not want to be *Blockältester.*" "How dare you want or not want!" He screamed at me and delivered a ringing slap to my cheek. The blow was very forceful and I was tossed against the barrack wall. I fell and my blood flowed, but I felt no pain and only heard: "This is an order! You are the *Blockältester* of Block three!"

This was unexpected trouble. I had a roaring in my head, an endless series of questions, and no answers. How was I to do this job? How could I control four hundred women? Should I refuse? *I quickly stopped thinking of that.* I asked for advice, but no one had anything to say. Whoever failed to obey Hans Moses was tortured. The victim was tied to a tree for an entire day, hands behind the back, and feet in the air. A frightening sight. Insulting!

*I entered Block 3 and blew the whistle as part of my duties. At that moment, it seemed to me that I had crossed the threshold of hell...* I met the four hundred after they returned from work and had eaten their soup. After that it was customary for the distribution of bread, cheese, and marmalade to take place, and this job fell to me.

"You saw what happened to me," I appealed, "and you know I did not want to be the *Blockältester.* This came about because you are late for the *Appel.* I ask you to help me so that I can help you. I will not raise my hand, but do not take advantage of this. Let us improve the conditions in the block for everyone's sake. From this moment on, I am one of you."

They listened to me and even believed me; they had seen what had happened to me earlier in the day....For two weeks the women got up in the morning without a shout being heard or a blow being delivered. The atmosphere had changed beyond recognition. In the evening the women gathered in a circle to sing. I learned *A Balade fun Zurisene Shich,* The Ballad of the Torn Shoes, and *Shtiler, Shtiler, Lomir Shweigen,* but discontent is the way of the world. This time, the *Stubendienst* were unhappy with me. I supervised the distribution of food so that not so much as a crumb was removed from a single portion, and I demanded things that no one had demanded of them before. I made them collect wood, light the stove in the block, and heat the water for those returning from the field. I also placed pails in the block so that the girls could urinate at night without having to go out into the cold. In the morning, the *Stubendienst* had to empty the pails and clean them. Unhappy as they were, they did not bear a grudge against me. Other blocks soon followed the procedures we had initiated. Instead of blows and screams, there was now an atmosphere of comradeship in the Gerdauen camp. No one died of hunger, either, and only one girl died of typhoid.

In all, we spent two months at Gerdauen. Three of those weeks I spent in the kitchen as the representative of the girls from Lodz; an additional three weeks I spent laboring in the field, and the final two weeks I spent as the *Blockältester* in Block three. The hardest days for me and the girls with me were the days when I worked in the kitchen.

When we left, all of us looked better than when we had arrived.

# From Gerdauen to Stutthof

❈ ❈ ❈

In December, 1944, the order was given to evacuate the camp. The *Appel* was held as usual; we were leaving, and none of us knew where we were going. We went on foot this time, and we were accompanied by the *Aufseherinnen* and soldiers. Hans Moses disappeared.

We walked and walked. Esta, who was the first among us to express the rebellion in her heart, spoke of escape. No one wanted to join her and she capitulated—as she had so many times before— for the sake of the family. When Marilka began to speak of escape, Lolka refused to leave and she dissuaded her from doing so. She, in fact, stopped her. Esta and Marilka continued on the march.

I do not know the distance from Gerdauen to Stutthof, but I recall that we walked on and on, seemingly without end. We had neither the strength nor the courage for such an ordeal, but a residue of hope remained—and we trudged on. From time to time we passed through a German town, stopped by a water tap, and drank like camels of the desert. The walk went on, and we had no food; we fell from exhaustion, and we were shot. One bullet, and the agony of the victim ended. We saw it all, but we could not react; we were numb. Nothing seemed to matter; we were one with the suffering, and that led to death.

Our legs were swollen and frostbitten, and yet we dragged them under our bent bodies. Our heads hung between our arms like the stuffed straw heads of scarecrows. The men's trousers were muddied to the knees, and the women walked barefoot because they had lost their shoes to the mud. We plodded on through cities and towns, all of us sinking deeper and deeper into mud. *I was about to collapse. Drops and drops of water dripped from the rooftops onto my head.* Esta brought up her proposal to escape from time to time, but I was among those who opposed the idea. I was afraid. I did not have the strength in me, but one of the girls did. "See you when the sun shines for us," she said.

The trials of the march continued until we got to Stutthof. We returned to the barrack we knew so well. The barrack of Katya Bozka and Alzinka, the two infamous sisters. The same barrack for one thousand women divided into twenty *Stuben.* The same twenty windows. During the day, the crowding; during the night, the twenty cold moons peeking through twenty windows, once on the left, once on the right, as if putting to sleep those curled up there.

Winter was in full force and the snow fell incessantly; it swirled and mounted until it at last reached the height of the window sills. There was no longer any way to prevent the deterioration of the girls' health. The cold and the starvation decimated the prisoners in the barracks. The nightly *Appels* were unimaginably cruel, and God help anyone who did not stand at the roll call according to regulations! Bozka inflicted severe punishments, like that of kneeling in the snow with one's arms uplifted. The victims of her whim generally froze, never to rise again. Those who lived through these and other perils had to contend with an outbreak of lice and one affliction after another.

Our girls were still healthy and our *Stube* still set an example for the others. If we chanced to sing at night, our lullabies and songs of longing could be heard throughout the entire barracks.... We lived by the principle: "All for all," and we shared everything among ourselves.

The end of December came and we counted the days, but we heard no news. A typhoid epidemic spread among us. The girls fell ill and lay in their filth, no longer able to get up. We relieved ourselves in the bowls from which we ate, and we threw the excrement out of the window. When a hand trembled and the girl did not have the strength to turn the bowl outside, the excrement spilled onto the heads of the others.

First Gutka fell ill. After her, Lonia, Lolka, Marilka, Bella, and Leah. The disease spared no one. The girls lay shivering on the floor, their eyes glistening with fever. I stood over them helplessly, only able to get a little water. I moved from one to the other, moistening their lips.

I was the last to get sick and I could not rest; I had to do something. According to the rules, those who fell ill did not eat. One had to be able to withstand the grueling *Appels* in order to get soup and since none of us could do so, we were deprived of food. A daring idea occurred to me. I had nothing to lose, and I decided to approach Bozka. "Come, see how the girls are lying here. They are sick. If they receive their rations, maybe they will recover," I said to her. I do not know where the courage to speak to her came from, but I went on: "Look. They are like flowers—girls 16, 18, 20, 22 years old. Help them get well."

Bozka's response was unbelievable. She not only promised to do something, but also kept her word. We got our rations every day, and every day another girl got up on her feet. Every day another girl joined those who went outside to stand in line for soup. Lolka was the quickest to recover and in addition to her ration, she was able to "organize" another portion of soup or a piece of bread....

It was a clear day in January. The sun shone and its rays entered the barrack to warm our bones. Suddenly, Katya, the *Blockältester,* appeared. She announced that there would be an inspection and she ordered us to open the windows; I suppose the barrack was malodorous and we had grown accustomed to it. We did not open the windows, however, and Katya left. A *Stubendienst* entered, a girl from Lodz. She passed through the center of the barrack and she, too, demanded that we open the windows. When she came to us and saw that we had not done so, she got furious, picked up a shoe, and threw it at the girls lying there, unable to move. The window was opened, but the shoe had hit Gutka on the forehead.

When I think about it now, I do not know where my strength came from. I stood up—for I, too, was lying on the floor—picked up the shoe, threw it back at the *Stubendienst,* and closed the window. I threw a shoe at the *Stubendienst!* The girl did not react. She left. We remained in silence, but there was no reprisal. Only those who were in a concentration camp can understand the restraint of the *Stubendienst* in overcoming herself.

The inspection began. The polished boots of the SS officer made their way slowly through the passage as we remained in absolute silence. Alongside him were Katya, Bozka, and Alzinka. They walked from one end of the barrack to the other, and then they left. Only the silence remained, and it was a while before we spoke.

Bozka continued to provide soup for the sick. We regained our strength, and Gutka got well. She was among the first to go out and stand in line. One day, one of the functionaries dealt her a mortal blow to the head. She had an open wound that filled with pus and would not heal. Gutka lay down again, never to rise. I do not know who hit her. Who knows? Perhaps it was Bozka, who saw to it that we had soup.

The cold continued. The snow fell. Lice dulled the mind and hunger gnawed. We died like sprayed flies. Those who recovered from typhoid sat cross-legged and swayed to the left and right like wheat in an open field. They were propelled by lice, gripped by despair and melancholy, and no longer fought. They closed their eyes and fell: one to the front, one to the right, one to the left. The floor was covered with corpses, and the commandos came to drag the dead out-of-doors.

One day Rivka Pliwecky, the bright lawyer whom I knew in Lodz, fell to the ground. A man in the commando came and took her away. The commandos filled their pockets with bread or anything else they could find among the dead, and they took from

Rivka as well. The next morning, the "dead" girl returned to the barrack. She had managed to "recover," and had dug herself out from under the snow. She looked like a skeleton, but she was breathing; her soul was still alive. When Rivka presented herself before God another time, however, He accepted her.

When all but Lolka were ill, Marilka annoyed her. The hungry girl did not seem to remember that she, too, received help when she needed it. Marilka wanted Lolka to help her and her alone, and Lolka agonized over the issue. Her dilemma was not an easy one, but she solved it according to conscience without abandoning the struggle.

The month of January seemed endless. The girls no longer got up, and Lonya refused Bozka's soup. She said: "Riva, you should eat. You are taking care of the girls." For two days Lonya ingested nothing, and the red circles around her eyes grew paler. Her hair, curled like the wool of a sheep, crowned her head as she lay quietly, neither demanding nor desiring anything. On February 2, 1945, a clear and beautiful day when the sun shone and snow covered the yard in the camp at Stutthof, Lonya asked me to kiss her. When I did, she closed her eyes forever.

Lonya was the first; Fella was the second. She had collapsed without saying a word while sitting cross-legged and she, too, was removed from the barrack by the commandos.

My beautiful Bella was suffered as none can imagine, and was the third to die. Her body literally fell apart; parts of her body dropped off, and there are no words to describe the agony she knew....*How did the girls hold on to their feelings when they parted from one another with warm words, hugs, and kisses? What experiences did they undergo?* Bella, like Lonya, said good-bye with kisses. I came to moisten her lips, but she waived my hand aside and kissed me; then her head sagged and her eyes closed.

Marilka died during the night; I found her in the morning, curled up, cold and dead. Esta still had a fever and had not recovered from typhoid, and Gutka was in severe pain due to the head wound. I did not stop trying; maybe there was something I could do for those who remained....

One twilight I went out into the camp yard. I found live coals—probably left over after the *Stubendienst* had cooked for themselves—and I decided to make use of them. I looked for and found a tin can, got water from the lavatory, and put the can and its contents on the coals. Suddenly, as if the earth had "opened up" and produced him, a man with a large dog at his side appeared next to me. He commanded the dog to attack me and it did; it jumped and bit me. Torn, frightened, and miserable, I returned to the barrack without bringing hot water to the girls.

The bite wound got infected and the lice tortured me. I lay still, the fight drained out of me. I refused to eat. The heavy burden of caring for the others now fell entirely upon Lolka's shoulders, and she performed her duties with devotion. Gutka and Esta accepted Lolka's care passively, but I rebelled. I was tough and refused to eat, but Lolka found a way....In those days, she said to me, *Zechishte Meluche,* or "What a piece of work you are!" When I refused to eat, she delivered a ringing slap to my face. My resistance collapsed. I swallowed a spoonful of soup between the slaps.

During this period the *Totenmarschen,* or death marches, began in Stuttof....We removed our clothes out of despair and lay naked, with the lice eating away at us. Then we were moved—however, I do not remember why we were moved. Perhaps the Germans decided to burn our block. Who knows? All I know is that after the war I found out that Esta had remained in the block. I do not remember anything. When I regained consciousness, I found Gutka next to me on the pallet. Lolka, it seems, had carried Gutka on her back like a sack of flour. What strength!

Gutka's last days passed in that block. Lolka brought the soup and was the first to drink; I came next, but only after being slapped, and Gutka drank last.

I remember how Gutka rose and sat down and how she held the bowl in her thin, untrembling hands. They still had strength, and one could see that she enjoyed the soup. She drank it to the last drop without pausing. She licked her lips and laughed, her beauty unmarred but for the loss of all her teeth. She lay down once more, and this I cannot understand—but it happened—Gutka, like the others, blessed us. She blessed Lolka and me with these words: "Rivale, Lolka, you will yet find goodness in life, and thank you for the wonderful soup."

Gutka died and I closed her eyelids with my own hands; after that she was lowered from the pallet to the floor. Lolka and I remained lying in the barrack. We did not cry. I only remember the strong winds blowing from every side.

One morning the Germans announced a "parade." I remember that I did not have the strength to stand for the *Appel* and that I did not seem to care, either. I lay down on a block of ice and could not get up. Lolka was frantic with fear that the commandos would collect me, for this is what they did with those whose strength gave out.

At the *Appel* we were given the "choice" of whether or not to go on the death march. Naturally, we declined....I do not remember how I was able to reach the barrack that had been "torn down," but I did it and even managed to lie on my pallet. Lolka lay alongside me. A girl passed by; she turned to me and stopped: "I remember those eyes," she said, and suddenly she shouted: "Riva Citrin!" "Yes," I answered. Full of pity for myself, I cried for the first time since the girls died. The girl cried and Lolka cried too. "I am going on the road," said the girl. "Take this, Riva. I have a down quilt here; maybe it will help you." Now, how can I explain the significance of a down quilt that played such an important role in our lives?

Another morning passed and we were still in the windy barrack open to the elements. Someone called me by name. Bluma Stav, who had been in the Lodz ghetto, discovered that I was lying in this barrack; she looked for and found me, and brought along with her a cup filled with cooked beets. "Take, Riva. Eat. I will come to you again." That was a good day for Lolka and me.

Bluma returned and decided to take me to her room. For some reason, that room was heated. *For some reason...*"I will come," I said, "but only on the condition that Lolka comes with me... *Only if Lolka comes.* I will not move without her." And Bluma agreed. When the *Blockältester* entered Bluma's room, she beat us mercilessly without asking for an explanation. More dead than alive, Lolka and I crawled back to the windswept barrack.

Lolka got a high fever and we were moved to the sick bay. I wanted desperately to help and I began doing things. My mind droned *I must do something, I must do something,* over and over again. I managed to crawl outside naked as I was, but I was intercepted. A well-dressed woman stopped and said: "Who are you? If you are going about like this, you will live!" And, suddenly, she recognized me. "Riva," she shouted. "Do not move. I will bring something to you." The woman, whom I could not identify with certainty, left and returned very quickly, handing me two baked potatoes. I twisted like a lizard until I crawled back to Lolka—this time, on all "threes," inasmuch as I held the potatoes in one hand.

We ate hungrily. The apathy left me but the fever did not leave Lolka. She began to mutter for water, and once more I crawled away in search of something hot for her to drink. I found Henka Ribovska. "I need hot water," I cried. She stared at me. "Riva?" "Yes." Without another word, she went into some room and brought out a can of hot water. This time, I navigated on my buttocks. I managed to return to Lolka with the full can of hot water in my hands. Not a drop had been wasted.

One day a woman who knew me in Gerdauen passed by. At that time she marvelled at me and asked me if I had a boyfriend. When I said that I did, she guessed that he was a doctor. The girls who were with me were amused by her comment and laughed, but I was flattered. Now I sat naked in the corridor, and she looked at me again and again unable to believe her eyes. "Are you really the one I met at Gerdauen?" "Yes," I said, and once more I pitied myself. When I began to cry, the woman gave me the soup she held in her hands. "You are young," she said. "You must live."

I brought the soup to Lolka and—who knows—perhaps the woman healed her. I became more energetic even though I crawled about naked and was wounded within and without, but I had been encouraged to keep trying....Since then Lolka and I have met this woman many times. We refer to her as the *Meshiach,* the savior.

# Liquidation

Stutthof was emptying and Lolka and I could not move. We lay on our pallet, miserable and despairing, hungry and weak. We were abandoned. Bluma Stav had seen us lying naked and had brought us dresses to wear. We covered ourselves with these, but we soon took them off and remained as before. The lice tormented us and we removed them by the fistful from the face and arms, legs and other parts of our bodies....The dog bite I had received was putrefying....

Next to me lay a girl whose chin was disintegrating. Rotted pieces fell from it but she lay quietly, without moaning and without removing the lice swarming all over her. From out of the lice crawling on her face, I saw her eyes ablaze like burning coals. A German guard passed by from time to time and once, when he passed near us, strange, inhuman sounds escaped this girl's throat. "Mr. Overseer, shoot me," said a voice from another world, but he continued to walk among the rows without saying a word.

*Diarrhea.* What is the meaning of diarrhea in Stutthof? Precisely this: it is a sign of the end of life. It means that at best one has two weeks to live.

...Lolka had diarrhea and a high fever, but I improved as she declined. It became my task to organize food and drink and I crawled about to do my job.

One day in mid-April, 1945, I sat at the barrack's entrance. I noticed that everyone behaved in an unusual way. Prisoners who still could stand ran in every direction; the *Stubendienst* ran; the uniformed Germans ran or fell flat on the ground, as if seized by a *dybbuk*. I remained where I was, petrified. I saw the sky covered with planes, like a flock of shiny gulls. Bombs fell, and I was no longer afraid. It was a marvelous spectacle. The metal wings glistened and, like birds on a beautiful spring day, cut through the air, filling it with hope. When the raid was over, I went to Lolka. She knew the end of the war was drawing near; we all knew, but we were afraid to allow our thoughts escape our lips.

Germans got up from the ground and came out of shelters; and *Stubendienst* returned to lord over us. Diarrhea plagued Lolka and lice drained our blood, but hope found a refuge in a remote corner of our souls. We knew the bombing of Stutthof brought with it tidings of liberation.

The days and nights passed, but I do not know how many. I did not know then and I do not know now; the days were long, and the nights very dark....*Could we make it?* I did not know that either, but I resolved to take better care of Lolka. We were all that was left of the thirty-three lovely people who had left Lodz together so long ago.

At the four corners of the camp the Germans still manned the watchtowers. Sometimes searchlights were used to flood the grounds. At such times, the light insinuated itself through the paneless windows and into every crack of the barrack....Lolka lay motionless and altogether like a wax doll, her illuminated face fixed in a peculiar expression. I heard her breathing heavily as I lay awake and in silence, waiting for the morning light. The morning star was my sign. When I no longer could see it through the window, I knew that I soon would be able to crawl outside to gather a little snow. I was determined to moisten Lolka's lips and relieve her thirst.

One morning I heard a strange commotion in the camp yard. The Germans had been moving about since dawn and the *Stubendienst* stood ready. A medium-sized flatbed wagon, hitched to a pair of horses, arrived. No one asked questions and no one said a word, but we knew something was about to happen. What would this latest affliction bring us?

That morning there was no *Appel* and a dense, strange silence hovered over us. The prisoners who could work removed those lying on the floor of the barrack and loaded them onto the flatbed wagon. Those who could get up climbed onto the wagon by themselves. The camp was being abandoned.

Lolka and I, still naked, did not have the strength to climb onto the wagon; we were among the last to be loaded on, like sacks of flour, and we lay at its edge. As the wagon drew farther away from the camp I gazed at the electric poles, the barbed-wire fences, the barracks, and the paths within the camp. At last, everything grew distant and dim until it disappeared from sight altogether. Now that no one was left in the camp, I tried to imagine the silence there. There is nothing and no one to be afraid of over there, I thought. The fear had left the camp together with us; it came with us. It was an inseparable part of us. Wherever we would go, it would be there as well.

*Where to this time? What awaits us? Why are we being moved?* The monotonous squeaking of the wheels added to the anxiety churning within us. We rode and rode. Finally, we reached a port. No explanation was given. It was April 22, 1945, and a boat moored at the pier expected us.

Those who could, entered the boat on their own; those who could not, were carried aboard and placed on the deck until it overflowed. There was no room for Lolka and me, but our "savior" appeared and said: "There is room next to me in the passage." And indeed she proved to be correct. There was enough room for two people to sit between the ship's interior and the deck. Lolka and I settled down. We had our down quilt with us, and we wrapped ourselves in it. The woman, the savior, saw to everything and even "made us up" so that we would appear "all right," but there was no food on board—nothing at all—not even the starvation rations of the concentration camp. We needed to "organize," but we had no strength to do it.

We knew we were at the Baltic Sea, but we did not know if we left from Gdansk or Gdynia. We did not know the name of the boat, and we did not know our destination; we only knew we were on a boat that was used for cattle. Before long, a rumor spread that we were sailing for Denmark.

Sky, sea, and boat. A day passed, and then a night. The sun appeared and disappeared with lightning speed. Clouds swept the skies and brooded overhead, and strong winds blew. The boat sailed on in darkness, thrashing about in a raging sea amid mounting waves. Were we about to capsize? The clouds unleashed their fury; they pelted us with hailstones and brought along with them a fierce cold. Moisture and mud spilled onto the ship's passage where Lolka and I sat exposed to the merciless elements attacking us on every side.

The boat sailed on. Another day passed, and then another night. Darkness and cold descended on us and clouds swept across the sky, occasionally allowing us to sight a solitary star. I could not keep track of those days and nights, but one morning our savior discovered bags of cattle feed in the belly of the ship and brought some of the grain to us. This was a great treasure and an enormous discovery, and the starved prisoners desperately tore the bags open to assuage their hunger. We drank sea water, Lolka no longer had diarrhea, and we began to feel better.

A new morning came and—there, in the belly of the ship, along a curved wall—I saw a man hopping about from place to place on his hands and feet. He was dressed in prisoners' clothes and wore a blue and gray striped cap. He hopped like a bird jumping from branch to branch, but his expression came straight out of the regions of madness. Like a wounded animal, like a tortured dog, strange howling sounds came out of him as if from within the bowels of a cavern.

An SS officer paced nearby and methodically made his way

toward him. He did not strike him, and he did not persecute him; he did not scold, and he did not shout. He merely held his whip under his arm and motioned toward the deck. The officer wanted the prisoner to leap into the sea—and that is what he did. His body sank like lead into the depths. When we looked, we saw concentric circles spreading out on the calm, blue waters. The "hopper," however, did not sink into oblivion. No, he did not "sink" in that way. Everyone had seen him touch life, and everyone knew that what had befallen him had created a bridge of sadness that would span all the generations of humankind.

Another new morning. The sea was calm; the sky was blue. The sun felt good, and our down quilt was nearly dry. We asked for nothing; we only wanted a little peace—but it was not to be. SS officers attired in their raincoats walked back and forth followed by *Kapos* in prison garb, and we sensed that something menacing was about to happen. Those lying on deck raised their heads; others tried to move their legs; still others attempted to sit. We who looked like skeletons still had eyes, still had feelings, and still knew both fear and hope. There is no doubt that we held on to that hope until the very last moment.

Lolka and I sat in the passage as if we were spectators. We watched as two "humans"—one a man in the SS and the other a prisoner—periodically lifted a human skeleton. One grabbed the arms, the other grabbed the legs—and both tossed the individual into the sea. The water surged and eddied a bit, and that was all.

One morning we heard an ear-shattering noise. We had been bombed and had taken a direct hit. Fragments flew in all directions. A girl was killed next to me and another was killed next to Lolka, but we two remained unharmed. The flying debris did not touch us, but rather became embedded in the down quilt in which we were wrapped. The feathers spilled onto the deck and intermingled with the blood of the injured. Sighs, moans, and death besieged us at every turn. Later in the day we were bombed and hit again, but this time we heard the shout: "The ship is on fire!" Panic ensued.

People pushed one another in order to reach the deck, and the number of wounded mounted. Lolka cried: "I will not go up! I fear water more than fire!"

I was pushed against the edge of the deck until I was half in the water, but someone grabbed my hair and pulled me out. When I got back on deck, I had but one aim: to return to Lolka in the passageway. *The fear mounted.* People's faces were covered with soot....Some fainted and others, pushing toward the exit, trampled on the fallen. The wounded held on to the last vestiges of strength left to them and tried to stay on their feet. When I caught sight of Lolka, I embraced her with these words: "From this moment on nothing will happen to us any more," but Lolka shouted: *"Zechishte Meluche,* we are sinking! Can't you see how close the water is to the deck?" "Yes," I said, "but the boat is moving forward. The engine is okay."

And so it was. The boat moved on and burned; smoke towered, and tongues of flame were reflected in the water. We did not cry; we did not shout or sigh. Silence overcame us. The waters of the sea swelled and the boat advanced. *"Shema Yisrael, Adonai Eloheinu, Adonai Echad."* The prayer had come from the deck. Did you hear it too, God?

A German rescue boat arrived in the evening. Once more we panicked; we ran and pushed. The strong moved toward the lifeboat; the weak remained where they were. Lolka sensed that I was gripped by apathy and went in the direction of the lifeboat, but I sat on the deck of the burning ship. After a while Lolka returned for me, pushing her way through to help me, but she fell into the water and someone pulled her out. She wept and pleaded: "Get up! Why could you stand before? Why did you say nothing would happen to us any more? Why are you sitting like an idiot? *Zechishte Meluche,* get up! Come!" I was not afraid of her; this time she was far from me. She was in the lifeboat, and I knew that she could not deliver a ringing slap to my cheek.

One day the Germans fired into the air to direct us to the

lifeboat. Everyone did so, but I alone sat on the deck. Suddenly a young, tall, handsome man approached me and asked: "Child, why are you sitting like that?" I did not say anything. It was almost dark, and he removed a flashlight from his pocket; he shone it on my face, looked at me, and said no more. He simply scooped me up in his arms and moved me to the deck of the lifeboat—but not before he had wrapped me in his sweater. The night and the cold and the darkness wrapped me as well, and I dozed off. When I awakened, I no longer was on the deck. Lolka hovered over me and whispered: "Riva, Riva, how did you get across?" She gave me a cup of real hot coffee and she placed me on a comfortable bunk. That same day— May 1, 1945—we reached the port of Kiel.

Kiel had been badly hit in the bombing raids of the war, and piles of brick from ruined structures were strewn throughout the city. We were put in the large hall of a building that still remained standing. There, for the first time since I had left Lodz, I sat at a table.

The Germans who "liberated" us could not control the situation, and no quantity of food was sufficient for the starved survivor. They threw food at us—onions, for example—as if to monkeys. Whoever was quick caught something. They threw beets, and I believe they also threw bread. They gave us drinks, too. Whoever stood on his feet received a ration, but I sat at the table and did not move. I was proud.

Lolka became enterprising on my account, and this is how it has always been with us. If I was helpless, she was helpful; the weaker was shored by the stronger. In this case she continued to organize. She looked after me with devotion; she divided her spoils, and she brought "all the best" to me—including part of a beet. When a girl offered me a cigarette for the piece of beet, however, I had no need to think twice about the transaction.

The survivors hopped from place to place in the hope of catching a bit of food. Some were satisfied with minor spoils, and some had managed to organize a storage place for themselves; they ran and pushed; they fell and rose. Others wanted justice. "You got something to eat! I saw it with my own eyes! I, too, want to eat!" There were a number of tables and chairs in the hall, but no one other than I sat. I watched what happened as I smoked.

Lolka arrived with a cup of coffee in her hands—but when she saw me in ecstasy over the cigarette, she flew into a rage. Almighty God! What anger! She sent the cup crashing to the floor. "Who do you think you are? Riva Citrin from Lodz?" "You bet I am! Riva Citrin is sitting at a table. You don't have to bring food to me. The war is over, and the Germans have lost. There will be a better world and we have survived to live in it, Lolka. We will never be hungry again."

Lolka had been left gaping, but the truth of the matter is that since the Germans were "our liberators," the taste of freedom had fallen flat.

# From Kiel to Friedrichshof Camp

✿ ✿ ✿

Our liberators' sleeves bore the identifying armbands of the SD; they were the *Sicherheitsdienst,* or intelligence wing of the SS, and they took charge of us.

We were put into touring boats and we sailed on the Kiel Canal. We sat on benches and we were comfortable. A German caretaker patrolled among us and from time to time asked if we needed anything. The weather was pleasant and the trees were turning green. We saw villages and towns that had become rubble, but we also saw flocks of birds. They warmed our hearts and calmed us as they dove to the surface of the water or uttered their cries. We were enchanted, and yet we spoke in whispers.

I cannot remember either my condition or Lolka's, because I was in some sort of a torpor or psychological twilight zone. We had been wounded horribly, and had not yet made the transition from war and servitude to wholesomeness. We were like clay in the Germans' hands; they transported us, but no one asked where we were being taken. We had grown accustomed to not asking questions, but we were physically and spiritually exhausted too. The end of the war had come and none knew what lay in store. Deep, deep within us we evidently repressed such thoughts, for we did not ask ourselves what we would do at the next destination.

When we landed we were told to disembark, however, the Germans assisted those who could not walk. We were now in Friedrichshof, a camp for Belgian prisoners of war. We received a room for four, with four bunks in it. The Germans brought us coffee and a little bread in the morning; soup at noon, and a drink, bread, margarine and jam or cheese at night. This time there was no discrimination, and the sick got their rations. Some of the survivors went out into the camp yard and organized all sorts of food and clothing. Some went to nearby villages and brought back vast treasures of food.

Lolka and I lay in our room. We did not move. The camp was infested with lice, but not to the extent of Stutthof. Once more we removed our clothing, but at a certain point a spirit of rebelliousness possessed me. I found a knitted garment that had been cast aside. I unraveled it, made knitting needles out of a sliver of wood, and knitted a garment for myself. Lolka and I took turns wearing this new garment, and on alternate days the one who remained naked lay in the bunk. Apathy settled in on us again, and we did not bother to get anything additional to eat.

On May 8, 1945, I had the knit garment on me when I crawled out into the yard. I was not far from the barracks and leaned against a barrack wall. It was a warm, clear, and beautiful day. A young man passed by, stopped, and began to talk to me in both French and Flemish. I understood very little, but we somehow managed. The fellow was Belgian and his name was Franz. I introduced myself and then he asked: "Riva, are you hungry?" "Yes," I replied. "I am."

Franz ran off and immediately returned with a bowl of pea soup. I navigated on my buttocks, holding on to the bowl in order to reach Lolka. "Where are you going," he asked. "To my friend." "Eat," he said. "There is more, and I will bring you as much as you want." "No. Lolka must first get her half. First I will share," I replied. Franz carried the bowl for me and I crawled to Lolka through the long corridor. She and I shared the soup and thanked him. "This was very good; very good," we said. When he asked if we wanted more, we said that we did. In a little while Franz returned with two full bowls of soup—one of which was carried by a friend who had come along to help. On that day, May 8, 1945, I had eight bowls of soup.

Franz and his friend brought us clothing and provided us with utensils, and Franz became our guardian—but he did not have to care for us for very long. Lolka's fever returned and was quite high; all she wanted was water. Meanwhile my arms got swollen; my body could not handle the huge portions of soup Franz had been kind enough to bring to me.

At about this time I heard two girls from Lodz chattering in the corridor outside of our room. They peeked in for a moment, but I heard one say to the other: "Did you see Riva? She will not live..." The following day a medical committee arrived. They examined us, and we were transferred to Schafstadt Hospital—midway between Kiel and Hamburg.

# Schafstadt Hospital

We were in a German hospital where only German was spoken, and we believed that the ninety women who survived the ordeal of the burning ship were among the last of the Jews because we had no access to news.

The suffering was not over and the sadness did not end. Girls died every day. Frieda, one of the girls who was a *Musulman* and little more than skin and bones, was placed near the window. She received a colorful, Gypsy-like printed kerchief, and with it she crowned her skull of a head. Her legs were folded under her in a manner we had seen many times before on the floor of the barrack in Stutthof. She was unable to straighten her legs; she was unable to hold a spoon in her hand, and she was unable to lift her head. She was fed but she could not swallow, however she could speak. "The war is over; soon I will go home. I will certainly meet my family," she said. When the head doctor addressed her, she spoke to him as if he were her father. When the nurse approached her, she stroke her and spoke to her as if she were her mother: "I promised you, mother, that I would survive the war."

On an early evening in the spring of 1945, Frieda died. She died with her legs forever locked, and her skeletal head wrapped in the flowers of the colorful Gypsy kerchief, happy and joyful in the belief that she had been reunited with her parents. That same night Frieda was removed from the room and we did not turn on any lights. In the dark ward the dams had been breached, and each girl spoke of what had befallen her. Among the stories I heard, I shall never forget what Lucy Elstein of Kovno had to say…Like a flowing fountain, Lucy related over and over again the story of Fort IX and the murders that took place there. We lay in silence as she spoke of the three years she spent as the secretary to Dr. Elchanan Elkes, the elder of the Kovno ghetto…

Many deaths followed Frieda's—but, with the exception of a girl named Rosa, I do not remember any of their names. I recovered quickly and gained weight—an unbelievable two pounds a day— but before being brought to the hospital, I weighed fifty-five pounds.

Lolka continued to have a high fever and was given a special diet. As always she wanted to share, or at least have me taste the delicacies she had been given. One day, her doctor whispered that she would like to speak to me privately. We went to her office, sat across from one another, and I waited for her to begin. "I am sorry to say that Lolka is very ill," she said. "She has open tuberculosis." The words struck me like lightning, and I understood that Lolka, who knew the implications of tuberculosis, could not be informed about her condition.

I had nightmares, and I still limped. I had difficulty walking, and I had a pain in my left hip because I had been made to lie on a block of ice during an *Appel.* Nevertheless, my condition improved daily. I could help the girls lying in my ward, and even go to the other wards where girls who had been rescued from the burning ship were in need. I said nothing to Lolka about her condition. When she offered me the special foods she received, I could not refuse. I did not want to arouse her suspicion.

The girls got well slowly; they began to walk and then to hike. A beautiful park surrounded the hospital, and we ventured farther into this area in order to acquaint ourselves with the vicinity. There was a broad field in the park, the gardens were filled with flowers, and their fragrances refreshed us. It was a place tended by skillful hands and we sat on the grass, enjoying the warmth of the sun.

One day as we sat on the lawn, we were distracted by an approaching figure. There were many German soldiers and Russian prisoners of war about, but this fellow somehow seemed different from the others with whom we sometimes exchanged banalities. For one thing, he was set apart by his broad smile, shy demeanor, and friendly eyes; for another, we neither could identify the khaki beret nor the uniform he wore. When he came closer, however, we saw the Star of David on his sleeve. His name was Yisrael Cohen and he was looking for his sister, Frieda, a girl who had been with us on the boat and was here with us now. Excitement, tears, embraces, and stories burst in on us at the reunion of a brother and sister.

We saw a Jewish soldier who spoke Hebrew and had come from *Eretz Yisrael*. We listened and heard, but that day Yisrael Cohen could not sate our curiosity. He was a fairy tale come true, but we could not quite believe it yet...That very day Yisrael took Frieda with him, and we never saw either of them again. They entered the landscape of dreams and inhabited tales of wonder. We had discovered that other Jews were alive; that there were survivors in Germany, and that there was a Jewish settlement, the *Yishuv*, in *Eretz Yisrael*.

Yisrael Cohen told us that in the city of Lubeck a Jewish committee had been established from among the survivors' representatives, and that the aid activities of the Joint Distribution Committee and the Red Cross were underway. Since I was healthier than the others, I was asked to go there and notify them of our presence here, to represent us, and to check up on the situation beyond the hospital walls.

I had gotten fat or was perhaps still a little swollen, but I felt I had the physical and emotional stamina to do the job. My hair had grown in and my head looked like that of a hedgehog; this frustrated me terribly, but I was determined to overcome.

I cannot remember how I got to Lubeck—but I do remember that I walked through the streets feeling quite alone and uncertain as to where to turn. I asked passersby about the Jewish community and I asked them about the Joint. The Germans, although polite, could not help me. I did not know what to do or whom to turn to, but I knew that I had to find some sort of a Jewish institution by the end of the day. As I stood there helplessly, a dark-eyed, moustached fellow stopped next to me. He looked at me and spoke to me in Polish: "Are you Riva Citrin's sister?" "No," I replied. "I am not her sister. I am Riva."

I am unable to convey the excitement of this meeting even though there had been no special contact between us in Lodz. This was the joy of one Jew meeting another after a calamitous war. I had been "recognized" by Greenberg, the streetcar conductor in the ghetto whom I sometimes encountered as I went about my business; this was an acquaintance.

Greenberg invited me to the house he shared with four young men from Lodz. I agreed at once and without fear, because I knew that I was on the right track. Among those living with Greenberg was Karol Schwarzbard, who had worked in the Kitchens' Office and whom I had known in Lodz.

The fellows helped me to connect with the Joint. I told them that I represented some ninety Jewish women patients in the Schafstadt hospital, and their attitude was positive. They promised to come to the hospital as soon as possible, but I did not agree to this. I informed them that I would not return until a Joint representative came back with me. I explained that the sick had no contact with the outside world, and that they were still at the Germans' mercy.

My hosts offered me a room and asked me to stay. From the point of view of my health this was a reasonable request, but I refused on two counts: I had promised I would return to report back to the girls; and I could not leave Lolka alone. We finally arrived at an agreement. I would be ready to move in if I could come with Lolka and if they could provide us both with a room and suitable amenities.

For several days I ran about among Jewish and non-Jewish institutions in order to arouse interest in the plight of the girls. The public servants were very busy, but three days later I managed to travel from Lubeck to the hospital with two Joint workers: Mr. Goldberg; and Bertha from England…This visit by the representatives of the Joint signalled a change for the better for all the inmates at the hospital—and each one of them was recorded on the list of survivors who were still in Germany at the time.

After many warnings from doctors and many entreaties from me, I managed to have Lolka released. The few days I had been gone seemed like an eternity to her, and she had become convinced that I had betrayed and abandoned her. What she had undergone in my absence was indeed hard to bear, but we traveled to Lubeck with the two staff people from the Joint in the knowledge that waiting for us was a home with good, warm-hearted Jews.

# From Lubeck
# to Bergen-Belsen

❀ ❀ ❀

$M$y acquaintances from Lodz lived in a two-story building and they provided Lolka and me with a room on the second floor. Because of my despair over Lolka's condition, I rarely left the house. I had no idea whether or not Helunia and Zosia were alive and I did not search for them; I did not believe.

Since the dining room was on the ground floor, Lolka and I met our new friends at mealtimes. The men were happy and told stories about the events of the day; they smoked cigarettes and spoke loudly out of exuberance. Someone told of his success in business; he patted his hand over his shirt pocket and said: "Here is my profit for today." I did not know if what he referred to were marks or dollars. Someone else took a diamond ring from his pocket. "Do you like it," he asked. When I said that I did, he offered it to me. For some reason this embarrassed me, and I told him that I do not wear diamonds. "Look, Riva," he said: "What has been, has been. I have money. Money is the passport to anywhere in the world. I have not yet decided where I am going. I only know one thing for sure. We have to forget. We have to forget everything. To live, that is my motto." He coaxed me: "Try to wear the ring. I want to see how it looks." I placed the ring on my finger as his hand trembled in mine. The stone in the ring glistened—and just so had the fellow's thoughts glistened in my mind. I removed the ring, finished eating, and went to my room.

It was clear to me that Lolka and I had to move. I contacted friends in the Zionist movement and marshalled my energies to-

177

ward getting us a room. I also contacted Bertha, who understood our predicament and with whom I had become friends. She helped me and several days later, some time in September, 1945, we obtained a room near the Lubeck synagogue.

While in Lubeck I met Norbert Wolheim, who has since emigrated to the United States. Norbert, a German Jew, was a Zionist who had passed through "the gates of hell" during the war. He was very active and cooperated with Yossele Rosensaft, who later became the president of the World Union of Bergen-Belsen survivors. I also met Hadassah Bimko, who married Yossele, and two sisters: Regina and Tsasia—who later married Karol Schwarzbard.

On the High Holidays all of us went to the synagogue. Rav Gothelf prayed and chanted from the *bimah,* and his pleasant voice still reverberates in my ears…I began to change, and I began to participate in all sorts of activities. On one occasion someone took a picture of me; due to that very photograph, I met Zosia and Helunia…

Once when I went to the synagogue toward the evening, a young man entered in a dark blue military uniform; he was a pilot in the RAF, and wore a lieutenant's insignia. He was blond and did not appear to be Jewish to us, but he made a point of approaching those present. He wanted us to know that he was a Jew, that he came from *Eretz Yisrael,* and that his name was Aharon Remez. How proud I was when, after the holidays were over, the pilot helped us move our things to our new room. Aharon carried steel beds, mattresses, and other belongings which we felt were too heavy for us to carry.

When we were settled in our room friends began to visit, and our place became something of a social center. I remember one evening in particular, when Aharon sat and wrote as another friend, Sylvia, talked on and on—and I wrote memoirs on every scrap of paper I could find.

Aharon taught us to dance the Israeli hora, which differed from the diaspora hora. He told us about life in *Eretz Yisrael,* and of public and political events. I got the impression that everyone there was great, and I remember asking him whether or not the people of *Eretz Yisrael* were more idealistic than others. I was concerned with whether they were able to forego materialistic objectives, which then seemed to me to be rather petty, and I wondered if the party system blocked the way to matters of principle. Aharon answered unequivocally that human beings were only human beings wherever they were, and that more should not be expected. From his response I concluded that there was no room for excessive idealism—but this realization did not in the least alter my determination, striving or yearning to go there. Not long thereafter, Aharon left Lubeck. We corresponded and, later on, when I went to Israel, his entire family befriended me.

In time, Lolka and I left Lubeck with the assistance of the soldiers in the Jewish Brigade...One day as we sat in our room, we heard a vehicle stop outside. We peered out of the window and saw that a military jeep had parked in front of the synagogue. Two soldiers jumped down. One was dark with a tangled shock of hair and the other was light, freckled, and red haired. We immediately went outside. To our great joy we learned that these were our soldiers...

There were no barriers between the Brigade soldiers and the survivors. We listened to them and they listened to us—and in this manner, we created a bridge of understanding between us. They reinstilled our faith in mankind and, because of them, we sensed our renewal in the belief that a new world awaited and wanted us in our land.

These two, Shmuel and Yehoshua, brought us news and told us of charting a new path, albeit illegal, to *Eretz Yisrael.* They did not promise a smooth journey, but rather spoke of unknown trials and a difficult trip. They kept nothing from us and nothing held us back. We did not experience a moment's hesitation; we did not have a second's doubt. We believed this was the way we must walk, and the news of the decision spread like wildfire. Some survivors became excited; some thought twice. One girl said: "I cannot join you. I ordered a suit from the tailor and it is not ready yet; I also ordered new shoes." This amazed me, but nevertheless I accepted her reasoning.

Time was short and we had little time to think. We had to drop everything and go to Bergen-Belsen, where both the illegal immigration center and the survivors' center were located. At that time, Mr. Bilauer and his two sons lived among the Jews in Lubeck. The younger son, Adam, was fifteen and wanted to join us—but the situation was fragile. Lolka was too sick to undertake the journey, and Adam was too young.

Shmuel Potic tried to persuade me to leave without Lolka. He promised to find her a sanitarium in Switzerland and vowed to bring her to me afterwards. I told him that I would not go without her, and Lolka was adamant: "If I am sick, you also want me to be alone," she cried. Shmuel grasped the situation; he saw that he did not understand and that emotional content overcomes reason—and he agreed that Lolka and I were to go to Belsen where the final decision would be made. On the strength of that, I told Adam Bilauer to join us and I assured his father that I would be responsible for him.

When I reached the illegal immigration center I asked to see Arye Wishniak, the regional head of the organization. Arye sat alone in the room. *This is the appearance of a man who works underground.* I entered. Arye's blue, dreamy eyes were fixed in a face hard as desert rock. I sat across from him and presented my problems. "Lolka has a condition," he repeated after me. "And what about Adam Bilauer?" "Adam is fifteen years old," I said. "If he remains in Germany he will fill his pockets with money from illicit profits, and he will settle in this accursed country."

Arye did not reply on the spot, but I knew that Lolka, Adam, and I would start on the road together—and so it was.

# Reunion

When it seemed to me that Zosia and Helunia were dead, I was in despair and found little meaning in life other than in caring for Lolka. She must recover and live, and I too must live if only for her sake. Such thoughts scurried through my mind.

A convention of the survivors in the region was about to be held in Bergen-Belsen, and it was my duty to be there in behalf of the Zionists in Lubeck. On the designated day, before leaving for the convention, I lay on the couch and daydreamed. In my dream I heard a strong knocking on the glass door in the house at 30 Franciszkanska Street. This is how Zosia would knock, I thought —and then I leaped from the couch. "Lolka," I cried. "Zosia is alive! I heard her knocking on the door a moment ago!" *"Zechishte Meluche,* you are talking nonsense; you are having hallucinations," she said. "Come back to reality." She did not hesitate at all before she slapped my face.

It worked; it always worked. I was afraid and I accepted Lolka's warning. I returned to the couch and thought: *Lolka is right. This is a hallucination; this is daydreaming.* That was the morning of September 21, 1945, and I was gripped by sadness as I set out for Belsen.

A truck waited in front of the house and the entire delegation from Lubeck climbed onto the canvas-covered truck. We drove and drove; the weather was good and my friends sang or joked with one another, but I withdrew into myself. I acted as if I had nothing in common with anyone or anything. My comrades understood and tried to cheer me; they asked me questions, but I only answered with a word.

When the truck approached the survivors' camp, we came to a large yard. As the truck stopped, a man with a familiar face came toward me. At first he walked; then he ran. "Riva, Zosia is alive! She is here in Bergen-Belsen!" The bringer of good tidings, whose name I no longer remember, helped me down from the truck and continued to run. I too ran and ran, but then I stopped and thought: Why do I run? Whom do I bring with me from the family? What good news can I give her? Not one sister who came with me remained, and out of my many friends only Lolka lived…The man urged me on: "Come, Riva, Zosia is alive! She is waiting for you!" Only then did I ask: "And Helunia? What of her?"

I entered the room quietly. I was miserable and ashamed—ashamed to be alive. I cried and Zosia cried and our tears intermingled; the others who were in the room left…Helunia was alive in Burgsteinfurt, and Zosia spoke of their tribulations, picking up her story from the time I had last seen her during the fateful selection in Auschwitz which had sent us on our divergent paths. "They took us back to Birkenau," she said. "We were registered by name, and both Helunia and I said *Citrin*. After that they took away the clothes we had been given earlier. We were stripped naked and in that state we were led into a chamber. There were pipes on the ceiling and on the walls, and two tiny glass windows opposite one another. Beyond the windows, and on each side there was some sort of a corridor where the SS walked back and forth. On the far side of each corridor there was a large window with shutters which appeared to us to be constantly opening and closing them. Each time the shutters were closed it became dark in the chamber, and we prayed for 'it' to come. But the shutters opened again; light filtered in through the tiny windows.

"The SS peeked at us through the tiny windows. The chamber was small, and the crowding great. Body touched body. Impossible to move. Every woman reacted differently. Naked and miserable, we rubbed against one another and looked in every direction. Up above was a ceiling with devices allegedly for showering, but there were pipes all around the walls as well....Some women lost their minds and scratched their faces with their fingernails until they bled. Some shut their eyes and fell silent, and some mumbled the names of their children and loved ones. Others prayed: 'Quickly. Oh God,' and others screamed.

"Helunia broke out in red splotches all over her body. I hugged her and prayed for the end to come—only quickly, quickly. Late in the evening, however, we were suddenly removed from the chamber. We did not know why we were put in or why we were taken out of there. After our ordeal, we were issued Auschwitz-style clothes and told to sit on the ground outside....Darkness. We waited. It was good to breathe the fresh air after an entire day in the chamber....We heard the roll call from the adjoining blockhouses, and we saw bread and 'coffee' being distributed.

"After everyone had entered the blocks, we were divided into groups for the various huts. Helunia and I were assigned to Block 19, which contained some twelve hundred women. We had gotten no food that evening. In Block 19 we again became 'numbers' and it was a relief for us, for we were now just like everyone else there: hungry prisoners in Auschwitz." At last our sobs erupted. The dams burst, and neither of us was ashamed.

Zosia and I left at once for Burgsteinfurt. When we arrived there and I saw Helunia, she truly surprised me. She was as beautiful as ever; she was happy; and she was involved with a young man in the British Army, Mickey Levy.

Helunia was full of life; her hair had grown and her laughter rang out. She had decided to remain in Burgsteinfurt with Mickey, and Zosia did not know whether to be happy or not. She found it hard to accept Helunia's decision, and I did not know how to react either. I only understood that we had to return to Bergen-Belsen without Helunia, and that I bore some resentment. Who was this Mickey, anyway? What does Helunia know about him? She understood a little English but she barely could say anything in the language, and we could not speak to him at all. What could we do? *We gave them our blessing.* Zosia and I stayed with them for two days before we returned to Belsen; Helunia and Mickey remained in Magdeburg; from there they went to London to get married.

On the twenty-sixth of September, the survivors swarmed into the square where the ceremony for unveiling the memorial was to take place. We went, made many stops, and saw the signs on new graves. Only yesterday and only today these people were alive, but their ordeals had triumphed. Among the graves, we discovered the new tombstone of Zosia Grossman—my friend Shifra's sister and the daughter of Elimelech and Ella Grossman.

Many others did as we did, and it was hard to reach our destination. Zosia and I held on to one another as wave upon wave of anxious people seeking someone known rushed across the grounds. Excitement filled the air. We heard the cries and the kisses, and we saw the rush to go on with the search. *The search.* I looked for no one. There was no one to look for any more.

The meeting that night was very emotional. The participants included Silberman, British Member of Parliament; Brodetzky; Meir Argov; Captain Arye Simon; and many others from *Eretz Yisrael* or other nations. Some were from the Jewish Brigade and others were emissaries of the Jewish Agency. Arye Olevsky served as the secretary of the Bergen-Belsen organization, and it was he who took the minutes of the addresses given at that time.

Zosia and I stood and watched the restless ones as they passed by or ran about. All at once, a fellow who had not said a word threw himself at us—kissing each of us in turn. A current of joy tainted by sorrow coursed through us as the fellow grew calmer and delivered a note to Zosia. She read its contents, burst into tears, and handed the note to me. I read the following: *Zosiu, I heard you are alive. There are rumors that you became involved with another man and went to Holland. I am in Lodz. Yehuda.*

The following day, Zosia and I returned to Lubeck. Zosia met with Lolka and then, on the next day, she set out for Poland. She was on her way to Lodz to rejoin Yehuda.

Zosia and Yehuda eventually left Poland illegally. When they crossed the Alps in the winter of 1946, Zosia was pregnant with their son Alex. They reached Italy, where they stayed until early 1949, and from there they went to Israel. In 1971, Alex was killed in an accident while serving in the Israeli Defense Force.

# Bergen-Belsen Revisited

Belsen was the place where the living encountered the dead and asked themselves or one another if survival was worthwhile. Remnants, solitary individuals without a framework and without a redeemer or home, looked for family, friends, and support. They asked: "What are we to do?" "Where are we going?" "What now?" If a man survived without his wife and children, without a home and without means, how and where should he begin?

As the representative from Lubeck, I had an opportunity to speak at the convention. Among other things, I warned that the plans for *hachsharot*—training farms—or any other forms of "temporary settlement" in Germany were dangerous. People were tired and very quickly would become attached to a room, a house and its walls, possessions, and perhaps even to the Germans themselves—who would claim they knew nothing...

The British forbade us to enter *Eretz Yisrael,* but I was aware of the saying: "Judah fell by fire and blood, and it shall rise by blood and fire." I wanted to participate; I wanted to join the fighters in Palestine. I wanted to *attain the privilege* of being a fighter. I was angry at the world that owed us such a huge debt and not only failed to repay the note, but also denied its existence. Despite such strong sentiments, however, I was ambivalent—for in a chance conversation with Captain Arye Simon, I argued that the survivors of the concentration camps should not be permitted to enter *Eretz Yisrael.* I was afraid of the question: "How did you remain alive," a question applicable to every one of us. Did we sin to preserve our lives at the expense of others? If so, we should not be allowed entry. Did we maintain integrity throughout? If so, why yes, we should be allowed. I wanted to maintain "the ideal" even as I felt: "Blessed is the man who was not there, and had no need to contend."

Arye rejected my reasoning entirely, and I needed a great deal of time in order to evaluate things properly. Today I see all the survivors as martyrs. Then I accused. I demanded the impossible.

When the convention was over I returned to Lubeck, and before leaving for *Eretz Yisrael* I returned to Belsen. This time I met Arye Schwartz who asked, "Where are you from?" "From Lodz," I replied. "Perhaps you know the Grossman family there?" "Which Grossman family?" "Elimelech and Ella," he replied. "My wife, Saba, is from Lodz; her parents were in the ghetto with their two girls, Zosia, the eldest, and Anya, the youngest. "I knew them; I knew them," I replied. "And how I knew them! Your wife was my closest friend! I was in the ghetto with them until it was liquidated!" I then told him how my sister and I had found Zosia Grossman's grave....We sat and shared a great deal; we became very close, and to this day we have a relationship that has never been broken...

Bergen-Belsen is a symbol of Nazi persecution and the place from which many survivors left for *Eretz Yisrael.* The threads of faith were spun by the Jews in the Brigade who inspired us in Belsen, and it was from there that we survivors began to think of a new life. The encounter of the Holocaust survivor with a soldier in the Brigade—or any other Jewish soldier for that matter—was tantamount to a connection with life. To their everlasting credit, they removed the barriers before us as we tried to reintegrate our fractured lives.

◆ ◆ ◆

We made our way to Belgium by roundabout roads and arrived in Antwerp, where we sat in a locked house for three months...Our daily menu included "fatling," or smoked fish, and each of us ate ninety during that period. We never tired of it...The soldiers in the

Brigade taught us Hebrew; we sang the songs of *Eretz Yisrael;* and we presented skits or conducted parties. We slept on three-tiered bunks, and everything was good. The people of the Brigade had provided us with the answers to the questions: "What now?" "What next?" They were the living bridge over which we crossed....When Meir Argov visited us in Antwerp he said: "I stand here in reverence. I was privileged to cross the threshold of the Holy Temple—and you are that Holy Temple." I, who had to respond to his statement, answered thus: "For us, you are the high priest."

In house "A," where we stayed in Antwerp, were the members of *Kibbutz Buchenwald.* I was attached to them as was Lolka, and we went to *Eretz Yisrael* together. These survivors are today the members of *Kibbutz Netzer Sereni,* a kibbutz they founded.

From Antwerp and hidden in British army trucks, the fighting Jewish Brigade of the British army took us through Germany to the port of Marseilles. We sailed from Marseilles on the ship *Tel Chai,* but on the 27th of the month, the ship was seized by the Royal Navy while on the high seas and its entire complement was taken to the Athlit internment camp.

We stayed in Athlit several days. During that time some of us received letters and some of us were visited by relatives. Lolka and I received nothing and no one visited us until one morning, when Lolka and I were asked to go to the gate. Standing on the other side of the fence was Dvora Potick, Shmuel Potick's wife. She introduced herself, looked us over, and handed us—through the fence—a parcel of sweets and a brief letter. On that occasion she invited us to her home, and later on I received a postcard from Saba Grossman-Schwartz. She had found my name on the lists of the Jewish Agency, and had written to say that they expected me in Jerusalem.

I was very excited at Saba's news, but I could not decide what to do. I knew that I had to find a place to live, and I did not want to be with the people of *Netzer Sereni* because of the question with which I was plagued: "How had they survived?" One morning, however, everything changed. Meir Argov appeared at Athlit with Golda

Meir, and it was she who helped me to find a home in *Kibbutz Ramat Yochanan*....Lolka, still very ill, had to go to a sanitarium and Adam rejoined his father, who had remarried and preceded us to Palestine.

I arrived at *Ramat Yochanan* on Friday, April 5, 1946, a very hot day. I had walked from *Kfar Ata,* some miles away, because I had been told that it was "not far," but to me it had seemed very far indeed. I was given a room in a wooden hut; I had a bed, a table, and a closet. Curtains fluttered from the screened window, and on the table stood a vase containing flowers. It was Friday night, and in the dining room the tables had been set with white cloths.

# Epilogue

Jerusalem, blessed with an abundance of greenery, rose up before my eyes. Tall erect cypress trees formed an avenue at the entrance to the building where we studied—two girls to a room—I and a sabra full of life, vibrant and laughing. Laughing from her heart and about anything; a nineteen-year-old girl, flourishing, joyous, happy. Each week she would expectantly await the parcel of sweets which her mother sent without fail.... This was Shoshana.

We went on hikes, crossing the Judean desert on foot, and we came to Kibbutz Beit Ha'arava. The earth was cracked and the clods were rimmed white with salt. The Dead Sea lay motionless, like a mirror reflecting the blue skies above. We climbed Masada. We continued on to Eilat. The Red Sea lay before us. There was no Egyptian border as yet, for everything was under British rule. We threw off our shoes and clothes; we collected shells, hiked and enjoyed nature. We went into Sinai desert. And this was Malka Levin and me.

Waves of loneliness washed over me. I missed my home, my parents and my sisters....

I went to Tel Aviv. A friend from Lodz told me that Shmuel Chirurg, who had been in the ghetto, lived at 20 Adam Hacohen Street—which was not far from where I stayed. I knew Shmuel, for he sometimes had come to my office, opened the desk drawer, and taken out a cigarette. I knew Rebecca, his wife, and his children, Ruthie and Zili. I knew his uncle, Pini Gershovsky, too.

Shmuel now lived on the third floor with his brother, Moshe

Gurari, and I began to climb the stairs very hesitantly. Virtually everyone in the ghetto had a tag, and Shmuel's tag had been that of "a decent person." I kept climbing, hesitating all the way, but suddenly Shmuel was there. We could not speak and fell weeping into one another's arms. We asked no questions; we knew the moment of inner touching had happened.

Two days after our meeting, Shmuel and I decided to get married. On the very day of our decision we were already sitting on the floor, looking at the pictures Shmuel had received from Rebecca's sister, Heniele. We looked at the photos of Rebecca and their daughter, Ruthie—there were none of Zili. They had left at the end of August for Auschwitz, and from there they were sent to Stutthof. On September 10, 1944, Rebecca and the girls went into a gas chamber in Stutthof, along with all of the women with whom they had come on the transport.

The wedding took place between *Yom Kippur* and *Sukkot,* on Friday, September 26, 1947. A friend from Lodz lent me a skirt and a white blouse, and I used mosquito netting for a veil. Aharon Remez was there and the Lembergs were there; Chana Gurari and her sister, Eva Carlebach, were there too. A modest dinner for five—including Shmuel and me—was held in Chana's home.

We found a place to live in *Yad Eliayhu.* (Shmuel and a friend opened a textile store on Lilienblum Street in Tel Aviv, and he worked from morning to night.) We used orange crates from the grocery store for a table and kitchen cabinets; our bed came from more veteran settlers; and our eating utensils were tinny and black, but we accepted everything with love. Almost all the women in the vicinity were pregnant, and so was I.

It was there in *Yad Eliayhu* that we stood by the radio and heard the votes cast by the United Nations on November 29, 1947, and it was there that Shmuel and I danced through the night, ecstatic with joy, hoping that the Jewish state would become a reality.

On Friday, May 14, 1948, at four in the afternoon, we stood outside of the museum on Rothschild Boulevard and listened as

David Ben-Gurion declared the establishment of the State of Israel. On May 15, the War of Independence broke out. Shmuel joined the army, but he had no rifle. The Israelis did not have enough guns for everyone—and yet he and others like him were out in the trenches....

We left our house after the Arabs attacked the Jewish quarter, while I was in my eighth month, and moved in with friends at 11 Gilboa Street in Tel Aviv....My daughter Rina was born at the Hadassah Hospital on June 19, 1948, during the first armistice of the War of Independence. For me it was as if the whole world had turned upside down. The sky was underfoot and I touched it in my overwhelming joy. In fifteen months, on Saturday, September 11, 1949, my son Michael was born. And so there was a son named Mishael! A *Brit* in Israel! The son of Riva and Shmuel who had lost entire worlds and had begun to rebuild.

6

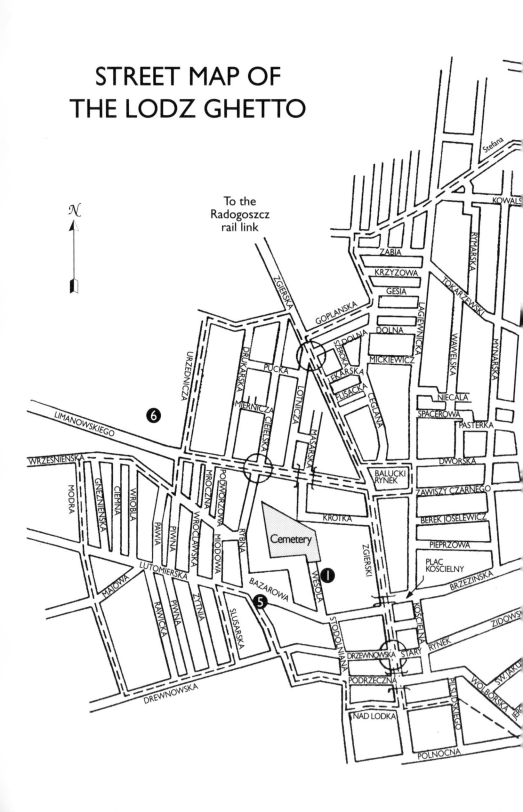

# STREET MAP OF
# THE LODZ GHETTO

N

To the
Radogoszcz
rail link

Strefana

KOWALS

ZABIA

KRZYZOWA

GESIA

RYMARSKA

TOKARZEWSKI

ZGIERSKA

GOPLANSKA

SZEROKA

DOLNA

DOLNA

LAGIEWNICKA

WAWELSKA

MLYNARSKA

URZEDNICZA

DRUKARSKA

PUCKA

LEKARSKA

MICKIEWICZ

MIERNICZA

LOTNICZA

FLISACKA

CEGLANA

NIECALA

SPACEROWA

PASTERKA

LIMANOWSKIEGO

CIELELSKA

MASARSKA

⑥

DWORSKA

WRZESNIENSKA

PODWORZOWA

MROCZNA

BALUCKI
RYNEK

ZAWISZY CZARNEGO

MODRA

GNEZNIENSKA

CIEMNA

WROBLA

PAWIA

PIWNA

WROCLAWSKA

MIODOWA

RYBNA

KROTKA

BEREK JOSELEWICZ

PIEPRZOWA

Cemetery

PLAC
KOSCIELNY

ZGIERSKI

①

BRZEZINSKA

LUTOMIERSKA

MAJOWA

ZYTNIA

BAZAROWA

WESOLA

ZIDOWS

RAWICKA

PIWNA

SLUSARSKA

⑤

STODOLNIANA

KOSCIELNA

RYNEK

STARY

DRZEWNOWSKA

STARY RYNEK

SW. JAKU

PODRZECZNA

WOLBORSKA

PILSUDSKIEGO

DREWNOWSKA

NAD LODKA

POLNOCNA

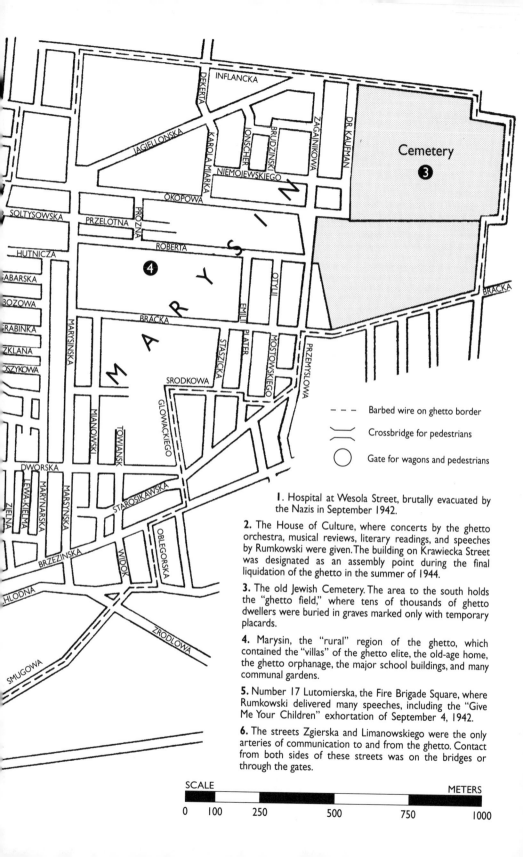

**Cemetery**

❸

❹

- - - Barbed wire on ghetto border

⌣ Crossbridge for pedestrians

◯ Gate for wagons and pedestrians

**1.** Hospital at Wesola Street, brutally evacuated by the Nazis in September 1942.

**2.** The House of Culture, where concerts by the ghetto orchestra, musical reviews, literary readings, and speeches by Rumkowski were given. The building on Krawiecka Street was designated as an assembly point during the final liquidation of the ghetto in the summer of 1944.

**3.** The old Jewish Cemetery. The area to the south holds the "ghetto field," where tens of thousands of ghetto dwellers were buried in graves marked only with temporary placards.

**4.** Marysin, the "rural" region of the ghetto, which contained the "villas" of the ghetto elite, the old-age home, the ghetto orphanage, the major school buildings, and many communal gardens.

**5.** Number 17 Lutomierska, the Fire Brigade Square, where Rumkowski delivered many speeches, including the "Give Me Your Children" exhortation of September 4, 1942.

**6.** The streets Zgierska and Limanowskiego were the only arteries of communication to and from the ghetto. Contact from both sides of these streets was on the bridges or through the gates.

SCALE

METERS

0   100   250   500   750   1000

# A

*Yardscapes*

# YEAR

# A

# Yardscapes

## YEAR

[ Ideas and Plants for Bay Area Gardeners ]

# MIA AMATO

## SASQUATCH BOOKS
### SEATTLE

Printed in the United States of America
Distributed in Canada by Raincoast Books, Ltd.
02 01 00 99 98          5 4 3 2 1

Book and cover design: Karen Schober
Cover and interior illustrations: Diane Bidga
Copy editor: Frances Bowles
Index: Sigrid Asmus

Library of Congress Cataloging in Publication Data
Amato, Mia.
     A yardscapes year : plants and wisdom for Bay Area gardeners / Mia Amato.
          p.          cm.
     First appeared in the San Francisco Examiner.
     Includes bibliographical references (p.     ) and index.
     ISBN 1-57061-178-5
     1. Gardening—California—San Francisco Region.  I. Title.
SB453.2.C3A43   1999
635.9'09794'6—dc21                                          98-47933

Sasquatch Books
615 Second Avenue
Seattle, Washington 98104
(206) 467-4300
www.SasquatchBooks.com
books@SasquatchBooks.com

Sasquatch Books publishes high-quality adult nonfiction and children's books related to the
Northwest (Alaska to San Francisco). For more information about Sasquatch Books titles,
contact us at the address above, or view our site on the World Wide Web.

*To Mom and Dad*

# Contents

# *Acknowledgments*

All of the material in this book first appeared in the *San Francisco Examiner* newspaper; along with the gardeners who so graciously allowed me into their gardens and the gardeners who read and enjoyed the columns, I owe much thanks to two editors at the *Ex*: Bruce Koon, who first hired me for the job, and Jo Mancuso, who was the reason I stayed.

I would also like to thank Dick Tracy and Terry Dvorak at the *Sacramento Bee,* and Karen Wilson of the *San Diego Union-Tribune,* who were instrumental in giving "Yardscapes" a wider reach into Northern and Southern California. This circle of friends and readers is now further broadened with this collection, published in Seattle by Sasquatch Books. My thanks to all the Sasquatch team for their help, and my thanks most especially to Gary Luke, for his vision, guidance, and simpatico good sense.

# Introduction

Northern California to me will always be the Terra Brava, the wildly beautiful western edge of America where eternal spring ignores the calendar, and where a deceptively mild climate for year-round gardening sows the hopes and dreams of gardeners who like to explore, push the envelope, and create their own beauty in a countryside that can mimic the best of Tuscany, Hokkaido, Quito, and Kew.

Lots of people say they leave their hearts in San Francisco; many gardeners break their hearts here too. Terra Brava is always a challenge to those who till and tend the earth, for climate and conditions are unique and often hard to understand. Weather is wacky from the word go, and soils are a complicated mix; rainfall is not to be relied on, and then there's the odd earthquake to tumble your laid-stone garden wall.

I am not a native of this land. I learned to garden in New Jersey, where weather is appropriate to four seasons. The spot where I grew up is, oddly, a hillside above a protected ocean bay. But any resemblance to my San Francisco garden stops right there, stops cold, as cold as the fog that creeps in and out each day, in certain degree or less, through the course of the gardening year—even on Potrero Hill.

Northern California's combination of bumpy tall hills and oceanfront peninsulas creates a weather unheard of anywhere else on earth. The city of San Francisco changes its season by the hour: Early mornings are foggy, damp and wintry cold; the sun pierces the clouds as much as it will do so by noontime, and green growth is as warm and sparkly as on any bright spring day. But an hour later the glare is harsh and the ground is dry, and by 3 P.M. a stiff, dry wind rises to sting your eyes and batter the rose petals. At dinnertime a calm signals a change in the wind direction, and the pall of night, with its blanket of damp and slightly salty air, drives everyone indoors but the slugs.

Television weathermen like to call this our "natural air conditioning," these conditions that suck up and dispel great draughts of moist sea air that move, in the course of a day, as regularly as a tide or the breathing in and out of some great animal.

And this is the "good weather." We pay for rainless skies from May to October with August days obliterated by fog, and droughts that come in seven-, ten-, and twenty-year cycles. Gardeners here never seem to get used to it. Each time we relearn our palette of unthirsty plants, but every time that palette gets broader. On the last round, lots of us discovered the charms of South African plants; I think we would see more New Zealand species in our garden centers today if the rains hadn't started up again in 1995, prompting everyone to go back to grass lawns and marigolds.

Do the right water thing and Terra Brava still throws curves: the earthquakes (such as the one dubbed "The Pretty Big One" in 1989), the massive flooding that also caused landslides (1997 and 1998), deadly wildfires (1991 and 1995), and freak freezes (1991) that browned bougainvilleas and turned the princess trees into purplish pulp. But there is no need to reinvent your own gardening wheel, or learn all the hard lessons by yourself. The information—and the technology—is out there.

In many ways I've been lucky. Long before I began writing my newspaper column, I took the Master Gardener certification class through the University of California Cooperative Extension's agricultural office, based in Hayward at the time. If you have gardened for a while in California, the names of my instructors are familiar to you: Dr. Ali Harvandi, an icon in the turf industry; Dr. Bob Raabe, the plant pathologist known for his pink socks; the trendspotting food maven Dr. Nancy Garrison; and many more experts from Davis, Fresno, Riverside, and the entire University of California system.

It was a journalist's dream: After every class, I collected a business card. This became the basis of a Rolodex of experts I could later tap for columns covering the state of the art in pest control, water management, and orchard technique. Becoming one of many lay practitioners in the Master Gardener program—the further extension of the Cooperative Extension, in the old days known as Farm Agents—also put me in touch with other expert home gardeners.

It's an old axiom that a reporter doesn't need to know the answers: she just needs to know where to ask the questions. Landscape architects, designers, nursery owners, contractors, builders, artists, and the officers of our many local plant societies helped with the information you will find on these pages. But I've rarely recommended a plant I didn't try to grow myself, never suggested a technique I myself did not attempt on the serpentine slope of Potrero Hill, where the sun shines a bit brighter and a glimpse of the Bay was my inspiration whenever I looked up from my computer desk.

At last count we had nearly 550 horticultural groups in the region between Mendocino and Monterey. Our gardening community is broad but shy and sometimes hard to find. Where possible you'll find a local address for the sources cited in these pages, and I hope you'll contact your brother and sister gardeners there to learn more. Gardening can be a solitary pleasure—as is writing—but I have found both so much more rewarding whenever I could reach across a fence or garden gate to find something I could later share with you, dear reader.

—Mia Amato

# I. Late Winter Awakenings

[ *Early Rambles Under Fog* ]

# [ Preparation: The Rites Before Spring ]

*Quick greens to grow for winter salads;*
*using shadows to determine where to put*
*your lettuce bed. Plus: saving*
*tomatoes over winter.*

I mark the start of my gardening seasons on the winter solstice, which is not spring but the first day of winter and the shortest day of the year. Because of the sun's angle in the sky, shadows cast by buildings and trees are all at their longest. But if the sun is shining as you look around your garden around noon, you will notice which areas are bathed in sun and which are in shadow. Mark the sunny areas—with sticks or a line drawn in the dirt—and you will have located the ideal spot for your first spring vegetables.

Spots that get sun around noontime at the solstice will always be the warmest parts of the garden in winter. This is where the ground will dry out first after rain, providing the most hospitable climate for your weatherproof garden chair, and where you may launch the winter gardening of lettuces and cold-weather greens.

For many gardeners in coastal California, the first crop of the new year is arugula. Sow seeds of this spicy green now and you'll be harvesting tender leaves in less than a month. Watercress, red mustard, and mizuna are others to try and, like arugula, they sprout in about a week. Having grown all these, I recommend them for quick results: You only need small pieces to liven up a salad of store-bought greens. Mâche, too, also called lamb's lettuce or corn salad, is easy and fast, but I found the flat rosettes of leaves hard to pick, and the taste as flavorless as any 'Iceberg' found in a supermarket.

So far, the biggest salad hit at our house has been the last of the 'Early Girl' tomatoes. In November, when the vines are pulled out, any large fruits that are still green are saved. These we store in the garage, in a paper grocery bag with one green 'Granny Smith' apple at the bottom. The apple emits ethylene, a naturally occurring gas that triggers ripening in other fruits.

One by one, the green tomatoes in the bag turn red, and every now and then we take a few out to add to a salad. The taste isn't as good as that of a sun-ripened tomato, but compares favorably with a supermarket tomato. Using the apple is a simpler, less messy method than ripening tomatoes on a windowsill, and in some years it keeps us in tomatoes until Valentine's Day. (Persimmon lovers note: An apple in a bag of persimmons will ripen these fruits quicker, too.)

The average yard harbors a variety of microclimates that can be put to good use by backyard farmers. The garage—frost free but cool—is a good stand-in for a root cellar. Any south-facing wall that collects the last rays of the sun on a winter's day is a good place to install subtropical vines and shrubs that are most cold tender, such as bougainvillea, princess tree, and citrus limes. Even a passageway that is cold, dim, and damp year-round can become a purposeful garden for mosses, ferns, or flavored mints.

Spring in coastal California gets the jump on most of the continent, beginning two months earlier and keeping that lead throughout much of the growing season. Roses that would be pruned elsewhere in March are pruned in January here—are your shears oiled and ready? Rosebushes will be in full bloom by April, and potatoes and tomatoes ready to pick as early as July. It's a lot to take in, even if you were born here. I was not, and so much of what I have learned about gardening was hard won by experience.

So, pausing between the last lessons of the old year and inspirations for the new, I start my garden on the winter solstice. It's well worth it to take some time now, to really notice where you are on the planet, the positive realities of your climate and weather, and to note the year's last roses and the first green tips of narcissus hurrying their way to spring.

# [Old Roses for Armfuls of Flowers]

*The most reliable rose cultivars*
*for fog-belt gardeners and a laugh at election*
*year bare-root offerings—'Desert Peace'*
*and 'Barbara Bush'.*

When you are selecting roses, the newest might not be the best, especially if you're looking for a rosebush that will reward minimal attention with armfuls of flowers. In California, January is the best time to plant new roses, and you'll find them available then as bare-root plants at nurseries, most for less than ten dollars each.

For some years I have followed the rose shows around the San Francisco Bay Area and could not help but notice that certain varieties tend to win the blue ribbon more often than others do. If you tour municipal rose gardens, such as Berkeley's Rose Garden, or the one in Golden Gate Park, or the one in the small courtyard outside the San Mateo Garden Center, you'll also find repeats of these same tried-and-true cultivars.

By and large, they are loose-flowered roses, with a low petal count (fewer than thirty). This makes them less susceptible to mildews encouraged by our cool and foggy summer nights. It dawned on me eventually that the thick-flowered red 'Blaze' that festooned walls and fences on the East Coast has its opposite number here in the bicolor rose 'Joseph's Coat'. Loosely petaled, this red-and-yellow climber is ubiquitous in the Bay Area simply because it succeeds where other roses fail.

Other local success stories include the bright pink rose 'Sexy Rexy' and the deep red 'Europeana'. I have yet to see a miniature rose win more blue ribbons locally than 'Minnie Pearl' does; and I've never seen any new gardener disappointed after planting some of the sturdier, older hybrid teas, such as pink 'Bewitched', white 'Pascali', or that best of the yellows, 'Helmut Schmidt'. Thankfully they are still widely sold, along with the legions of brand-new roses introduced every year.

How does one judge new roses? The All-America Rose Society (AARS) attempts to do it for you by designating several as "best" each year. Winning cultivars are judged by test panels around the United States, which doesn't necessarily mean they will do well where you happen to garden. Still, a certain amount of disease-resistance and ease of care can be expected from AARS roses. A 1992 winner of note, for example, was the coral and cream bicolor rose 'Brigadoon'. This is an offspring of 'Pristine', a white rose that's a frequent prize winner in our local rose shows. The petals on 'Brigadoon' have a rich pink tone on the outer edges, with white touches within.

As with racehorses, picking a rose by its parentage and breeding guarantees a winner more than making your choice by name. Still, commercial distributors tend to lean toward topical names—even political names in election years. In 1992 Wayside Gardens offered 'Desert Peace', a red and yellow rose, or, to quote the catalog, "a brilliant desert sunset reflected above golden sands . . . to honor the peaceful conclusion of conflict in the Middle East." That same year you could get a pale pink 'Barbara Bush' tea rose from Jackson & Perkins. A year later (postelection) I could walk into the two large retail nurseries on Bayshore Avenue in San Francisco to find the aisles lined and jammed with bare-root 'Barbara Bush' overstock that had been marked down dramatically. They couldn't *give* those roses away.

My advice would be to start, at first, with the older cultivars proven to work in the Bay Area. That would mean easily grown floribundas, among them the fragrant, plum-colored 'Intrigue' and 'French Lace', a rose that starts pink in the bud, opens white, then ages to a wonderful ivory. Both are great roses for old-fashioned bouquets.

Wayside's catalog and many local nurseries now carry the heirloom roses developed before the twentieth century, and the "English" roses that are very recent hybrids created in England by David Austin. Most of these are dense, many-petaled roses that respond best to long periods of bright sun and deep watering. They are not easily tended but grown for their romantic or historical associations. The sweet pink 'Souvenir de la Malmaison', for example, was named after Empress Josephine's country place. It has a squashed bulldog kind of face and a wonderful fragrance, but like many tight-petaled roses, may not open well in foggy neighborhoods. Austin's roses have the same type of heavy, flat blossom: 'Abraham Darby', a coppery pink Austin rose, is one that I know grows well throughout the East Bay.

Among "old" roses, single-flowered species such as *Rosa rugosa* are making a stylish comeback here, as they are on the East Coast. One single-flowered (five-petaled) rose to look for is the yellow 'Father Hugo' *(R. hugensis)*. I have seen this thriving in coastal gardens from Mendocino to Carmel.

*SOURCES:*
*Jackson & Perkins, Medford, OR 97501.*
*Free catalog. (800) 292-4769.*

*Wayside Gardens, Hodges, SC 29695.*
*Free catalog. (800) 845-1124.*

# [Outdoor Orchids Are Easy]

*Cymbidiums are
the beginner's orchid
for mild-winter
gardeners.*

Late January is prime time for climate smugness. On most of the continent, your friends are knee-high in slush and snow: They call and tell you just how bad the weather really is. They ask how things are in California, and smugness overdrive kicks in. "Well," you say, "we haven't had all the rain we wanted, but the orchids are blooming on the back deck."

Cymbidium blooming season starts around December and can last well into March. According to Jeff Britt, the Director of Orchids for Rod McClellan Company in South San Francisco, they're an ideal outdoor potted plant for the Bay Area, because they prefer summertime day temperatures eighty degrees and below, and nighttime winter mercury drops to about forty degrees. "They'll take it down to thirty without much difficulty," Britt adds. Other orchids—masdevallias, laelias, and some dendrobiums—can survive as outdoor plants but the cymbidium can be practically foolproof.

"They may be planted in the ground in a raised bed, but that's not common," Britt says. "Most people like to have them in pots, so they can be brought indoors for display or if we get a freeze."

Many of the Acres of Orchids at the McClellan Company's green-houses are devoted to cymbidiums. Although not as showy as the hot pink and passionately purple cattleyas, they have true orchid-shaped blossoms, which grow in clusters on a stem called a flowering spike. Flower color can be pink, white, yellow, brick red, green, or bronze.

"Cymbidiums need a lot of bright light to bloom," says Britt. In foggy coastal microclimates, such as those of Pacifica and San Francisco, the plants benefit from direct sun; in hot inland summer zones such as Lafayette or Palo Alto, direct sunlight is too hot and will burn the leaves. "The further away you get from the coast, it gets more difficult, because the orchids need cool temperatures at night to set flower spikes. The new miniature cymbidium hybrids tend to do better in those areas. With shorter leaves, they are much more heat tolerant."

Years of experience have taught Britt that the bulbous base (pseudobulb) of a potted orchid must sprout at least twelve leaves to produce a flower spike. "That's why it's so very important to use a high-nitrogen fertilizer during January through July, which is when the plant makes all its leaf growth," Britt explains. "You know the old saying, 'Corn knee-high by the Fourth of July' to get a good corn crop. Well, twelve leaves by the Fourth of July is a good rule of thumb for orchids."

Britt recommends fertilizing once a month, "or fertilize twice a month with a half-strength solution." At McClellan's, plants are fed automatically and almost constantly with a small quantity of fertilizer that's applied every time the plants are watered. "The old adage, 'weekly/weakly' works too," says Britt. "Home gardeners might try a quarter-strength fertilizer solution applied three times a month."

The most common questions Britt gets from novice orchid growers concern dividing and repotting plants into fresh chipped bark, the pre-ferred soil medium for these semiterrestrial plants. "Something about repotting seems to terrify people," he notes. "They think the plant is delicate. Cymbidium has roots like agapanthus, as tough as that. You have to be firm when you pull it out of the pot, manhandle it a bit."

The best time for repotting is just after bloom has finished, March through May ("June at the very latest"). If you've had a cymbidium for a number of years, and new growth is spilling over the pot, the plant should be divided into sections with at least three pseudobulbs and some current-year growth per division.

For the skittish, the company will, for a fee, repot the cymbidium for you, then babysit it to the point of blooming fitness at the in-house Spa for Orchids. Fearless do-it-yourselfers can find complete instructions for division and cymbidium care in a free brochure available at the nursery.

*SOURCES:*
*Rod McClellan Company, 137 Hickey Blvd.,*
*South San Francisco, CA 94080; (650) 871-5655.*
*The McClellan Company has another store located at*
*914 S Claremont, San Mateo, CA 94402*

## [Orchid Calendar]

JANUARY–MARCH Purchase plants in bloom. Place in bright location and water every other day, feed with high-nitrogen fertilizer once a month. Aphids and spider mites may be controlled with an insecticidal soap spray. Protect plants from snails by surrounding pots with diatomaceous earth or copper strips.

MARCH–JUNE Repot and divide old specimens. Scale insects, which appear as hard, crusty bumps on leaves, are best dislodged by scraping them off with a nail file: Most insecticides are useless against scale, because their hard shell protects them from sprays.

JULY–DECEMBER Switch fertilizer to 0-10-10 to encourage flower buds. Reposition plants during summer and fall to a cooler, northern exposure in hot microclimates. In cool areas, move plants to where they will get the most sun.

## [Freeze Damage Is Not Forever]

*How your garden*
*plants may have survived the*
*"Big Freeze," despite outward*
*appearances.*

Is your bougainvillea brownish? Jade plant drooping? Are you worried about whether your lemon tree survived the coldest weather in years? You're not alone. Jack Schwegmann, a Master Gardener volunteer for the free telephone advice line at the University of California Cooperative Extension in Alameda County, says that the phone service gets swamped with calls after the first freezing temperatures in December. Many counties in California have such a service (see numbers below) staffed by Master Gardeners, expert gardeners who have received training from the university to provide the latest horticultural advice.

"People are distressed by the appearance of dead-looking plants, and they ought not to be," says Schwegmann. "Most plants will come back."

Callers from Alameda County have reported temperatures as low as sixteen degrees (in Castro Valley) and most were concerned about their citrus trees. With university pamphlets close at hand, Schwegmann tells callers that it may be several weeks before freeze damage is noticeable. When it comes, it is in the form of blackened, burnt-looking leaf tips and stems that may extend down to the woodier main stems of the tree.

"It's the tender, new growth that's been killed off," Schwegmann says. "If the tree has been in the ground for several years, or is woody at all, it will survive." Fruit now on the trees, especially thick-skinned oranges or 'Meyer' lemons, may be okay to eat. Schwegmann suggests cutting one in half to check it out. "If it looks normal and juicy, it's fine," he says. "Damaged citrus will have a mushy-looking pulp that's an off color." Gardeners don't have to remove damaged fruit because it will fall off on its own.

Other landscape plants may soon show blackened branch tips, especially if they were pruned in the fall. Eugenia, a common hedge plant, can really suffer in a hard freeze, notes Schwegmann. Tropical succulents, especially jade plants used for outside landscaping, succumb when water in their fleshy stems freezes, bursting plant cell walls. Slightly droopy jades might recover if watered, but devastated plants may have to be cut back hard to make them resprout.

Schwegmann's best advice comes straight from the University of California, which strongly recommends that homeowners resist the urge to prune off dead-looking plant parts for between four and six weeks after they appear. "Wait till it's warm enough, when you see new buds breaking on the part of the plant that is still alive," Schwegmann says. "Then take each branch and work backwards to the first breaking bud. Make your cut a slanting cut, close to the bud, and don't leave a stub."

Another reason to wait is that plants that lose all their leaves in a freeze may not have any dead branches. Figs and roses and many street trees normally loose leaves in colder climates. A good rule of thumb is that, if your relatives in snowier parts of the country grow the same plant in *their* gardens, your garden plant will survive. "Azaleas and rhododendrons may lose some buds but they'll be okay," says Schwegmann. "Very early blooming camellias may have some damaged flowers. Camellias still in tight bud will be fine."

The university also recommends resisting the urge to add fertilizer to "help the plant along." Wait till buds break. Feeding flowering plants in winter, when the days are too short for adequate photosynthesis, will only result in a mess of weak, spindly branches that will not produce flowers.

Those browned bracts of bougainvillea will eventually drop off and be replaced with new growth. Garden geraniums, bush fuschias, and other plants shriveled to ground level should sprout new growth from the roots. Geraniums and fuschias in pots that froze solid may not be so lucky. Give them water when the pot soil is dry but don't overwater, says Schwegmann, and wait a month or two to see if the droopy stems fall off and are replaced with new growth.

Some good news: Richard Molinar, the urban horticulturist for Alameda County Cooperative Extension, says that there's evidence that a hard freeze, such as the one in 1991, kills off colonies of fuschia gall mite, the tropical pest responsible for the deformed flowers that plague fuschia growers especially in the Bay Area.

There's a real silver lining in a freeze for homeowners who have apple, pear, plum, apricot, almond, or cherry trees. To set fruit these all require a minimum of three hundred and preferably more "chilling hours"—weather below forty-five degrees. In our normally mild winters, some backyard gardeners in warmer zones rarely accumulate enough chilling hours to get a good crop of fruit.

### SOURCES:

*Cooperative Extension Master Gardener Programs exist in most counties in the western states. San Francisco County residents are referred to Alameda County (510) 567-6812, San Mateo County (650) 726-9059, or Marin County (415) 499-4204.*

# [The Magnificent, Misused Magnolia]

*Saucer magnolias*
*need their space: Michael Barclay*
*suggests a few for smaller*
*backyards.*

Well before streetside plum trees wave their pink-flowered branches, magnolias are in bloom. Their large, leathery flowers can be as wide as a dinner plate, with petals silvery pink on the outside, pure white inside. Their languorous boudoir fragrance hangs on the wind and stops people in their tracks. When the magnolias are in bloom in Golden Gate Park, joggers swivel their heads as they run by, and tourists look about in wonder and delight.

Alas, the graceful magnolia is ill used as a home landscape tree in California. Because they are such tall trees, the most beautiful deciduous species, which bloom in winter on bare stems, inevitably wind up lost as parts of property-line shrubberies. Of the evergreen magnolias, the less said the better: They're overused as street trees in San Francisco, trimmed to ugly mop tops, and drop their rubbery tan blossoms on the sidewalk sporadically through the year.

The popular saucer magnolia, *Magnolia soulangiana,* "is a bad tree for urban gardens, because it grows to the point where it shades everything else out," says Michael Barclay, a local landscaper. The Bay Area climate is one of the few that can support the frost-sensitive Asian magnolia species that thrive in Golden Gate Park but, he says, these are also too large: "Unless you've got an estate, forget it."

Magnolias need their *space.* Figure a distance from the trunk on all sides that equals the trunk height (which is usually between fifty and seventy-five feet) to see the tree properly, to appreciate the fine vase shape of the branching and each year's smoky cloud of white flowers. Trees may bloom as early as November in a mild winter; unusual frosts will dim their display. "When it gets [to] twenty or twenty-five degrees, the flowers start to blacken and the buds fall off."

In New Zealand, Barclay notes, new magnolias are being bred with the emphasis on hardier, smaller trees for urban gardens.

I asked him to suggest a few that would be suitable for us. For a small city backyard, the dwarf magnolias 'Iolanthe' and the yellow-flowered 'Elizabeth' can be showstoppers, he said, if planted where they will stand out as a ten- to fifteen-foot-tall specimen tree. Near the front door is a good spot. In a mixed border, Barclay likes to see them backed by dark evergreens, and perhaps set off with another early, white-blossoming shrub, such as the white form of flowering currant.

Star magnolia, *M. stellata,* is another choice. The petals are thin, like white ribbons, giving double forms the look of a white ribbon bow. Even in very small gardens one can achieve the proper viewing distance from a star magnolia by training it flat (espaliered) against a brick wall. Star magnolias can also be grown in large pots, if kept well watered in a sheltered spot. "A single stellata with large flowers, like 'Royal Star', looks very good in a garden setting," said Barclay. "In a perennial border it makes a wonderful background plant, putting on a wonderful show before anything else is in bloom."

For the magnolia look with a longer season of bloom, another choice would be the michelias. Native to Asia, michelias are part of the magnolia family tree and, in fact, hybridize so readily with the latter that some botanists now think that they are simply a different form of magnolia. Evergreens, michelias grow upright, up to about fifteen feet. "Mrs. Louise Davies has an *allée* of them," noted Barclay. "Several hundred, I think, on both sides of her main driveway."

The most common type found in nurseries is *Michelia figo*, also called banana shrub, because the blossoms smell a bit like that fruit. I remember seeing one at Robin Parer's geranium nursery Geraniaceae, in Kentfield, where the cooler climate had kept it blooming through May. Unlike the magnolia, michelias are best appreciated up close and personal, and you do not need an estate to see them at their best.

*SOURCES:*
*Michael Barclay's Really Special Plants and Gardens,*
*Kensington, CA; (510) 524-0888; by appointment only.*

*Geraniaceae, in Kentfield, CA; (415) 461-4168,*
*is also open by appointment. Catalog $4.*

# [Martini Gardens and Pipe Dreams]

*Martha Stewart visits Havana;*

*California bans smoking in public places.*

*Now just how easy would it be to grow*

*your own cigars?*

A brief news item—that Martha Stewart would broadcast live from Havana on the week of the pope's visit—was enough to send the mind of this rain-idled gardener racing. What would television's most elegant how-to gardener do in Cuba? Teach us how to grow our own tobacco and show us how to hand-roll our own cigars?

The actual television program was nowhere near my fantasy of Martha tilling the fabled "Cuban seed" into her Connecticut flower borders, curing the big leaves by hanging them, on leftover Christmas twine, over a smoking kitchen woodstove while the kids hand-paint the little paper rings. But in early spring all of us are fantasizing about the gardens we are planning for this year. Why not a cigar garden? What could possibly be more trendy?

Then I found out that they already do grow tobacco in Connecticut, and not very far from Westport. Two centuries ago, enterprising farmers brought the crop up from Virginia, and the state is still a source for high-quality leaves that are used as the outside wrappers for cigars made with blended tobaccos. "The General Cigar Company makes cigars up there, and they grow a lot of cigar wrappers in Connecticut," said Niki Singer, a senior vice president of the Manhattan-based *Cigar Aficionado* magazine. She said that the cultivar 'Connecticut Shade' was world famous. "It's considered one of the best as far as we know."

If New England can grow tobacco, so can we. Given California's antismoking fervor, there might be something racy, something end-of-the-century decadent, about growing tobacco plants in your own backyard. The foliage is large and tropical looking, the plants typically five feet tall. The flowers of some of the tropical tobaccos are spectacular, strongly fragrant, rosy red, yellow, or white trumpets. Their blossoms attract hummingbirds and, at night, large exotic moths.

Some smaller *Nicotiana* species (pronounced neeko-shee-A-nah) have already made their way into our gardens. At garden centers you can usually find hybrid annuals with starry flowers, but these lack the sweet scent of the species, which is as easily grown. *N. alata,* sometimes known as jasmine tobacco, sends up a two- to three-foot flowering stalk of fragrant white trumpets from a base of velvety, pale green leaves. It is a tender perennial; in my San Francisco garden it has wintered over and usually self-seeds. *N. sylvestris* is a taller, rangier plant, with flowering stalks that reach five feet, and it usually has to be staked to keep it from flopping over. I've also grown the annual *N. langsdorfii,* for its odd, pale green trumpet flowers.

You can get the smoking kind, *N. tabacum,* easily enough. In Southern and Midwestern states, gardeners of an older generation still grow a few rows of tobacco for their personal use, and the older seed companies still offer them seed. Henry Field's, for example, sells seeds of 'Burley 21', described as an "all-purpose plug tobacco for chewing and wrapping cigars," and a packet to try is only $1.15. You'll find the biggest selection of tobaccos in J. L. Hudson's Ethnobotanical Catalog of Seeds. This Redwood City firm offers several different cultivars of Burley and darker-leaved Havana types (the catalog notes this that seed comes from a source in Wisconsin). The Havanas are short-season crops, sixty-five days to maturity, so these might do the best in our cool summers. Some gardeners might be more interested in the Central and South American species listed there, plants grown for ceremonial or medicinal purposes. Hudson's catalog also offers enthnobotany books on tobacco culture. For the curious, there's a $1 reprint of an 1892 USDA pamphlet with instructions for growing, harvesting, and curing tobacco for smoking use.

I thought it might be interesting to try to cure a few leaves, to be later crumbled into a man's potpourri, to add that perfume note the French call *tabac*. But why stop there? Maybe I will make a martini garden, with an olive tree and a juniper bush. You see how easy it is to get launched into a garden fantasy.

If you're going to try them, the larger tobaccos will need about two feet of clearance on all sides, in a sunny spot with moist soil. Put them at the back of the border or give them a bed in the vegetable patch, to amaze your friends and delight the hummingbirds. All *Nicotiana* seeds need light to germinate, so it is best to scatter the small, fine seeds lightly onto a planting flat or directly on the soil. Young plants should be protected from snails and slugs until their leaves get furry enough. Their other nemesis is the tobacco budworm, also known as geranium budworm, a green caterpillar that's also a pest on petunias. The biological pesticide BT *(Bacillus thuringiensis)* usually takes care of them. The nicotine content of tobacco leaves, which were once crushed to make homemade insecticidal dusts, keeps most other pests—including deer—away.

### SOURCES:

*Ethnobotanical Catalog of Seeds, annual; $1.*
*J. L. Hudson, Seedsman, PO Box 1058,*
*Redwood City, CA 94064; phone unlisted.*

*Henry Field's Seed and Nursery Co., 415 North Burnett,*
*Shenandoah, IA 51602. Free catalog. (605) 665-9391.*

# [Fragrant Orchids]

*Who says orchids have no scent?*
*Here are a half-dozen species, fragranced*
*like "chocolate covered cherries" and*
*"static-cling dryer sheets."*

Were you to walk into a room filled with ten thousand orchids—as you certainly would if you visited the Pacific Orchid Exposition, held at Fort Mason in San Francisco every February—you would notice a funny thing. The room would be alive with tropical color and hubbub, the air humid, and yet the fragrance of flowers would be barely noticeable, an undercurrent scent that's not languid, but freshly green. Most show orchids don't have fragrance; it takes some hunting to find those that do.

Odd—because you use a scented orchid in the kitchen all the time. It's the vanilla orchid, which is grown commercially for its fragrant seedpod, the source of vanilla extract and vanilla ice cream. The flowers of the vanilla orchid also smell like vanilla—if you can get them to bloom.

"It's a hard one to grow, and it really needs a greenhouse," said Jean Lee, an orchid hobbyist and past president of the San Francisco Orchid

Society, which has hosted the orchid show for over forty-five years. In that time, few of her fellow members have managed to get a vanilla plant to bloom. "It grows on a long vine and it takes many years to get a flower," she explained. "And then the flower only lasts a day or two."

But an orchid that smells like chocolate is dirt-easy to grow, according to Tom Perlite, the owner of Golden Gate Orchids, a wholesale nursery in San Francisco. This one is an oncidium—one of the "dancing lady" orchids that can be grown on a windowsill. "*Oncidium* 'Sharri Baby Sweet Fragrance' really smells like chocolate," Perlite said, adding that the scent is stronger than that of the chocolate cosmos *(Cosmos atrosanguineus)* many of us attempt as a garden plant. "The fragrance of 'Sharri Baby' is enough to fill a room. It's a nice flower, too, a dark burgundy color."

Scott Zalkind, a horticulturist at Rod McClellan's Acres of Orchids outlet in South San Francisco, reports that the nursery keeps a blooming vanilla orchid in a greenhouse open to visitors. The huge vine is very old, purchased from the estate of the late actor Raymond Burr (also known as Perry Mason), who was an orchid hobbyist.

But Zalkind's favorite orchid for fragrance is a small plant with puckery yellow blossoms that smell like cinnamon. "The name is *Lycaste aromatica.* You can smell it four feet away." This, too, would be a candidate for the windowsill because it takes the same culture as oncidiums. "It's a cool grower, so the most important thing is to keep this orchid out of direct sunlight from 11 A.M. to 3 P.M., otherwise it will fry."

Many tropical orchids have fruity scents. *Maxillaria tenuifolia,* a small-flowered species, reeks of coconut, "but some people say it just reminds them of tanning oil," said Jean Lee. *Vanda coerulescens* has a fragrance variously described by its fans as "grape soda" or "bubble-gum."

Generally, the more colorful the orchid, the lighter the scent. *Dendrobium kingianum,* a small white creeping orchid easily grown outdoors in the Bay Area, has a noticeable perfume in the open air. Most of the larger-flowered greenhouse dendrobiums do not. Cattleyas, the big corsage orchids, can have a citrusy or jasmine scent (especially the white ones), but you really have to stick your nose in.

The common cymbidium, a popular outdoor container plant here, has a fragrance you will only catch if the plant is moved into a closed room and has at least two blooming spikes.

The purpose of scent is not, however, to attract humans but pollinating insects. As Perlite pointed out, "if a flower has strong scent, it's not likely to have a large, colorful flower, because then it doesn't need one." A good example is the night-scented brassavola orchid known as Lady-of-the-Night, which is pollinated by long-tongued moths. The greenish white flowers on this orchid aren't flashy, but many grow this plant for its scent alone.

Among orchid fanciers, the latest rage is for zygopetalums, mottled brown flowers with a dark purple lip. This fragrant orchid is so easy to grow that even I have no trouble getting double flower spikes from the plants I have in pots on the back porch. Their culture is the same as that of cymbidiums, but they flower in October and November. Brought indoors during the bloom period, zygopetalums release a strong floral perfume.

What do zygopetalums smell like? Mine remind me of hyacinths. To Tom Perlite, they smell of roses or potpourri. To Jean Lee, "it's a lot closer to the smell of those sheets you put in the clothes dryer to prevent static cling. But it's a sweet smell, and it's one of the easiest fragrant orchids for a beginner to grow."

### SOURCES:

*San Francisco Orchid Society, (415) 546-9608. Call for show dates.*

*Rod McClellan Company, 137 Hickey Blvd., South
San Francisco, CA 94080; (650) 871-5655. Open daily, retail.*

*Golden Gate Orchids, San Francisco, CA; (415) 467-3737.
Wholesale only, by appointment.*

*Orchids of Los Osos, 1614 Sage Avenue, Los Osos, CA 93402;
(800) 55-ORCHID or (805) 528-0181. Mail-order catalog $3.*

# [Stepping Stones Are a Piece of Cake]

*A recipe for*
*home-made pavers will*
*take your mind off*
*mud season.*

In about the middle of mud season, a gardener's mind turns to hardscape: stone or brick walls to shore up slippery slopes, firm and dry pavement to walk on, perhaps a patio. Working with stone and concrete is not hard for the do-it-yourselfer, yet it's surprising how many gardeners who love to dabble in mucky potting soil imagine that mixing concrete is somehow beyond their skill.

A quick project for the beginner is stepping stones. Wally Hennessy, a Master Gardener in Castro Valley, has a simple recipe for concrete pavers that's as easy as baking a cake. He's made dozens of homemade stepping stones for his hillside property, in many shapes and sizes. Most are round and have a surface of shiny pebbles over poured concrete set into molds he made himself. One mold is simply a thin metal band curved into a circle, the two ends crimped and held together by wing nuts.

To me, the mold looked very much like a springform cake pan. When I mentioned this to Hennessy, he agreed with a laugh. In fact, if all you need is an eight- or nine-inch stepping stone, Hennessy says that the ring from such a cake pan could certainly be used. Like a cake pan, the stepping stone molds "need to be greased on the inside, so the hardened concrete will slip out easily later," Hennessy pointed out. "I use motor oil, and I set a piece of heavy plastic trash bag down on the ground first."

After protecting the soil from the oil, he prepares some quick-drying, ready-mix concrete, whipped up in small batches in a wheelbarrow. "I think some people believe you have to mix up things like sand and lime, but all it takes is a bag of ready-mix," he says. "All you add to that is water, which I work in a little at a time until I've got the consistency I want, smooth but not runny."

Like cake batter?

"Yes."

The first shovelfuls are usually enough to fill his wider molds about a half an inch deep. Then Hennessy tosses in a few scavenged metal rods or a bit of chicken wire, his substitute for rebar, the metal reinforcement used by professional masons.

"I'll fill up the mold to the top and take a flat masonry trowel to smooth it off," he explains. "Then I might add some pebbles. These are polished Yuba quartz, from the Yuba River." Similar aggregates are easy to find at masonry supply stores. The pebbles are sprinkled a single layer deep ("just like a cake topping") and tamped down with the trowel "till the concrete starts popping up between the stones."

Then you let it bake—er, set?

"Let it harden for two days at least," Hennessy advises. Then the mold can be opened and, thanks to the oil, will slip off easily to be used again. "Concrete costs about two dollars for a sixty-pound bag," he points out. "That can make a quite a few stepping stones."

For some years, Hennessy generously held "open days" in his backyard, so other Master Gardeners and curious friends could get a closer look at the paths and a small patio made by this process, along with terracing and fountains creatively crafted of poured and reclaimed concrete. The stepping stones have all sorts of things on their surfaces: brass letters, handprints, leaf prints, sea shells, stones collected from a lifetime of family adventures. Mud season may come and go, but a paver cast in concrete is a bit of garden art that's built to last.

# [If It's Still Too Wet, Start Seeds Indoors]

*Step-by-step*

*instructions for*

*starting vegetables*

*from seeds.*

It's time to get moving on spring vegetable gardens, but the rain we all prayed for may be holding some gardeners back if the ground is too wet to dig. One solution is to start vegetables from seed indoors and set them out later, after you've had an opportunity to work in fertilizers and spring soil amendments.

Stick your trowel in the dirt and grab a handful. Squeeze it in your hand. If the clod crumbles easily through your fingers, it's okay to begin digging. If the soil clump sticks together, it's too wet. So start some seeds indoors.

Milk cartons, rinsed clean and cut lengthwise, are easy to start seeds in. Cut a few slashes in the bottom with a knife or scissors for drainage. I always use a sterilized potting mix, and dampen it with water from a spray bottle before adding the seeds. If you're new to this, just follow the directions on the seed packets. Generally, you can press large seeds down to three times their depth; sprinkle very fine seeds just on top of the potting mix. Mist the seeded containers again, enclose the entire container in a clear plastic bag, and put it in a sunny window.

If you are sowing warm-season vegetables or flowers, such as tomatoes, marigolds, zinnias, or peppers, place the containers where they will get some bottom heat for about a week—perhaps on the top of the television set, or on top of the refrigerator. The seeds will germinate very quickly and can be put in a sunny window with the others once they have sprouted.

As the seedlings grow stronger, give them plenty of light and remove the plastic bags, watering when necessary. Because seedlings bend toward the light, turn cartons that are set on a windowsill around every few days so that the tiny plants grow straight. If the seedlings are growing too thickly, pull about a third of them out when the second set of leaves appears. A sharp tug with tweezers will dislodge them, or you can snip the extras away with nail scissors. Leave the strongest plants, and remove the weak ones.

Leggy, spindly, and pale seedlings are simply either getting too much warmth or not enough light: Move them to a cooler, brighter window. Sturdy, dark green seedlings with at least two sets of leaves can be set outside (water thoroughly first) in their containers for an hour or so daily. This is called "hardening off" and prepares them for life outdoors.

Seedlings of cool-weather plants (leafy greens, most annual flowers) can be transplanted as soon as the outdoor beds are ready. Keep tomatoes, peppers, and eggplants indoors until late April; if you want to transplant them any earlier, put the seedlings under a cloche to protect them from cold air. A simple cloche can be made by cutting the bottom off a plastic gallon milk jug. Or cut the bottom off a quart- or gallon-sized glass jar with a bottle cutter kit (follow directions carefully). Transplant your vegetable and settle the cloche over it, leaving the top of the jug or jar open to the air. The cloche serves as a minigreenhouse, keeping warmer, moister air close to the baby plant.

It's also important to protect your transplants from snails and slugs.

Surround the plants with copper stripping or a sprinkling of diatomaceous earth. If you prefer to use poison snail baits, put them out now, early in the season, to keep the numbers down. Handpicking any snails you see as you check your vegetables or walk the garden on an overcast day also helps, especially if you do it every day.

# [Dandelion Wine]

*Dandelions blooming in the*
*open fields are a rousing spring tonic*
*and indicate it's safe to set*
*out your tomatoes.*

We've already seen the robins, and daffodils are blooming in the rain. True beacons of spring are sometimes hard to find in mild-winter climates, but this is a sure one: It's spring when the dandelions bloom. An Italian tradition says that, when dandelions bloom in open fields, the time is right to at least start thinking about setting out your tomato plants. Frost is not usually a problem for coastal gardeners, but a tomato planted out too early tends to languish for lack of sunlight in winter's shorter days.

In theory the dandelion is a seasonal indicator because its bloom coincides with increasing day length. Check a farmers' almanac and you'll notice that days are an hour longer at the end of February than they are at the beginning of the month. It's a big enough change to prompt a growth response in the dandelion, with mechanics so subtle that the plant will even adjust itself for extra gloomy hours caused by days of pouring rain.

Of all spring's yellow flowers, the dandelion is one that even school-children learn to recognize by its fluffy bright yellow flower and rosette of jagged leaves (our name comes from the French *dent-de-leon,* or lion's tooth). The plant is a tenacious perennial: Even if you dig it up, so vigorous is the dandelion that as little as an eighth of an inch of root left in the soil can make a new plant. Repeated spraying with a translo-cating herbicide for broad-leaf weeds will eventually kill them off in a lawn, but such herbicides should not be used in a vegetable or flower garden. And new recruits keep parachuting in from the fluffy seed-heads that form after the yellow flowers fade.

Gardeners who curse the dandelion might be surprised to know that it came to North America not as a despised and freeloading weed but as a warmly invited guest. Europeans who settled here brought *Taraxacum officinale* with them as a staple in their herb and kitchen gardens.

Medicinally, dandelion was used as a diuretic, and was so well known for these properties that its common name in Merrie Olde England was piss-a-bed. The roots, like the roots of chicory, were dried, roasted, and ground as a coffee substitute, drunk as a mild stim-ulant and probably as a laxative. The young green leaves were gath-ered in the early spring for salads, prescribed "to cleanse the blood."

Science now tells us that dandelion leaves are chock full of vitamins and minerals, including high levels of calcium—the perfect spring tonic. Jeanne Rose, who is a herbalist in San Francisco, says that the whole plant can be dug up, chopped, and brewed into a tealike infu-sion, for a healthy drink. "If you've got dandelions in your yard that haven't been visited by dogs or cats, you can use the fresh leaves in a salad," said Rose. "It's a bitter green, so it's better just mixed in. Or you can buy dandelion leaves at [some] markets; I've seen them for sale in Andronico's."

There is another use for this pesky and enduring perennial: You can make dandelion wine. My friend Ellen, who also happens to be my sis-ter-in-law, tried this for the first time last year. The recipe, from one of her neighbors in rural Pennsylvania, called for eight quarts of dande-lion blossoms, or about two mop buckets' worth. Even with several acres of fallow pasture at her disposal she says it took quite a while to pick them all.

Though some of the bottles exploded in her cellar, we all got to taste the finished product over the Christmas holidays. The liquor turned out a lovely shade of topaz yellow, and was slightly bubbly like champagne. Sitting in Ellen's living room, in the warmth of a crackling fire, drinking dandelion wine while big snowflakes swirled in the darkness of the windowpanes was the perfect treat to end a gardening year.

Folks in Pennsylvania still have some months of snow and ice to go before their spring arrives. The dandelions will not bloom in Ellen's fields until late April or even May. But in the Bay Area, dandelions are blooming in late February—a sure sign that spring is really, truly on the way.

# [The Grass Is Always Greener at the Ballpark]

*The Giants and A's play on natural
grass, just like little kids do. "Sod Squad"
managers reveal their secrets, from
fertilizers to field paint.*

While many baseball teams play on artificial turf, the San Francisco
Giants and the Oakland Athletics play on natural grass—just as little
kids do. Candlestick Park and the Oakland Coliseum have preserved the
tradition of the grass playing field, to the envy of the leagues and any
home gardener faced with keeping a grassy play area in good shape.

Real heroes, it seems, don't mind giving up their trade secrets. Mark
Razmun, the Oakland A's sports turf manager, and Jim Delfino, who
supervises the grounds at Candlestick Park, told all to a standing-
room-only crowd of two thousand at the thirtieth Annual Turf and
Landscape Expo, held for landscape professionals at the Santa Clara
Convention Center.

First off, if you're planning to refurbish your lawn as a field of
dreams for your own little slugger, the choice of grass is probably the
biggest difference between pro fields and play yards. At Candlestick

Park and the Oakland Coliseum they use bluegrass. In warmer cities, as in Texas and Florida, pro teams play on Bermuda grass, according to Tom Del Conte, who is the president of the Northern California Turf Council. Bermuda grass is the sod of choice at Stanford's stadium in Palo Alto and is also used in the refurbished Kezar Stadium in Golden Gate Park. "What blue and Bermuda have in common is that both are easier to mow short," said Del Conte. During baseball and football season, Candlestick's field is mowed daily to a height of one inch; at the Coliseum, Razmun's crew trims to three quarters of an inch. Infield work is done with a hand mower.

No league regulations define choice of grass or mowing height. But Ali Harivandi, a turf expert at the University of California, Berkeley, and an advisor to the Turf Council, cautions that homeowners might prefer one of the new dwarf fescues, which require less water than do the thirsty bluegrass and Bermuda. Harivandi also suggests mowing higher (three inches) to shade the roots and save both water and time.

Ballparks, of course, have grounds crews to do the work. Candlestick is resodded each January, after the 49ers football season, using giant rolls of sod measuring forty-two by seventy feet held in place by squares of honeycombed plastic grid. Sod pavers, as these are called, are also used at San Francisco's Balboa Park ballfield and can be found under the rooftop lawn at the Yerba Buena Center.

Among baseball players, Candlestick has a reputation for its "soft" infield, Delfino said. His recipe for pitcher's mound, home plate, and baseline is a fast-draining mix of 70 percent cinders, 20 percent fired clay, and 10 percent sand that's firm yet yielding to the grinding twist of a pitcher's toe. Sod and clay both sit above a twelve-inch base of pure sand. Below this is an ancient network of plastic and tile drains, which wick away excess moisture the way a two-ply sports sock wicks away sweat.

"Candlestick is *not* below sea level, no matter what John Madden says," Delfino pointed out. The frequent puddling on the field is caused by failures in the drainage pipes. "Every time we replace a part of the field, we replace the pipe as well," he added. To remove morning dew, he and Razmun top-dress their turf after sodding with calcinated clay dust. "Most people have that around the house," Delfino said. "It's kitty litter. It absorbs excess moisture and tightens the sod."

The two men differ on fertilizer. Delfino prefers liquid fertilizer injected through the irrigation system (home mixing devices, attached between the faucet and hose to an oscillating sprinkler, cost between ten and sixty dollars). Razmun uses granular fertilizer and a spray-on product called Roots, an organic blend of liquid humus, marine algae, and enzymes.

Stadium "sod squads" have tricks that anyone can use to perfect a fine looking lawn. If you're planning a wedding, barbecue, or other special backyard event, try this tip from Razmun: Before every extended series of home games, he orders the entire field sprinkled with chelated iron, a mineral supplement that turns the grass a brighter green. "It looks better for the TV cameras," he said.

Stadium crews will even paint the grass green if they have to. Field paint, a sprayable, water-based latex, is rapidly replacing chalk or lime as the way to mark lines for both baseball and football games. When Delfino's crew has to convert a field from Giants baseball to 49ers football in less than twenty-four hours, lines that don't easily wash off are painted away by hand. Field paints are also used to color end zones and paint league emblems directly onto the grass. Permanent paints are used when the Giants and A's host playoffs and the World Series; the color "grows out" with the grass, in about ten days.

# [Wisdom About Wisteria]

*A Southern gentleman*

*recommends you start pruning*

*the vines in March, but*

*don't stop there.*

In some gardens wisteria is blooming in March; in others it is still in hard bud, and in others the drooping racemes of purple blossoms are already faded and dry. That's the way of wisteria, a vine much loved for its fragrant and elegant flowers, and a plant much misunderstood.

Bill Abeel knows his wisteria like the back of his own trowel. It is one of the crowning glories of his spring garden, tucked into one of the cooler streets around San Francisco's Pacific Heights. He's trained the vine like an arbor, across a second-floor bedroom balcony and over the doors that lead from the house to the garden. In bloom the wisteria suspends three-foot-long ropes of purple blossoms that hang like a curtain in the doorway, perfuming indoors and out for about two weeks. Peak time for this brief but spectacular show "should be April 14," he notes. An anticipatory smile lights his eyes and his slight southern drawl mellows deeper as he speaks of this, his garden's jewel. "I've charted the bloom time each year, because we usually throw a special garden party dinner to celebrate it."

Such delights are within the grasp of any average gardener, for wisteria is a hardy perennial, long lived and adapted to both freezing winters and hot, dry summers. But for many, wisterias give spotty bloom or none; a vine that's pampered may not bloom at all.

It turns out that pruning is the key to a lush wisteria, and not just once, but twice, if not more. As Abeel explains, "The runners go out at two different times during the year."

Most garden books tell you to trim wisteria in midsummer, after the flowers have finished and the vines shoot out into long, leafy new growth. But Abeel trims his wisteria in winter as well, just before the first leaf buds emerge. "I try to wait and trim them just before the bud looks like it's going to do something," he says. "And I will trim it back enormously, down to hard, old wood." Unless he's planning to have a bud develop into a runner that will extend the balcony arbor, he cuts the vines down to a sturdy main framework. Over many years, these main trunks develop what he calls "knuckles"—and from each hard old knob a cluster of flower buds springs forth, spread out like the fingers on a hand.

The cutting begins in early March, and he usually makes several passes over a period of weeks, observing buds and trimming here or there at leisure. And he also trims any leafy green runners that sprout during or after the bloom time, leaving only a shoot or two to extend the arbor's woody frame. "It's only by hard cutting that you force an enormous amount of blooming," he says, his voice now firm and authoritative. "Otherwise the energy of the plant goes into runners you would trim off anyhow." Abeel's other advice is to water wisterias copiously and fertilize them lightly. He sticks one plant-food spike into the ground when the flower buds begin to color up, "but I make sure it gets all the water it needs."

A wisteria that does not bloom is probably getting not enough water or too much fertilizer. Although wisteria are cited as being drought tolerant, they do need lots of water, up to and during their bloom period, to create long, full racemes. Nitrogen fertilizers (especially the overflow from lawn food) create too many leafy shoots at the expense of flowers. Because flower buds form in late summer, a sprinkling of bonemeal or phosphate, and a teaspoonful of Epsom salts (for mineral magnesium) then can induce a shy bloomer to give a bigger show next year.

It's also important to know that two types of wisteria are commonly sold in garden centers: Chinese and Japanese. Abeel's specimen is the Japanese vine, *Wisteria floribunda*, also labeled *W. multijuga*. The flowers are two-toned, light blue in the center with a darker blue violet outer petal, and hang in long, narrow bunches that easily reach three feet. (White or pink forms are known, but they are rarer and less hardy.) Planting Japanese wisteria where the flowers can be suspended, as Abeel has done with his arbor, encourages the length of the racemes.

Chinese wisteria, *W. sinensis,* creates an entirely different effect, with chunkier, grapelike clusters of flowers that open all at once. This is the best one to use if you'd like to run a vine more casually up a house wall, or create a flowering tree. Weeping Chinese wisteria standards in pink, white, or shades of blue purple also make good potted plants, provided they get lots of water and attentive pruning. Planting a standard slightly on a slant, and encouraging a few low branches, will give your tree-shaped wisteria a more graceful look.

## SOURCES:
*Young plants of Japanese wisteria in white, pink, and blue are available by mail order from Forestfarm Collection, 990 Tetherow Road, Williams, OR 97544-9599; (541) 846-7269. Catalog $4.*

# II. Eternal Spring

[ Sunshine on the Border ]

# [Designing with California Native Plants]

*Monkey flowers with roses,*
*currants with tulips: choosing native*
*perennials for various border schemes*
*in a San Francisco backyard.*

Of all the reasons to add native plants to a California garden, beauty seems to run a distant last, after practical concerns. Some folks add local species to attract birds and butterflies; others are drawn to the low-maintenance possibilities of natives, which require little or no summer irrigation and hardly any fertilizer. California's rugged species are not generally bothered by garden snails, a star quality for any flower, but there's nothing wrong in planting natives just because they're pretty.

Every plant family has its member among California natives: roses, peonies, orchids, bleeding hearts, clematis, even dogwoods. This is one way to get started: Mix them in as you might use any cottage-garden plant. If you've had luck with garden columbines, you can probably grow our native version, *Aquilegia formosa*. If you enjoy roses, why not add *Rosa californica* to your collection?

A second way to integrate is simply mixing plants by flower color. In my own garden, I found a good match to a buff yellow rose in the tangerine trumpets of sticky monkey flower, *Diplacus* (now *Mimulus*) *longiflorus*. Sticky monkey flower blooms from June to November, its low, rambly stems a perfect skirt to hide the gawky base of a rosebush. New hybrids crossed from other California species extend the color range into apricot, pink and ivory shades; you might imagine how they match other roses. Wild species grow on windy slopes along the coast, so they're perfect in windy balcony gardens and make good pot plants.

I rarely see garden flowers color matched to native shrubs; people are so used to letting natives fend for themselves in waste places. Yet the pinky purple of flowering currant, *Ribes sanguineum*, made a great backdrop to pink and purple tulips in my garden. You could add something blue—perhaps primroses or garden borage, to create a spring picture, or extend the show taller and later with a redbud tree.

A third method is to pick plants by site conditions. A west-facing slope, brutalized by dry winds, is the perfect spot for California poppies, the seeds sown in late September, followed by summer-blooming wild buckwheats, with their umbels of creamy white. Domestic partners in this case might be white rockrose *(Cistus hybridus)* and Spanish lavender. Shady, low spots around your house might welcome wild ferns or redwood sorrel *(Oxalis oregana)*, which is a native, pink-flowered relative of the pesky yellow sorrel we grub out of our gardens every spring.

Native plants can be a lifelong study, but their garden use is getting easier as plant nurseries now carry more local species. To get acquainted, check plant tags: Key words to look for in the second Latin name are *californica, occidentalis*, or *canadensis*, which identify western species, or *douglasii, menziesii*, or *fremontii*, which identify plants named after pioneer explorers.

Members of the California Native Plant Society have been especially helpful in making species available in the Bay Area. To learn more, I recommend two books by a local botanist, Glenn Keator, each with extensive lists of plants for particular uses. These are *The Complete Garden Guide to the Native Perennials of California* and *The Complete Garden Guide to the Native Shrubs of California*. You'll find both in the bookstores at Strybing Arboretum in San Francisco and the University of California's Botanical Garden in Berkeley—two public gardens also known for well-marked displays of native plants.

*SOURCES:*

*California Native Plant Society; for local chapters call the headquarters in Sacramento; (916) 447-2677.*

# [Stop and Smell the Lilacs]

*Freak weather of the previous*
*year produces an unheard-of abundance*
*of lilacs in the Bay Area;*
*the secrets of scent.*

The conversation started when Charlotte-Anne noticed the lilacs next door. They'd never bloomed so fragrantly before, and reminded her of the southern gardens she knew, where lilac smells seem to tint the evening May air nearly purple with their heavy sweetness. Charlotte-Anne's neighbor told her that a cold snap the previous winter was what prompted the lilacs to smell so nice this year. Not exactly true, of course, as there are many factors that unlock the secret of flower fragrance. Some of these are beyond the gardener's control, but some can be manipulated to increase flower scent.

Botanists will tell you that the purpose of flower fragrance is to attract pollinators, usually insects. But people are also attracted to flower smells. Does this mean we are also potential pollinators? (Anybody who has ever gotten ineradicable lily pollen on a white shirt is far more likely to curse the flower.) Plant leaves, too, have smells attractive to us. The essential oils in leaves of herbs do us good, but what good does it do the plant when we pick it? (Think of mint and how it roots from any piece of stem; you can well believe that it might be so programmed to travel on a mammal to colonize a new place.)

Fragrance oils in herbs are said to be more concentrated just before the flowers bloom. Actually, the determining factor is not so much maturity as it is the weather. Most of our fragrant Mediterranean herbs, such as thyme, oregano, sage, and rosemary, come into bloom, like the lilac, just as summer's hot dry season begins. The increase in scent is caused by lack of water; the oils are less diluted in the plants, so more concentrated. A sure way to increase scent in leafy herbs is to hold back water as they begin to show their bloom. In rainy years some gardeners may find their mints and oreganos less fragrant. In such years it may be better to wait until hotter weather to harvest leafy herbs for drying.

Cold weather doesn't trigger flower fragrance, but it does trigger flower bud production in temperate-climate deciduous trees and shrubs, such as lilacs, that set their buds in winter. Scented plants that set buds in summer, such as citrus and wisteria, prefer warmer weather then. So the combination of a very warm summer and an unusually chilly winter would make the following year a banner year for many flowers. It's also likely that Charlotte-Anne's neighborly lilac smelled better that year because it had rained more. With a climate to its liking, the bush may have put out an extra effort to attract insect pollinators—seizing a window of opportunity to set seed.

Soil pH and soil minerals also affect scent. Lilacs, roses, and lavender need limy soil to take up the minerals they use for flower production. These scented flowers smell better if given a touch of lime when they are fertilized at the bud stage with bonemeal or 0-10-10. It's not always possible to mimic a plant's preferred habitat, but it helps to make them feel at home. They too, may have memories of scented evenings in another place.

# [A Paradise Not Lost]

*The renovation of an Olmstead-Church*
*garden reveals the Bay Area's rich landscape*
*heritage that remains after the*
*Oakland hills firestorm.*

Sometimes you have to lose something before you recognize its value. In the 1991 firestorm in the Oakland hills, many old homes with landscaping of historic value were lost to the flames. As new homes rise in the burned-out areas, bulky modern architecture and strict relandscaping rules are painting a twenty-first-century face on the hillsides, and a way of life—a way of gardening—has disappeared.

For Paul Sundstrom, a landscape contractor in Berkeley, the conflagration meant a change of mission: to help preserve landscapes that still exist. "Berkeley, especially, has so many fine old gardens," he said. One in particular won Sundstrom an award for Best Large Garden in the Berkeley Horticultural Nursery's annual gardening contest, a restoration of a formal garden that escaped the scorched path of the firestorm by a mere half-mile.

That property has a rich horticultural pedigree: It was subdivided from an estate landscaped by Frederick Law Olmstead, the designer of New York's Central Park. The five-story home was built in a Mediterranean stucco style in 1936 by the Bay Area architect William Wurster, who also designed the balustraded terrace for a formal rose garden, which now contains a pool and patio with hot tub. "Thomas Church, who was one of the great modern landscape designers in California, took out the rose garden and put in the swimming pool in the late 1950s," said Sundstrom. "The pool has a cloverleaf shape. I'm really glad he did that instead of a rectangle, because it works as a water feature as well as a functional swimming pool."

A lower garden, reached by a steeply stepped path flanked with a parade of eighty-foot-tall Lombardy poplars, is screened off by a dense, tall hedge that on closer inspection turns out to be trifoliate orange, *Poncirus trifoliata*. Nobody knows if it's a legacy of Olmstead or of Church; both landscape architects used the spiky barrier plant. Whoever planted it was certainly gifted, because the sheared wall of dark green leaves, studded with fragrant white flowers and small orange fruits, is a marvelous piece of work. But when Sundstrom took over the maintenance in 1990, both this hedge and the Lombardy poplars were choked with ivy; what climbing roses remained on the balustrade were gangly and weak.

"We're putting in new climbers now, 'Climbing America', 'Charlotte Armstrong', 'Golden Showers', and 'Climbing Peace'—taking out the harsh reds like 'Blaze', and replacing them with roses in soft pinks and golds. One thing other gardeners can learn from this," he added, "is not to be shy about removing old, unproductive roses. I have two-year-old climbers that are already up to the top of the pillars."

Pink crabapple trees, star magnolias, and the ancient wisteria that wraps around a second-story porch have responded well to hard pruning. Sundstrom replaced frost-killed bougainvillea with espaliered evergreen magnolias that hug the white stucco, and he replanted the entrance walkway with more flowers than Church ever did. The masses of fragrant white blossoms here were requested by the owner, as was the columnar cypress by the front door. "In Italy, planting a cypress by the front door is a symbol of hospitality," Sundstrom explained. "A lot of the design work we've been doing is to make the garden softer, more people-friendly."

The lower garden is blessed with many existing fruit trees: plums, apples, persimmons, and citrus, also restored by hard pruning. The family had raised vegetable beds installed there, following the lines of an old floral parterre.

Sundstrom and a crew of two work here one full day a week, with much renovation still to be done on the hilly lot. Fire safety remains a big concern, so removing brushy debris is always on the schedule. The owners also suggested that the Lombardy poplars be pruned in a candle style that they'd seen on a visit to Italy. The lower branches were removed "so the tops just wave feathery in the wind," says Sundstrom. The effect is certainly striking—and the poplars are far less of a fire hazard now that their ladderlike lower limbs are gone.

Born in Berkeley, Sundstrom studied landscaping at the University of California before putting out his shingle as a licensed landscape contractor. Estate work soon became a specialty. "So many people want to become landscape designers," Sundstrom points out. "Nobody wants to do the real work, the old-fashioned craftsmanship that has to be done to keep up these gardens."

*SOURCES:*
*Paul Sundstrom, Landscape Services Company,*
*Berkeley, CA; (510) 524-9572.*

# [Lawn's New Look Is Natural and Relaxed]

*A bellis-studded lawn*
*like the one in Golden Gate Park*
*is part of the trend to low-*
*maintenance lawns.*

After many years of drought, turf front lawns are beginning to pop up again. The new-fashioned greensward is, however, a far cry from the clipped, tense spears of bluegrass or Bermuda grass that made up the old-style front lawn. The "natural look" is in. The natural lawn is actually a national phenomenon, sweeping from coast to coast. Homeowners who secretly enjoyed not having to take care of grass during the drought years will never again have to submit to the tyranny of weekends spent in pursuit of a perfect lawn. The new mood is relaxed, the emphasis is on low maintenance. Turf is allowed to grow taller, it looks greener and lusher, and flowers are allowed to grow in the grass.

The first step to your new low-maintenance lawn is to decide where you really need a lawn. If the only person who walks on the grass is the person who mows it, I would suggest you get rid of the lawn entirely and plant a ground cover instead. For a nice, emerald green alternative to the so-called ceremonial lawn in front of the house, try *Myoporum parvifolium* instead. Some *Myoporum* species are trees, but this prostrate form grows no more than four to six inches tall. The dime-sized rounded leaves are a shiny dark green, and from a distance of about fifteen feet a patch of it might easily be mistaken for bluegrass. It works well in shady spots, too, where grass is hard to grow. Look for this at your garden center in the ground cover section. Place a flat of it on the ground, view it from a distance, and judge for yourself.

In the backyard, grass is still king. It's the best play surface for children and easily springs back from foot traffic. Nothing sets off a flower bed like a small patch of thick green grass. Where grass is desired, try these tips for a low-maintenance lawn:

• If installing a new lawn, get one of the new, slow-growing dwarfed tall fescues that don't need to be mowed so often. One of the best is 'Bonsai', developed by Pacific Coast Seed, a turf wholesaler in Livermore. It's available as seed or sod from many garden centers.

• To prevent bare spots in high-traffic areas, put down stepping stones. Set them flush with ground level, so you can run a lawn mower right over the stones. No extra hand trimming will be needed.

• If you want the look of an English meadow, look for grass seed mixes that include flowers. Pacific Coast Seed has a grass seed mix that includes the 'Bonsai' fescue and tiny, low-growing wild flowers such as *Bellis,* the white English daisy. The company president, David Gilpin, told me that he got the idea because so many people asked him how they could replicate the bellis-studded turf in Golden Gate Park. You'll probably find yourself mowing less to enjoy the flowers, but the floral carpet effect does bounce back after you've mowed.

• Consider overseeding an existing but exhausted fescue lawn with white clover. The advantage here is that clover literally pulls nitrogen out of the air and into the soil, acting as a natural fertilizer for any grass blades nearby. White clover also mows well when you want a crisper effect, and it takes foot traffic in stride. It should not be confused with the weedy yellow oxalis or wood sorrel that has a cloverlike leaf. True clover spreads in low drifts of soft green leaves that make a fine foliage texture complement to thin-leaved grass. I have seen small packets of clover seed in garden centers; this is the easiest way to transform an existing patch of grass into the softer, natural turf effect that is in vogue right now.

## SOURCES:

*Pacific Coast Seed sod and seed mixes are available at garden centers. For a brochure on current offerings, contact Pacific Coast Seed Company at 6144 Building A, Industrial Way, Livermore, CA 94550; (925) 373-4417.*

# [Hay Fever Is Nothing to Sneeze At]

*Where*

*the pollen is coming*

*from, and where*

*it's not.*

An artist friend passed on a clipping about some guy who uses plant pollen as a sculptural art form. Wolfgang Laib had a show in Santa Fe that featured little cones and even rug-sized floor squares of bright yellow pollen painstakingly collected from hazelnut, pine, and dandelion flowers. The powdery stuff looks stunning in the photo, but I have to admit that my first thoughts were alarm and worry for unsuspecting hay fever victims who might have stumbled into the show.

Allergy to pollen—hay fever—isn't a pretty sight. The nose gets red and sneezy, the eyes itch and tear, and the symptoms appear almost immediately upon exposure. I had visions of folks walking into the Santa Fe art show and then fleeing, red in the face and doubled over as if they were Jesse Helms and had just seen a Mapplethorpe.

Many gardeners suffer from hay fever, and sometimes set such traps for themselves by planting around their houses the very trees and shrubs that will give them an allergic reaction.

The San Francisco chapter of the American Lung Association offers some brochures on allergenic plants of the Bay Area. Because of our long growing season and mild winters, they say, hay fever reactions can occur year-round. A person may be allergic to several kinds of pollen and so have symptoms year-round, too. Pine trees and acacias, junipers, oaks, and olive trees produce prodigious quantities of pollen in their flowering season. Grasses, too, especially the annual bluegrass overseeded in lawns and even many of the recently introduced ornamental grasses, cause strong allergic reactions.

It's not always easy or even desirable to remove the established oaks or other big trees that cause hay fever, but the gardener can learn to be selective about adding new plants, avoiding those known to be troublemakers. Safe plants are usually those with bright, colorful flowers, or extremely fragrant blossoms. This is true because highly noticeable flowers are those that have evolved to attract birds, bees, or other insects. The pollen on those flowers is typically sticky, so it will adhere to the critter visiting the flower and so be transferred to another blossom, on the next branch or down the road, to complete the pollinating process.

Hay fever sufferers need to watch out for plants with insignificant flowers that disperse their pollen on the wind. Grasses, with their waving florets, and ornamental trees prized not for flowers but foliage— such as maples, sycamores, and most conifers—are wind-pollinated plants. The pollen is dryish and loose and, especially in the case of pine trees, can often be seen drifting into the air when a branch is moved by wind.

And weeds that cause hay fever are more often introduced plants than native species. It's not easy to tell these apart, and a good example is our native American goldenrod. Scorned by many as a hay-fever plant, gardeners tear it out ruthlessly, despite the beauty of its abundant, gold-yellow flowers in late summer. The bright blooms alone should be a clue. It turns out that goldenrod is not considered allergenic. The real culprit for years has been a European ragweed, which opens shabby small flowers at the same time and often in the same naturalized sites as goldenrod. In Europe, goldenrod is a prized perennial, known by its botanical name, *Solidago,* and hybridized there as a commercial florist's flower.

### Hay Fever Top Ten:

| | |
|---|---|
| Acacia | Olive |
| Annual bluegrass | Plane tree |
| Juniper | Pine |
| Oak | Privet |
| Oat grass | Walnut |

*(Source: American Lung Association)*

# [May Time Is Tomato Time]

*A definitive discussion*
*of the best tomato cultivars for*
*fog-belt gardens, with plenty*
*of technical advice.*

The weeks of May are when gardeners across the United States transplant their tomato seedlings into the garden. Whether you live in Novato
or New Jersey, whether you carefully coddled your tiny tomato plants
from seed sprouted on the windowsill or bought them in a six-pack at
the garden center last weekend, it's time to get those tomato starts in the
ground.

We all know some hardy souls who set out their tomatoes in
February or March. Swaddled in plastic against a late freeze (the tomatoes, not their owners) these plants may, just may, bear their sweet red
fruits a week or two earlier than transplants set out when the ground
has fully warmed up. This is a lot of fuss and bother just to get a jump
on your neighbors.

Why then, do gardeners in the Bay Area pursue short-season varieties (those maturing in sixty days or less) such as 'Early Girl', 'Ace',

and 'Early Cascade'? It's not because winter chill cuts short our tomato season, as October or November are usually productive months in our mild climate. The reason for the big rush here is always to get the crop going by July and August, when dense fogs cut the sunlight and heat needed to grow and ripen tomatoes properly. Heavy fog in summer can cheat everyone out of tomatoes: From the East Bay to Monterey, home gardeners can sometimes wait until Labor Day to get ripe red beauties.

Good harvests start with the right cultivar. True, 'San Francisco Fog' or 'Ace' will give you red fruit, but their flavor is poor and mealy. It's my own feeling that no one living in an area that gets regular, coastal fog in summer should bother planting anything else but 'Early Girl', a consistent performer even in the worst weather.

Renee Shepherd, the founder of Shepherd's Garden Seeds down in Felton, disagrees. She favors 'Oregon Spring', a short-season variety developed by Dr. James Baggett at Oregon State University. Last year, her own group of test gardeners got hearty crops with this one, "even in Pacifica," she said.

A few years back Pam Peirce, working with the San Francisco League of Urban Gardeners (SLUG), tested varieties for both yield and flavor; the nod went to 'Early Girl' and to an heirloom variety dubbed 'Visitacion Valley' for its neighborhood roots. Peirce told me she suspects it is an open-pollinated descendant of 'Early Girl'. Seedlings of 'Visitacion Valley' were later distributed to other members of SLUG to see how it would fare in other neighborhoods.

One year, well before the fog rolled into my own Potrero Hill tomato patch, I tested five different early-season cultivars, transplanting them on May 5. The experiment included 'Early Girl', two French imports, 'Carmello' and 'Dona' (both introduced here by Shepherd), and two from Baggett's laboratory, 'Oregon Spring' and 'Early Cascade'.

Struggling in the summer fog, 'Early Girl' still provided the first edible fruits, on July 12—a week ahead of 'Early Cascade'. Through the rest of that meager season 'Early Girl' was the most prolific. But, in blind taste tests, friends and family liked the flavor of 'Carmello' best, and I found this French market tomato closest in flavor to the juicy 'Rutgers' and 'Beefsteak' long-season varieties I grew up with on the New Jersey shore.

Tomato plants like it hot and humid, which is why they grow so famously in New Jersey. They want plenty of water and ground heat during their growing season. In a cooler bioregion, drip irrigation and black plastic mulch at the base of the plants can do a lot to help approximate the climate of the Garden State.

Two of the most successful gadgets for tomato growing capitalize on the heat-plus-humidity factor. The Automator, around for years, is basically a plastic place mat the tomato grows up in, black to attract and retain the sun's heat, with some wells in it to hold water. The Wall-o-Water, designed by a man in Portland, is a plastic cone of translucent tubes that are filled with water from your garden hose. Sunshine on the tubes provides heat not only in the daytime but also at night, when the still-warm water within keeps your tomato plant cozy. During the day, when the plants are actively growing, the water evaporating from the open tops of the tubes supplies a helpful humidity.

Homemade variations are legendary. Setting transplants in the ring of a black rubber tire works because the dark rubber draws and stores heat. Sticking a gallon jug of water neck-first into the ground, so that water slowly trickles down, predates drip irrigation by a few decades at least. Recently I've been trying the latest infrared, red-colored plastic mulch, which is supposed to draw heat waves into the soil. I always use some Wall-o-Waters to get the humidity up. I may even play some Bruce Springsteen music from the back porch, to get the plants in the right mood.

*SOURCES:*
*Automators, black and red plastic mulch, and Wall-o-Waters are available by mail-order through Gardener's Supply, Burlington, VT 05401; (800) 863-1700.*

# [Big Rhody: The Super Shrub]

*Peninsula gardeners offer*

*their insights on selecting and*

*siting these colorful spring stalwarts.*

*Cal colors, anyone?*

The rhododendron manages to be both romantically old-fashioned and strikingly modern at the same time. Borne out of the Himalayas at the turn of the century by no less than Rothschild heirs, our familiar garden rhody is a never-fail bloomer among broadleaf evergreen shrubs. Their spring with us is a long one, for deciduous types from the Far East extend bloom from early March to late June, with a color range from royal purple to golden yellow.

Azaleas are botanically rhododendrons too, and their fiery reds and pinks can light up a shady city garden. Keith and Lurline Elliot, two Woodside gardeners well known in the American Rhododendron Society, say that pastel shades are more popular with home gardeners than the neon hues seen in older gardens, although 'Hino Crimson' remains a favorite with landscapers. Keith Elliot once confided to me his favorite rhododendron combination: two species, pale blue

*Rhododendron augustinii* with pale yellow *R. lutenscens,* "because they're Cal colors." It is a lovely combination, and one I have never seen anywhere but in the Elliots' yard, for the plants are not easy to find at a garden center. But as Keith Elliot notes, yellow rhododendrons, while rare elsewhere in America, include many semitropical shrubs that California's climate can support, and such plants are well worth seeking. For native plant lovers California has several native rhododendrons, including the pinkish white *R. occidentale,* which is heavily fragrant.

The Elliots led me to Jan Mountjoy, who prefers the old-fashioned, big-headed rhododendron hybrids. But she uses them unlike most people I know, her painterly mixed borders resulting from fearless juggling of large plants. "You don't have to worry about moving rhododendrons," she pointed out. "They're shallow rooted. Even if they are twelve or fifteen feet tall, you can transplant them in the spring." A starring combination in her own garden were the pink gold flowers of the hybrid 'Unique' on a bush placed just in front of a pink-flowered dogwood in the exact same shades.

In Ernie Kolak's garden in Portola Valley, the rhododendrons are in raised island beds in a front yard that used to be a cherry grove. Two old cherry trees are still there, and their ballet pink spring flowers help set off the amethyst shades of *R. davidsonianum* and *R. maddenii,* two Chinese species that tolerate the Peninsula's strong sun. Rhododendrons do well under oaks, so Kolak added oak trees, "to give the area some shade and structure," he explained. "At first, I could only plant rhododendrons on the northeast side of the trees, but as they grew, and their leaf canopy spread, we could put them all around."

It's only recently that Kolak began adding perennial flowers to his rhododendron garden. "Something was lacking—and I realized it was companion plants," he said. Now, spring bulbs add their complementary colors while the rhodies are in bloom, and ferns, hosta, coral bells, low iris, heather, and green and red maples add texture and interest year-round.

In the rear yard there is a stand of old redwood trees, and in their shade Kolak has planted large blooming Exbury hybrids. These shrubs are nearing their mature height of twenty to thirty feet, and their round flower clusters, called trusses, were each as big as a basketball. Had I a redwood grove, I would not hesitate to plant Exburys there— not after I had seen how the afternoon sun, slanting through the trees, painted the flowers in glowing reds, like the light that shines through the stained glass of a cathedral.

To integrate rhododendron color in your landscape, the Elliots suggest buying nursery plants when you see them in bloom. But check the pots first. Ideally the shrub you buy should be sitting in a loose, fibrous soil mix, not in hardpan. "Some cheap wholesale nurseries will field-grow rhododendrons in clay soil, just cut them out, and plop them in pots when they bloom," warned Keith Elliot. "All it takes is for the nursery help not to water the pots one time, and the clay dries hard as a rock and kills the roots. This is why a lot of people buy blooming bushes and wind up seeing them die after planting them in the yard."

Well started in a planting hole rich in organic matter, and slightly raised to assure good drainage, rhododendrons will grow anywhere in the Bay Area if their needs are met: light shade, summer water, acid fertilizer, and a mulch to keep their shallow root systems cool. Pruning should be done after flowering.

### SOURCES:
*Your best bet for finding unusual species or specific, named hybrid rhododendrons is your local chapter of The American Rhododendron Society. For local contacts write to Dee Danieri, ARS, 11 Pinecrest Drive, Fortuna, CA 95540; (707) 725-3043.*

# [Old Roses and Where to Put Them]

*Lots of*
*good advice about*
*heirloom roses in*
*the landscape.*

One of the flower fads sweeping the country is the rediscovery of "old roses." These include romantically named hybrids such as 'Fantin-Latour' and 'Reine des Violettes', and historic roses such as the striped *Rosa Mundi* or the Apothecary Rose, *(R. g. 'officinalis'),* used for medicine in the Middle Ages. At first prized for their rarity, the old roses were gradually reintroduced to the marketplace as familiarity bred demand. Now it's pretty easy to find a 'Cécile Brunner' or an eglantine at better nurseries or through mail-order catalogs.

Much of the romance of the old roses involves their poetic names and classical associations. But after you've fallen in love with a bourbon or a gallica, the problem remains of what to do with it in your yard. Most vintage roses bloom only for a few weeks of the year. In California's climate, early summer heat and drying winds can cut that flowering time by half.

Eleven months of anticipation for two weeks of bloom doesn't make much sense in a small garden. Once the flowers are finished, antique rose bushes can look pretty scraggly. Experienced landscapers usually hide them in a mixed border, with the rosebush foliage providing a medium green backdrop for later-blooming perennials. Some gardeners train sprawling, summer-flowering vines, such as clematis, over the bloomless bushes.

Some old roses do repeat their bloom, on and off over the summer and quite reliably in early fall, as the weather cools. Marlea Graham, the knowledgeable editor of *The Rose Letter*, a quarterly publication of the nonprofit Heritage Rose Group, recommends 'Sombreuil', a scented white rose that flowers most of the summer in her garden near Martinez.

Other repeaters include the autumn damasks, which Graham feels make unattractive shrubs out of season, and 'Souvenir de la Malmaison', a popular variety that she cautions doesn't do well in fog zones.

It might be argued that short bloom, dowdiness, and lack of disease resistance are the reasons why many old-fashioned roses were superseded by vigorous, flashy, modern hybrids. Yet the fragility and seasonality of the antiques are for many gardeners—including this one—the essence of their charm. Many old cultivars have a deep fragrance missing in modern roses; this alone is a good reason to add one or two bushes to the garden.

Like a crop of peaches or prosaic green beans, antique roses pour forth their beauty all at once. This makes them ideal as a source of petals for homemade potpourri, a traditional way to capture the essence of a briefly blooming rose. Old roses can also be "preserved" by using unsprayed petals to make rose jellies and jams. So, both history and practicality suggest that a kitchen garden—that place where you grow your garlic and green beans—may be the best place to situate these old beauties; their shabby off-season will not be noticed, and their fleeting glamour can be savored by the gardener whenever he or she marches out to pick the peas on a fine spring day.

*SOURCES:*

*A fine collection of old roses is open to the public at the University of California's Botanical Garden on Centennial Drive in Berkeley.*

*For more information on old roses, contact the Heritage Rose Group, 100 Bear Oaks Drive, Martinez, CA 94553.*

# [Bouquets in May]

*Get out*

*your secateurs*

*and a can of*

*Sprite.*

May marks the true midpoint for this gardener's year. Roses, flowering vines, shrubs, and perennials set out last fall or early winter are in bloom, and the warm-weather vegetables set out recently are still small enough to be undemanding. With the heavy work done, I can relax to literally smell the roses and pick some—along with border flowers—for indoor bouquets.

Vases at the ready and secateurs in hand, the immediate problem is how to make bouquets last in a house that doesn't have air conditioning. Most gardeners have a trick they use (add an aspirin to the vase water, or a copper penny, or a spoonful of sugar) but, until recently, very little scientific research was done on making cut flowers last longer.

William R. Woodson, Associate Professor of Horticulture at Purdue University in West Lafayette, Indiana, has been tackling the problem on behalf of home flower arrangers and the florist industry, which Purdue estimates has a $4.5 billion annual market in cut flowers in the United States.

"Despite the size of the industry, the biology of flowers hasn't received as much attention from scientists as the biology of fruits," said Woodson, whose discoveries include the finding that cut carnations produce ethylene, a natural chemical that agriculturalists know controls and hastens ripening and rotting in fruit.

Woodson said that his current goal is to genetically engineer a carnation that produces less ethylene, so it would last longer as a cut flower. In the meantime, he offered these tips on how to make cut blooms last:

• Trim the stem ends by one-quarter inch every two or three days. Change the water in the vase at the same time, so it doesn't breed bacteria and start to smell.

• Put a commercial flower preservative in the water. This contains food for the plant (in the form of a sugar) and a chemical agent that kills bacteria. You can buy packets of this from your florist or you can make a preservative at home. Woodson's own recipe is a mixture of one part lemon-lime soda, such as Sprite or 7Up, and one part water in each vase. "The soft drinks contain enough sugar to feed the plant," he said. So, diet soda won't work. But only lemon-lime will work. Why? "These flavors contain enough citric acid to help slow the growth of bacteria."

• Keep flower arrangements in a cool spot, out of direct sunlight. If the arrangement is small enough, it can be kept overnight in a refrigerator.

### SOURCES:
*You know where to get the soda.*
*Commercial flower preservative is available in bulk at the San Francisco Flower Mart, Sixth and Brannan Streets. The Mart is open to the public after 9 A.M. Smaller packets of preservative are sometimes sold at florist shops or crafts stores.*

# [The Case of the Missing Marigolds]

*Who stole the Pezzatti Perpetual*
*Trophy from the Oakland Rose Society's Mother's*
*Day Show? Why is it that copper stripping*
*repels slugs and snails?*

Oakland Police are still looking for the Pezzatti Perpetual Trophy, swiped from the East Bay Rose Society's Mother's Day Rose Show at Lakeside Park. The engraved silver tray is the prize given annually to the best example of a particular pink floribunda known, ironically, as the 'Pride of Oakland' rose.

Similarly puzzling thefts often plague first-time gardeners in the Bay Area, who may plant out a bunch of marigolds one evening and find them gone by morning. A crop of new peas or a row of basil may vanish under cover of night. Delphinium seedlings may be cut down in their prime.

Nine times out of ten, the culprit is the night-feeding European brown snail, *Helix aspersa*, also known as the escargot snail. Setting out a few pans of stale beer to drown them or picking them out at night with a flashlight won't stop a heavy infestation. Even a small garden may harbor hundreds, if not thousands, of snails.

Historical detective work by researchers at the University of California identifies an A. Dumas as the enterprising Frenchman who first "seeded" colonies of escargots near San Francisco, San Jose, and in Southern California during the 1850s. By the turn of the century, the snails were ranging fifty miles from their original drop-off points— a mile per year, not bad for a snail's pace. By the 1920s, the invaders were up to the snow line and causing serious damage in Southern California orange groves, eating holes in the fruit and stripping trees bare of leaves almost overnight.

Decades later, the university found a way to repel the snails: A thin strip of copper foil, wrapped like a collar around the trunk of a citrus tree, keeps snails from climbing up and ravaging leaves and fruit.

How does it work? According to UC Berkeley entomologist Carl Koehler, snails won't cross copper because it gives them a mild electric shock, caused by a reaction between the metal and an element in the snails' slime.

"When a snail touches copper it appears to get an electric charge," Koehler said. "If you watch one closely, it will put out an antenna, touch the barrier, and recoil."

UC Riverside researcher Theodore Fisher, who first tested copper-strip collars for commercial citrus growers, said that the idea came about when someone noticed that a copper sulfate solution prescribed for a citrus rot appeared to keep snails from climbing up the trunks. Today, he noted, "thousands of acres" of orange trees in the state now sport copper collars.

A similar collar for the trunk of a home citrus tree can be made with flexible copper stripping sold in garden centers. Under the brand name Snail-Barr, made by Custom Copper of Ventura, California, the stripping is available in twenty- and one-hundred-foot lengths. Four inches wide, it's thin enough to be easily bent by hand or cut with scissors. Copper strips can be wrapped under the lip of a clay pot holding herbs or flowers, or stapled to deck supports, planter boxes, or the sides of raised beds. Circles of copper strip inserted into the ground will keep snails away from especially tempting perennials such as hostas and delphiniums.

For home gardeners, copper barriers make good alternatives to the metaldehyde-based snail baits that can be toxic to dogs, birds, and other wildlife. If the aim isn't to kill but to repel, copper strips are more effective than other types of barrier favored by organic gardeners, such as swathes of wood ashes, crushed egg shells, lime, or diatomaceous earth. The only disadvantage to the copper strips is that they have very sharp edges. Wear garden gloves when placing the strips, and don't use them near children's play areas.

### SOURCES:

*If you can't find copper stripping at the garden center, a mail-order source is the Natural Gardening Company, 217 San Anselmo Avenue, San Anselmo, CA 94960; (415) 456-5060; outside the Bay Area, the company's mail-order number is (707) 766-9303.*

# [Snail Kept South (To Avoid a Slugfest)]

*More on slugs*

*and snails: Predatory mollusks*

*are no match for the banana slugs*

*in Bay Area counties.*

I've had some inquiries regarding the decollate snail, a predator snail that is a natural enemy of the European brown snail, a common garden pest in California. In the southern part of our state, the decollate snail has been introduced as a natural control for the brown snail. It's not yet allowed in the Bay Area because it also eats banana slugs, which I referred to recently as an endangered species.

Several readers wrote in to assure me that banana slugs appear to be in no danger of extinction, at least in their gardens.

"I live in Inverness and it is hard to get down my front steps without stepping on one of the dreadful creatures," wrote Mike Lipsey. "They crawl across the windows and lurk at the thresholds. . . . Are you okay?"

"Please elaborate," was the message from Buff Harding Jr. "They couldn't possibly be endangered. They all live in my backyard and feed regularly at my kitty bowls."

After diligent research (special thanks to Rezsin Jaulos) I have a correction to make—and a far more interesting story to tell. Common banana slugs—the nine-inch-long, yellow slimers capable of taking out an entire delphinium bed in a single night—are not endangered, but, according to wildlife experts, among them Barry Roth of San Francisco, who makes his living as a snail biologist, some banana slug species are considered by our state's Fish and Game Department to be potentially endangered. "There are about 300 species of native snails and slugs in California," Roth noted. "Some are what the Department of Fish and Game call 'candidates' for extinction or endangerment."

One such "candidate" *is* a smaller species of banana slug found nowhere else but on the slender peninsula that includes San Francisco. The creature has no common name; its scientific name is *Ariolimax californicus brachyphallus.* "That just means it has a small penis," said Roth. "It's one way the experts can tell it apart from other banana slugs."

The most commonly seen banana slug, *A. columbianus,* is definitely not endangered. "That one is pretty well distributed through California, and north as far as Vancouver," he said, adding that it is most likely the slug species encountered by Mr. Lipsey in his Inverness garden.

"Unfortunately, even if Marin County decided to allow the decollate snail, it still wouldn't help the guy," Roth explained, "because the decollate snail only eats small slugs and snails, and *A. columbianus* is too big for it. In fact, once brown garden snails get larger than about a half-inch, the decollate snails leave them alone. They will eat the baby brown snails, though."

Roth said he thinks it's unlikely that the decollate snail will ever be released in San Francisco County merely to accommodate home gardeners, because the predator would eat the young of *A. californicus brachyphallus,* thus threatening a species known to have a limited range. Such a slug's value to the world at large is undetermined, Roth added, but that doesn't mean it doesn't have any. "It's still part of the food chain, and part of the unique ecology of the Bay Area," he said.

"It might have an important chemical use that we don't know about yet, like the bark of the West Coast yew, which is now thought to hold a potential cancer cure."

Gardeners "need to take the long view" when considering biological controls that may have an impact on the ecosystem, Roth said. "We know the healthiest ecosystems are those that have the greatest diversity of life forms," he added.

# [Five Senses and Four Seasons: The Why of Bonsai]

*The elegant and well-groomed trees seen*
*at a bonsai show offer delights to those bold*
*enough to bend wires. And J. procumbens*
*smells just like a gin and tonic.*

The general public usually sees bonsai only at shows. Well-trimmed and set on a polished-wood stand ("shoes for the bonsai"), they strike us as elegant works of art. They seem remote from the natural world of living plants, and a far stretch from the day-to-day container gardening lots of us do. But bonsai isn't just something to look at. Bonsai work is pot-plant gardening that engages all your senses, an intense horticultural experience far beyond simply plopping some petunias in a planter box.

The sensuality of bonsai isn't talked about much. But it's always there, and treasured especially by city gardeners who relish the chance to get up close and personal to any plant. The smells, for example. The burnt-vanilla whiff of katsura is elusive, while a bonsai wisteria's scent can be traffic-stoppingly heavy and strong. Chinese garden juniper, when cut, smells exactly like a gin-and-tonic.

Touch is integral to bonsai work. Bark is rough under your hands and the same garden juniper "bites" your fingers with its sharp tips. Japanese black pine has needles that are cool to the touch; like the wet nose on a dog, this indicates the health of the tree. You need your fingers to search for the caterpillar larvae of the maple moth (yuck) and of course, you stick a finger into the soil mix to see if it's too saturated or too dry.

There are sounds, too: the snip and click of your cutting tool; the heart-rending snap that says you wired a branch too hard. There's a ringing tone when you rap a knuckle against the wall of a Japanese-made *tokoname* pot—like fine crystal, the tone is characteristic of these handmade, imported ceramics.

Bonsai offers gardeners a way to be in the moment and enjoy nature on a small scale, which is why apartment dwellers and many folks with small yards get drawn to it. You can have a private redwood grove in a pot the size of a fish platter, or enjoy a New England–style display of fall color on a balcony—maybe six feet of assorted maples, ginkgos, elms, and oaks. A beginner's collection might rightly be four seasonal trees: one conifer, one deciduous tree, one winter-bloomer (sasanqua camellia or quince, both easy to bonsai) and an autumn-fruiting specimen (cotoneaster or dwarf pomegranate).

As pot plants, trees can be a challenge to grow, but perhaps no more than rare alpines or certain orchids! You can find all the basics in *Sunset's Bonsai,* a cheap paperback that explains the craft far better than many more expensive books do. It's fun to do it yourself, and the book shows how to start with gallon-sized nursery stock.

A ready-made bonsai is costly only if it dies for lack of care. The most common beginner's mistake is to keep the trees indoors. Most species used are outdoor growers that need outdoor air and sun to thrive. Keep them in the backyard or patio, and bring them inside only for display: a few days on the coffee table, then back out. Watering can be tricky (daily is recommended) but pruning and transplanting follow a schedule nearly identical to that of similar yard trees.

Refining a tree's artistic design is a repetitive process that takes a decade or more, because any tree will only grow so much in a single year. For some gardeners, this seasonal work becomes part of the year's rhythm, like planting peas in spring or lifting dahlia tubers in fall. A lot of bonsai work is done indoors during our winter rains; many a bonsai conifer doubles as a dining-room Christmas tree.

As for taste, bonsai fruits are rarely eaten, but bonsai clubs are known for the lavish buffets served to members behind-the-scenes at bonsai shows. Club volunteers put a great deal of work into mounting artistic displays, but perhaps it's time to engage the public more, to reveal the joyous sensuality of home-growing bonsai that results in the fine trees displayed in their company "shoes."

Toward that end, the Bonsai Society of San Francisco usually offers free docent-led tours of its annual exhibition. Visitors who take the docent tours are able to touch, smell, and get a good close-up look at trees in all stages of design. Bonsai as a kind of pot-plant horticulture is no more esoteric than any other, and well within the reach of any good gardener.

### SOURCES:

*The Bonsai Society of San Francisco can be reached through its voice mailbox, (415) 273-5509; recorded notices of meetings and shows are also available.*

*Bonsai books, pots, and tools are available at Soko Hardware, 1698 Post Street, San Francisco, CA 94115; (415) 931-5510.*

# [Splendor in the Accent Grasses]

*An introduction to
ornamental grasses in East Palo
Alto separates the chaff
from the clumpers.*

Ornamental grasses are the trendy garden plants of the decade. Already a big deal in the East and Midwest, accent grasses were slow to catch on in the West. But there is an excellent source for grasses close to home: Baylands Nursery in East Palo Alto. The nursery is owned by Day and Yuki Boddorff; Day is a landscaper who opened the retail outlet when he found it difficult to obtain certain plants for his clients. "People like the texture, the form, the showy seed heads," he points out, "and they're also attracted to the fact that these grasses are low maintenance. If you're looking for a tall, vertical form for a landscape, try a fast-growing grass instead of a slow-growing shrub." Many of the grasses can grow five or six feet tall in a single season. "And," he added, "you can get any color—brown, red, purple, orange, blue, yellow, white—and green, of course."

Boddorff's way with grasses has a distinctly California twist that owes little to the prairie-inspired grassy borders seen in magazines: In his own backyard, he's used them to landscape an outdoor spa to mimic a tropical desert island. On a mound of earth to one side of the spa's weathered decking, tufts of blue oat grass, miscanthus, and dwarf fountain grass half conceal a rock-lined miniature stream that feeds water into the hot tub. In the rear, fifteen-foot-tall elephant grass makes a privacy screen. "Around the edge I've added small native shrubs that complement the grasses," Boddorff explained. For example, the round leaves of manzanita 'Paradise' have a blue sheen that brings out the blue color of the oat grass.

Grasses at the nursery include tall, ribbony fountains suitable for specimens and spiky tufts that might edge a walk. Some, such as zebra grass, have striped leaves; others, such as the corkscrew sedge, whose wiry leaves grow in odd curlicues, would make wild pot plants. "Most," adds Boddorff, "sprout interesting seed stalks that can be dried and used for indoor bouquets."

For perennial borders, Boddorff recommends types known as bunch grasses, such as feather reed grass (*Calamagrostis* x *acutifolia* 'Stricta'). Unlike grasses that spread by underground runners, bunch grasses are easily trained to remain tidy clumps. Many sedges *(Carex)* or fescues *(Festuca)* are small enough to fit in a small space, like a rock garden. He suggests avoiding certain plants, such as fountain grasses *(Pennisetum)* or rattlesnake grasses *(Briza)* unless you have a meadow in mind. "Those two are really heavy self-seeders. Feather reed grass is popular with landscapers because it doesn't readily self-seed. And anything in the miscanthus family generally will not self-seed."

Some grasses are drought tolerant, but most look better with a little summer water. Maintenance is minimal. Dry leaves and seed stalks can be left in place, to provide interest for a fall or winter garden. Once a year, around February or when danger of frost is past, ornamental grass plants should be cut back to within four and six inches of the ground to allow for new growth. An exception to this are fescues, which should be cut back after they bloom in July.

Boddorff recommends consulting a book or two on the subject: One we both like is *Ornamental Grass Gardening* by Thomas and Martina

Rheinhardt and Mark Moscowitz. You'll learn even more if you visit him at the nursery, which has also expanded to include a large selection of proteas and California natives.

*SOURCES:*
*Baylands Nursery, 965 Weeks Street, East Palo Alto,*
*CA 94303. For directions call (650) 323-1645.*

# [A Boulder Idea]

*A rock garden in the*
*Seaview neighborhood has lots*
*of stealable ideas and a*
*masculine whimsy.*

They say if life hands you lemons, make lemonade. And if fate hands you a quarry—well, you make a rock garden. Massive shapes of large, reddish boulders decorate Nelson Barry's corner lot at Lake Street and 30th Avenue in San Francisco. It's worth a trip to see it, because the stones rise above a shaggy landscape of matching reddish plants. The overall effect is ruddy—warm and welcoming in this foggy neighborhood known as Seaview, where front yards typically run to cautious clipped lawns and mind-your-manners hedges. "I used to have a plain old lawn, just like everyone else," said Barry, who has lived here since the 1960s. "But you kind of get the seven-year itch, you want to do something different. I wanted to make the property stand out, kind of put my name on it."

So, when California was in the middle of one of its routine and multiyear droughts, he dug out the front lawn entirely, to replace it with a low-water landscape. "At the time I had a financial interest in a company in Arizona that owned a quarry that produced these rocks," said Barry, an attorney in the city. The pink stone is called rhyolite, a volcanic rock with a high mineral content. "There's a lot of iron in it, which gives the rock a red color," Barry said. "If you go to Phoenix you would notice that many residents use small reddish pebbles of the same material for their front yards, instead of lawns. The quarry ground most of its rock down to half-inch size for this purpose, but there were also these big boulders."

An idea began to form—an idea that had nothing to do with the boring expanses of gravel often considered for a droughtscape. He hired Phil Johnson, a local contractor, to bring in some boulders by truck, and credits Johnson for placing them artistically around the yard. Many of the rocks are placed so that their surface grain runs in the same direction, as it would in a natural outcropping. Some are slightly submerged in soil. "They had to use a crane to move them around the street trees," Barry remembers.

Freshly cut from the quarry, the rocks were a bright flesh pink when installed. Neighbors were horrified. "The attitudes ranged from sheer hostility to cautious praise," Barry recalls. "Now that the plants have grown in and the stone has mellowed, people tell me they like it."

The lesson here is that believable rock gardens can be made on the flat surfaces of former lawns. Come to this corner and you can study how this garden is planted with flowers, grasses, and low shrubs that pick out and highlight the reddish color of the boulders. Barry asked Barbara Stevens, a friend and one of the city's best-known amateur horticulturists, to make the selections. In her color palette, the most striking flowers are hybrid variations of our native Douglas iris, in shades of buff, peach, and burgundy to match the red rock. "The collection includes 'Soquel Bronze', from the Sierra Azul Nursery in Watsonville, California, and most of the rest came from native plant nurseries around the state," Stevens said. "There are so many hybrids now, in these soft, peachy colors."

When the iris finish blooming in late spring, summer color is supplied by the fluffy, pink-tinged seed stalks of red fountain grass, *Pennisetum setaceum* 'Rubrum', which ripple softly in a breeze. Year-round, the garden has a red brown cast, with the stiffer, grassy foliage of bronze and orange *Carex*; a low ground cover of creeping beach strawberry has brownish red stems and similarly toned fruits. Supporting players at the back are strawberry tree, *Arbutus unedo*, and a species of tea tree with a deep burgundy leaf, *Leptospermum brevipes*. For contrast, there are plantings closer to the sidewalk of gray santolina, a very pale pink rockrose, purple Spanish lavender, and little puffs of bright green lime thyme.

I asked Stevens how she might design a garden around gray stone. "I'd probably use more blue flowers or those of darker purple," she said. As a ground cover, instead of strawberry, she'd use snow-in-summer *(Cerastium tomentosum)*, a low, fuzzy plant with gray leaves and white flowers.

Surprisingly, large boulders in varying colors are not hard to find for garden use, though Barry's red rhyolite is rare. Masonry supply companies offer buff colored rocks with fancy names like "Desert Rose" or "Cabernet Quartz," and boulders in blue gray tones. These are usually sold for pennies per pound, weighed on huge scales at the stoneyard. Some outlets will deliver and place the stones, for an extra fee.

In a smaller garden, a single large boulder might be used, its color tones matched with flowers, leaves, and stems of more common garden flowers. Some planting ideas for red rocks: peach-colored bearded iris, copper-colored roses, and red-leaved Japanese maples. For gray rocks: blue campanula, silver-edged lamiums, and a blue spruce.

## SOURCES:

*Local sources for stone include Maccon Masonry, 367 Bayshore Boulevard, San Francisco, (415) 285-5025; and American Soil Products, 2222 Second Street, Berkeley, CA; (510) 540-8011.*

*Sierra Azul Nursery is located at 2660 East Lake Avenue, Watsonville, CA 95076; call for hours and directions: (408) 763-0939.*

*Many other native plant nurseries are listed in* Where on Earth: A Gardener's Guide to Specialty Plants in California, *by Barbara Stevens and Nancy Connor. The book is available at the Strybing Arboretum book kiosk in Golden Gate Park.*

# [The Flavorful Loquat]

*One man's trash tree is another*
*man's pleasure fruit; everything you*
*need to know about this exotic*
*streetside tree.*

One man's trash is another man's treasure—that old saying couldn't be more true when it comes to the loquat tree. The tropical-looking loquat, with its broad, gold-netted leaves and pale orange fruits, is common everywhere in the Bay Area. You can find them in backyards and vacant lots and even decorating the sidewalks as a street tree. The fallen fruits are messy underfoot and at this time of year the Master Gardener desk always gets two or three calls from people asking, "Is there anything I can do to keep this tree from fruiting?"

But, ah, the fruits. Have you ever tasted one? When a loquat is well ripened and soft to the touch, the flavor hovers between that of a peach and an apricot, with a bit of the tartness of strawberries.

Most folks don't know that there are two different species. You can identify the sweet loquat, *Eriobotrya japonica,* by the stiff, toothed, and deep green leaf. It has fragrant little white flowers in the fall, and can grow into a large, sturdy shade tree. The bronze loquat, *E. deflexa,* is shrubbier, with softer leaves that are copper-toned as they emerge. It has bigger white flowers that come out in the spring. The late-summer fruit of the bronze loquat is not as fleshy and sweet, so it's used more as a landscape tree.

Some folks do know the difference. In fact, one of my neighbors has to put a sign on his streetside loquat, begging passersby not to pick the fruit. Loquat is a delicacy in both Asia and Italy, which probably explains how both trees migrated here. It's native to China and southern Japan.

Once, returning from a trip to Italy, my mother brought back seeds of some very sweet loquats she had enjoyed there and sprouted the seeds indoors as houseplants. She had high hopes of planting them outside in rural Pennsylvania, but the snowstorms got them. Loquat can survive only to 20° F, and her hopes for fruit were dashed. When I said that loquats were as common as dirt in San Francisco, she refused to believe me until I sent her two pounds of fresh fruit, courtesy of another neighbor and Priority Mail. But Mom's experience does show how easily the tree can be grown from a seed. The fact that seedlings sprout so readily is probably what gave loquat the reputation of a trash tree.

Lately I have seen loquat sold in nurseries. That's a good sign. After strawberries, and aside from citrus, sweet loquat is our first spring fruit, and it's easy to grow at home. When you think of all the trouble it takes to grow apricots—the extra water, the pruning, the brown rot, the chill factor—it seems so much easier to have a sweet loquat. Once established, the trees are drought tolerant, like figs, and need no summer water. Nor are they susceptible to insect pests beyond the occasional bout with spider mites and the chance of a wasp or bee hovering around dropped fruits.

If you find a tree with sweet fruit (ask permission to taste if you need to), simply dig up a seedling nearby for your garden. Or plant a seed in a pot. The young plant will look something like an avocado, with its wide leaves. You can plant it out in the fall and expect fruit within five years.

For faster results, buy a grafted tree. Two named varieties are 'Champagne' and 'Gold Nugget', but fruit quality can still be highly variable in size and flavor. For a good crop, water the tree when it is in flower in the fall if autumn rains are late. For bigger fruit, thin out clusters; sometimes loquats bear so bountifully that the branches bow or even break.

You can eat a ripe loquat out of hand, like an apricot, or peel it and toss with a sprinkling of sugar for an exotic fruit salad. Or eat them as the neighborhood kids do, from the Mission to the Marina: suck out the juicy pulp and then discard the skin and the pair of brown seeds. Our city kids may have no childhood memories of picking strawberries out of tall grass or of gathering blueberries along a lake. But their urban adventures do include scrounging streets and back alleys for loquat—the secret, tasty treasure that most adults pass by.

### SOURCES:

*For more information, the California Rare Fruit Growers Golden Gate Chapter may be reached c/o 2209 McGee Avenue, Berkeley, CA 94703, or through its web site, http://www.crfg.org.*

*Outside California, a mail-order source for sweet loquat is Raintree Nursery, 391 Butts Road, Morton, WA 98356. Write or call for a catalog: (360) 496-6400.*

# [Whither the Weather?]

*More freak weather (rain in late June)*
*turns out to have been predicted by the* Farmer's
Almanac, *an agricultural magazine, and my*
*neighbor's arthritis.*

Don't talk to me about freaky weather. Earthquakes, drought, unseasonable summer rains—we've had it all. What's a gardener to do? It's not as if you can predict the weather. Or can you?

As the rain drizzled down so oddly on a Monday in the last week of June, I leafed through my edition of the *Old Farmers' Almanac.* 1992 marked the two-hundredth anniversary of this oddity, with its old-timey yellow cover promising "planting tables, zodiac secrets, recipes" and "weather forecasts for 16 regions of the United States."

The prediction for our part of California for June 29–30 was terse: "Sunny, drizzle south." How far south? The National Weather Service reported rain as far south as San Jose. The next nearest *Almanac* region, which covers the Pacific Northwest down to Eureka, was a bit more on target for June 26–30: "Cloudy, scattered showers, turning cold." Upstate did get drenched.

Richard Head, a meteorologist who used to work for the National Aeronautical and Space Administration (NASA), is the full-time weathercaster for the *Almanac*. He still uses the "secret formula" developed back in 1792, which is "kept in a black tin box," though he admits taking into consideration sunspots and solar activity. He claims an accurate prediction rate of between 65 and 70 percent a year, and gardeners throughout the country consult his forecasts. The *Almanac* survives because long-range weather forecasts are of great interest to farmers. One modern agribusiness publication, *The Grower*, gives monthly weather predictions as well. Their consulting meteorologists, Bruce and Frank Watson, forecast a warmer-than-average June for our region, predicting rain for that last week in June.

Actually, I should have known the rain was on its way, because several older friends, also gardeners, had all begun complaining about how their arthritis was acting up terribly, and all on the same day. (I wish I'd paid attention and not deeply irrigated my own garden the day before the downpour.) Many gardeners know people who say they can predict the weather. My dad, who fell off a three-story scaffold doing construction work one day, claims that he can predict a change in the weather from a twinge in his arm that dates from the fall.

*Ring around the moon, rain soon.* When it comes to weather, it's just as easy to trust in bodies (our own or the heavenly ones) as it is in the weather report. One of my favorite weather telecaster's typical forecasts gives a temperature range "with highs from sixty-five degrees to eighty-five degrees." A lot of help this is, especially if you're trying to sprout lettuce or coax along subtropical plants.

These uncertain weather times make it useful to add two new garden tools to your inventory: a minimum and maximum thermometer, which records actual high and low temperatures on a daily basis, and a manual override for the automatic watering system. Technology isn't everything, though. You can still find out the outside temperature in degrees Fahrenheit by counting the number of chirps a cricket makes in a minute, then adding thirty-seven. Try it sometime.

# [Plums Aplenty]

*Pat Cacio,*

*connoisseur of plums,*

*offers a walking tour through her*

*Bernal Heights plum orchard.*

The easiest fruit to grow at home may well be the plum. In the Bay Area, the most reliable plums for home growing are the mild-climate Japanese plums, which were developed for local farms by Luther Burbank and other researchers in California. 'Satsuma', 'Santa Rosa', and 'Shiro' are popular, but there are many others with juicy black or red or green or gold summer fruit.

Pat Cacio's garden, on the eastern slope of San Francisco's Bernal Heights, is a veritable thicket of plum trees. Some were planted twenty years ago, and almost all of them are thick with fruit.

"I consider myself a connoisseur of plums," says Cacio, reaching a gnarled hand into her 'Santa Rosa' tree to pluck me a ripe red one. It's juicy-sweet and considerably larger than the 'Santa Rosa' plums found in a supermarket. This and the 'Satsuma' ripen first here, the latter so big "you can't close your hand around one," followed by the even larger 'Elephant Heart'. Her favorites, though, are the old-fashioned varieties that ripen later, such as 'Nubiana', a large, purple black plum, and the yellow plum called 'Howard Miracle'. "It's yellow with red cheeks, just like a 'Royal Ann' cherry," she explains. "The flavor is much sweeter than other yellow plums like 'Shiro'."

Casio gardens organically, attributing the vigor of her standard-sized trees to feeder roots that run beneath a chicken coop and former rabbit hutch. "Japanese plums are generally very fast growers any-way," she says. "Over the years, I've tried trees on dwarf rootstocks, but to me the taste is not the same." She uses a pole with a basket on the end to pick the fruit; her yard has such a steep slope that she can often stand above the tree to get to the ripe plums.

Casio has a mystery plum in her garden, a tree that was there before she moved in. It's greenish yellow and she suspects it may be a green-gage type—a European plum that, reportedly, does not do well in low-chill zones like San Francisco. "My neighbor down the street has a prune plum, probably a 'Stanley', that has good fruit, " she says. "I think more people should give European plums a try."

Besides the plums, many wreathed with bramble blackberries, this expert gardener also grows loquats, cherries, apples, and seedling apricots grown from pits. Casio has tried many named varieties of apricot, both dwarf and standard, but doesn't recommend any. "It's always worthwhile growing a seedling apricot, because at the very least you get a nice flowering tree in spring," she notes. "It is very difficult to grow good apricot fruit in our area, because the tree wants such extremes of temperature, freezing winters and hot summers. San Francisco weather is too mellow for apricots."

Gardeners with small yards will be glad to know that apricots, cherries, and plums, being related stone fruits, will often cross-pollinate, though European and Asian plums don't cross-pollinate well. For the best harvests, two or more trees should be planted, unless there are trees in a neighbor's yard. If there's room for only one tree, 'Santa Rosa' is a good choice because it's self-pollinating. For the adventurous, named varieties of apriums and pluots are also available and take the same care as a plum (which is to say very little care at all).

Cacio does recommend yearly pruning and "attentiveness" as the fruit gets ripe. "You have to watch some, like the 'Satsuma', because the fruit will drop to the ground once it's ripe," she counsels. "The other good thing about the 'Howard Miracle' is that, because it's yellow, the birds don't discover the fruit before you do."

A new garden plum tree should be planted in January or February, so take the time to peruse catalogs and consider where it should be sited. If you want to do a little field research in July and August, however, visit local farmers' markets to taste different plum varieties to find the ones you like best.

### SOURCES:
*Sonoma Antique Apple Nursery,*
*4395 Westside Road, Healdsburg, CA 95448.*
*The highly informative catalog costs $2, refundable with your first order.*

*One Green World, 28696 S. Cramer Road, Molalla,*
*OR 97038 (503) 266-5432. Free catalog with useful information*
*on growing plums, apricots, apriums, and pluots.*

# [Summer Stock: Daylilies]

*Interviews with daylily breeders*
*Dolly and Cheryl Sloat, on color trends and*
*how to get the best blooms from*
*this border standby.*

When it comes to "summer stock" it's hard to beat the daylily as an easygoing performer that blooms its head off from June through August, then provides encores well into September. Daylilies in all their tawny beauty are in bloom in the fields of Alpine Valley Gardens, a specialty nursery run by the Sloat family. The two-acre show is free to the public at peak bloom time, from late June to early July. The nursery specializes in about twelve hundred varieties of *Hemerocallis* hybrids, most field grown. You can actually buy them right out of the field. The Sloats will dig them up and pack them for your garden.

Yes, daylilies may be transplanted any time, even while in bloom, which gives you some idea of their ruggedness as a garden flower. Simply plop them in the middle of that bare spot in your flower bed where you took up the faded tulips and it will look as if you planned their pretty effect months ago. One reason that daylilies can be planted in our dry season is that they are somewhat drought tolerant. But the flowers will always do better if you give the clumps summer water. "The more they're watered, the better they look and the more flowers you get," said Cheryl Sloat. "But if you can't water them because you're on summer vacation or we're having a bad drought year, they will still survive. Very few people ever lose them because of drought."

Her mother, Dolly Sloat, says that water "is even more important than fertilizer" to get good blooms. That's because a daylily flower only lasts one day (hence the name), but the plants set buds repeatedly and rapidly. "If you're having a party Friday night," said Dolly Sloat, "you should water your daylilies on Tuesday, Wednesday, and Thursday. On Friday, the flowers will be huge."

Many garden books also list *Hemerocallis* among plants that can grow in partial shade. This isn't exactly true. The blooms and stems will stretch out to seek sun, eventually toppling the whole clump forward. In foggy summer areas, Cheryl Sloat recommends planting daylilies in full sun. "In areas where it gets over a hundred degrees consistently," she added, "they should have a little shade."

Daylilies come in two types: evergreen and deciduous. Native to Asia, they are cold tolerant. "In the Bay Area, most people do well with the evergreens," Cheryl Sloat said. "But, if someone likes the flower on a deciduous plant better, those will work fine too. They don't stay dormant long, and they're clean: when the leaves die, you can just pull them out at ground level."

Colors are typically orange, yellow, or tan, with hybrid excursions into peach or purple tones. Fashions in daylilies also run to dwarf forms and flowers with a dark center or eye. "Melon colors were in for a long time," Dolly Sloat said. "Now they want white, although there is no pure white, and pinks and lavenders. Red's still in." The slim-petaled "spider" types are enjoying a comeback among collectors. 'Kindly Light', a lemon yellow spider type, is recommended.

The nursery still gets many requests for old-fashioned varieties, especially an old fragrant yellow whose common name is lemon lily, and the tawny daylily, the long-blooming, orange-flowered type that grows wild in many places. "Another old-time one is 'Kwanso', a double orange,"

Dolly Sloat said. "The main disadvantage to the old ones is that they send underground runners, and new plants may come up five or ten feet away. They're good for naturalizing, though."

Most daylily flowers fade with twilight, but certain varieties known as Nocturnal or Extended daylilies hold their bloom through the evening, which makes them a good choice for gardeners who work late. 'Stella d'Oro', 'Babaloo', and the old 'Olive Pauly' are some to look for. For deck gardeners, dwarf types do well in pots. For yard gardeners, the best way to plant daylilies is to set them out in volume: at least six of one kind, or at the very least, clumps of three. A single plant alone has no visual power. In groups, their strappy leaves complement most other perennials and help anchor flower borders.

## SOURCES:

*Alpine Valley Gardens is now closed to the public. The daylily cultivars propagated by the Sloat family at Alpine Valley Gardens are now sold through Amador Flower Farm, 22001 Shenandoah School Road, Plymouth, CA 95669. This nursery has a display garden open to the public and offers a free mail-order plant list. Call (209) 245-6660 for more information.*

# [Propagating Roses]

*It's so easy to start a*

*rosebush from a blooming cutting*

*that everyone should try it once,*

*just for the practice.*

Propagating roses from cuttings is something professionals don't talk much about. Nursery owners, rose growers, and mail-order suppliers prefer you to buy rosebushes, not make them yourself. Many new rose hybrids actually come with a plant patent—carrying with it the unmentioned threat to send the lawyers after anyone caught multiplying said rose and selling it to other people. The industry also does a convincing job of saying that modern roses don't grow well on their own roots, although if that were true, why do 'Tropicana', 'Joseph's Coat', and others grow so vigorously from cuttings?

Gardeners must give hybridists their due, but it's so easy to start a new rosebush from a blooming stem cutting that I think everyone should try it once, just for the practice. A new plant from cuttings is often the only way to perpetuate the beloved rosebush that grew in grandma's yard, and it's the most cost-effective way to assemble a collection of heritage roses, those beautiful hybrids dating back a century or more. (Don't worry, those lawyers are dead.)

The simplest method requires only a cut stem with a bloom on the end. If your roses are blooming now, why not try it? Cut a generous length of stem, remove the lower sets of leaves to reveal the bud eyes (which appear as moon-shaped scars), and stick the cutting into a pot of moistened, sterilized potting soil or sand. Place the pot in a generously sized plastic bag, seal the bag, and leave it in a warm place that gets light but no direct sun. Rooting hormone or bottom heat will improve the odds. The old bloom turns into a black blob, but when you see new growth on the stem (check weekly), unseal the plastic bag—but keep the stem misted and the sand moist for a few more weeks as growth continues.

A second method, perhaps more foolproof, is passed on by Mike Cevola of the San Francisco Rose Society. For this method, the rooting medium is Oasis, a brand name for blocks of porous foam that florists use in flower arrangements. Along with the Oasis, you'll need a few cardboard milk cartons. Cut the Oasis into two-inch-square blocks and soak them thoroughly; cut the milk cartons in half horizontally and reserve the lower part.

Cevola recommends taking a cutting eight inches long, with at least three bud eyes. Stick the cutting in the foam square almost all the way through, and set it into the carton. Fill the carton with water until the foam block is half submerged.

Check the carton daily, adding more water to make sure the block is always half covered with water. In three or four weeks, you should start to see some roots appearing through the foam block. Once you see roots, transplant the foam block into a pot of good soil. Next winter, you should be able to transplant the new rose bush directly into the garden.

If this fails, try a third method: In January, when you and your friends are pruning roses, trade a few pencil-thick cuttings. Strip the remaining leaves off and stick the stems three-fourths of their length directly into the ground. With normal winter rains, some cuttings will root where they stand, and can be dug up gently and transplanted to flower beds by May.

# III. Summer of Sorts

[ A Dry Heat ]

# [Blueberries in the Garden]

*A practical discussion on*
*growing blueberries for your*
*breakfast cereal, in gardens and*
*in patio pots.*

Birds in my garden have been enjoying a laugh and a treat at my expense. Through much of the early summer I was expecting my first crop of home-grown blueberries, but the fruits never seemed to ripen dark blue enough to eat. I finally realized the birds were getting all the ripe ones first. The plant is in a pot, so I moved it up to the kitchen deck, which doesn't get birds. Now we've been having blueberries for our breakfast cereal for several weeks. Blueberries are very easy to grow in the Bay Area, but they do have their tricky points.

Deciduous in the east, blueberry bushes don't drop all their leaves in our mild climate zones. Flowers arrive earlier, as early as March, but you still don't get your crop until summer, usually after June-bearing strawberries are done for the year.

Another tricky part: Blueberries grow best in extremely acid soil (pH around 4.5) that is moist, loose, and rich with leaf mold, pine needles, or shredded bark. Because they are shallow rooted, however, blueberries will grow well in containers. Growing them in pots lets you keep the soil highly acid without affecting surrounding plants. If you've got a small city garden where planting space is limited, pots are the answer.

In a larger landscape, blueberries can be mixed with azaleas, rhododendrons, pines, and other plants that need acid soil. But blueberries enjoy full sun, so move them to the front of your border, out of the shade. A hydrangea planted nearby can serve as a soil monitor, because hydrangea flowers turn a bright blue in acid soil. To acidify soil, add cottonseed meal, Miracid fertilizer, or aluminum sulfate.

Once settled in, blueberries are easy to care for, requiring almost no pruning but welcoming regular watering; plants in pots need to be watered daily in the summer or the developing fruits will shrivel. No sprays are ever needed. Yellowed leaves may occur but can be quickly cured with a fertilizer high in iron, nitrogen, and acidity.

Experts recommend setting out at least two different varieties for the best pollination. Some, such as my 'Sharpblue', seem to be self-pollinating. The fruits are ripe when they are dark blue with a waxy silver bloom on them. Really ripe ones are easily detached from their stems. Bird-netting, nylon net (tulle), or old sheer curtains can be draped over the plants to keep birds from eating the fruit as it ripens.

Mature bushes more than five years old can be renewed by cutting the oldest branches down to the ground. Gardeners buying new plants should select bushes labeled as two or three years old. One-year-old plants are cheaper but you'll have to wait that extra summer or two before any fruit appears.

Of the many cultivars available, tallbush hybrids offer the largest, sweetest fruit. Landscapers might be interested in the newer lowbush hybrids, which stay about two feet tall. Several gardeners in our bioregion also report success with rabbiteye blueberries (such as my 'Sharpblue'), native to the American South. Huckleberries, a tart wild relative, are native plants in California.

I expect my one small bush to supply fruit well into August, as the berries don't get ripe all at once. Then in the fall, I can count on attractive red leaf color—another reason a gardener might look about to see where a bush or two might be tucked in. Blueberry bushes may be planted at any time but are easiest to find at garden centers in January, when the bare-root plants are sold.

# [Fountains that Weep and Seep]

*If fake boulder waterfalls leave*
*you cold, the Morales family recipe for a*
*water wall offers a calmer approach more*
*suited to city gardens.*

One of the biggest trends in garden design is a water feature, usually a fountain. While loud splashing water and bubbling jets may enhance Old World landscape styles, they often don't look right if the home has a casual design or if the garden is planted in a naturalistic style. Even boulder-type waterfalls, with a fake stream cascading through a tumble of rocks, often look and sound unnatural, especially in a small yard.

Garden designers in California now offer an alternative—they build fountains that weep and seep, where the water flow mimics the slow trickle of a natural spring. Tony and Jolene Morales, who jointly run Redwood Landscape Inc. in Millbrae, a small town near San Francisco, explained how it's done. A "weeping wall" that was part of their company's display for the San Francisco Landscape Garden Show one season helped introduce the concept to many people, and it's been widely copied since.

"The intention is to give the idea of a naturally occurring spring, perhaps one that is romantically trickling over an old house foundation," Tony Morales says. They prefer to make their water walls of stacked stone, with the low walls sometimes angled. The water collects in a basin that may simply be a depression in a corner of a garden patio, lined beneath the pavers with 30-mil PVC plastic pond liner. (In the garden show design, the basin was appropriately dotted mossy green and appeared to be a naturally sagging corner of an old stone floor.) For such a design, water circulates through a standard, electric-powered fountain pump; a ball valve on the pump can be used to manually adjust the water flow. "It's a waterfall that's quiet," says Jolene Morales. "People have no idea how loud a waterfall can be—sometimes so loud as to be maddening."

Creating the weeping effect is so easy you could do it yourself. The Morales simply run plastic tubing across the back of the wall, parallel with the top row of stones. With a knife, they slash a few cuts in the tubing, then plug the far end. A piece of garden soaker hose might also serve, they say. "Once you've got a good pump, what you have to do is play around with the ball valve until the water runs evenly," Tony Morales notes. As the water recirculates, a pump filter like that used in a fish tank will keep sediment from clogging the tubing.

Existing retaining walls of concrete or brick can be turned into weeping walls in similar fashion. "In a real garden, you'd put plastic liner behind the wall as well, or redirect drainage from behind an existing wall, to prevent natural runoff from muddying the stream," said Tony Morales.

Weeping walls are also water efficient. "The garden show design took only ten gallons to fill up, and that's about the equivalent of a single flush of a toilet," he says. "Boulder waterfalls, even small ones, need a few hundred gallons."

Eventually, the wall might grow mossy, adding to the charm and natural look. Mosquitos could be prevented by adding biological control tablets to the water basin. "And anytime you add any water feature, birds will come," says Jolene Morales, "even to the smallest city garden."

*SOURCES:*
*Redwood Landscape Inc., Millbrae: (650) 347-1523.*
*Electric fountain pumps, PVC pond liners, filters, and mosquito tablets are available at better garden centers or by mail-order through Van Ness Water Gardens, 2460 North Euclid Avenue, Upland, CA 91784; (800) 205-2425. Catalog $3.*

# [Junipers: Give Them Respect]

*Placing and pruning junipers*
*correctly can make them an asset to*
*the garden, not just landscape*
*background noise.*

Junipers get no respect. Some folks laugh to see them tightly pruned to pom-poms out on the Avenues; most of us just ignore them as landscape background noise. Even in better neighborhoods you see juniper hedges festooned with spiderwebs, or ground cover plantings of junipers baking and miserable—transplanted during California's last drought, now patchy and ragged from lack of care and lack of irrigation.

Take another look at these useful evergreens—the ones you may have in your garden and what you can find at a local garden center. Does your mixed border need a backbone shrub? Would you like a tall spire accent for your front yard? Have you got a terraced hillside to fill? For all those reasons, explore junipers in their wide range of colors and forms.

California has several native junipers, long-lived denizens of the high desert and the hot-zone foothills, where you find our rugged digger pines or piñon pines. In nature, California's junipers grow as multi-trunked trees, often with twisty trunks of great character. *Juniperus californica* and the blue-tinged Sierra juniper, *J. occidentalis,* are rarely used in landscaping. Sometimes wild trees are dug up (with permits, of course) and transplanted to be used as a single picturesque specimen in a desert-themed landscape or Japanese garden, but that practice is more common in the Pacific Northwest than it is here.

The spreading mat juniper, *J. communis saxatilis,* is easier to find, and makes a fine, drought-tolerant ground cover if you're looking for a native plant to range over a rocky bank. Less than a foot tall, mat juniper has green needles with a silvery reverse and fleshy blue fruits that resemble trapezoid blueberries.

Most of the ground cover junipers at the garden center are variations of *J. horizontalis,* an alpine native to the chillier regions of North America. There are lots of pretty colors—bold yellows, powdery blues, even a few such as 'Bar Harbor' that turn a pretty purple tint in winter. With feathery branches trailing and creeping, these junipers are drought hardy, and excellent choices for a rock garden or terrace planting. Unfortunately we often see poor *horizontalis* planted in baking-hot sites; eventually the plants lose their leaves, leaving bare, spindly stems along the ground. These actually prefer a bit of light shade in summer, though in fog zones they will take what sun you can give them. A little summer water doesn't hurt either. Given good drainage and a gravelly planting bed, they might be used in a mixed border that includes other low evergreens, such as dwarf spruce and mugho pine.

If you're looking for a hedge plant, many varieties of Chinese garden juniper, *J. chinensis,* will suit you. Shrubbier sorts such as San Jose, Hollywood, and Pfitzer are the common ones sheared to lollipops, pillows, and pom-poms. It's a testament to how well junipers as a group respond to hard or frequent pruning: An old, rangy foundation plant can be rejuvenated by cutting it back hard in early spring. Prickly Chinese junipers make good barriers; if you'd like a softer hedge, look for plants with elongated, scaly foliage, not needle-shaped leaves. If you're looking for a tall hedge, choose *chinensis* varieties that grow upright; many with golden or blue-toned foliage never get higher than two or three feet. Upright, columnar varieties make nice, tight spires that can merge into a hedge or be planted as tall garden accents, standing in for a water-thirsty yew or slower-growing cypress.

Browned tips on junipers are danger signs. If the tips are brownish black and soft, that's root rot, caused by giving the plant too much water. Stop watering immediately and the plant may recover; trim off the dark tips. If browned patches on junipers are stiff and hard, the culprit is usually the larva of a tip moth. Break open the tip and you may find it hollow or be able to spot the nearly microscopic brown worm wriggling within. BT *(Bacillus thuringiensis)* is an organic pesticide that may be sprayed on to kill the grubs.

Landscapers like junipers because they are nearly maintenance free, and if you choose them well, they can be solid backbones of your garden design. But don't ignore them, or at least sweep them of cobwebs now and then.

### SOURCES:

Sunset's *most recent edition of the* Western Garden Book *(1995) lists five pages of juniper cultivars for your further research.*

*If you're interested in exploring the use of collected California and Sierra junipers as specimens or accents for Japanese or desert-style gardens, Dan Robinson, a landscaper in Washington, is considered the expert on the West Coast. He may be contacted at 4394 Panther Lake Road West, Bremerton, WA 98310.*

# [Trumpeting a Crinum Revival]

*Reintroducing the crinum lily,*

*a summer amaryllid once popular in California*

*gardens. Luther Burbank's work in this*

*genus can still be seen.*

An old-fashioned summer flower that's getting attention again is the milk-and-wine lily, or crinum. Pronounced CRY-num, its praises are being lustily sung for its explosions of giant-sized trumpets, on three-foot stems, just at the time when other garden perennials are starting to lose their pep.

Crinums are fancier relatives of the common pink *Amaryllis belladonna*. These fall-blooming amaryllis shoot up on bare stems (hence the common name naked lady); because they are drought hardy, they have even escaped old gardens to colonize California roadsides. (Magic lily, *Lycoris squamigera*, does similar tricks in climates not frost-free.)

Crinums at least have the grace to retain their strappy leaves as a base for their trumpet flowers. Like the other two they have a sweet perfume and thrive on neglect. Flower color has a broader range, however, from pure white to rose plum. Crinums grow in big clumps that you might stagger through a flower border—as you would clumps of iris, daylily, or peony—for a showy display that runs from late July to past Labor Day. The size of crinums gives them a tropical look: Even a single specimen can be the star of the August garden. The true milk-and-wine lily is *Crinum latifolium,* which gets its common name from slender flowers striped burgundy and cream. The species grows shorter than the hybrids but will bloom the longest—throwing scapes into November if it likes the locale. All crinums appreciate moderate summer water and fertilizer and can take a bit of shade.

At the turn of the century, crinums were hugely popular. Santa Rosa's famous hybridist, Luther Burbank, developed many named varieties. Most of them have been lost, but the Luther Burbank Home in Santa Rosa, open to the public as a historic site, maintains a nice if incomplete collection. The site's garden curator, Cheryl Harris, says, "The main reason we're excited about crinums is that Burbank had been able to cross the crinum with *Amaryllis belladonna,* which had never been done before." The result, she adds was a plant that kept its leaves, had larger flowers, and was exceptionally fragrant. "We have six or seven of his modern varieties," adds Harris, "plus examples of the parent species Burbank used in his hybridizing."

Fashionable gardeners these days are seeking out all sorts of amaryllis family members, including late-summer nerines and the white *Pancratium maritimum,* also called sea daffodil. All are enjoying a revival in catalogs. Get some before they disappear again.

Harris suspects that crinums fell out of favor originally "because they look a bit shabby in winter and don't bloom all year round." They are also hard to move. "They form huge tubers," she points out. "When we dug them up to transplant last year, some of the tubers weighed almost ten pounds." Despite this, she recommends them for planting in big tubs (so they might be wheeled out of sight in the off-season, or stored over winter) and considers them pest-free. (But, like agapanthus, they can harbor snails.)

Along with the sunniest flowers of late summer, including dahlias, marigolds, zinnias, and cannas, crinums are in high bloom each

August at the Burbank Home, where visitors may wander the grounds freely from dawn to dusk. Or, you might wander around to the hardware store parking lot behind 1722 Walnut Street in Berkeley. An ancient crinum hybrid, many decades old, is holding its own despite drought and neglect, lifting masses of pale pink trumpets and channelling waves of sweet scent across the blazing black asphalt. Last time I looked, it was still there.

## SOURCES:
*At the Luther Burbank Home, at the corner of Santa Rosa and Sonoma Avenues in Santa Rosa, guided tours of the house and greenhouses are offered for $3; access to the garden grounds is free. For open hours, special events, and tour information, call (707) 524-5445.*

# [When Plants Eat Insects]

*A visit to Marilee Maertz and
Peter D'Amato at their nursery, California
Carnivores, and their tips on growing
insectivorous plants.*

Insect-eating plants have always been a popular curiosity. One day, while walking past Eliza's, a fashionable Chinese restaurant on Potrero Hill, I noticed that the windows and tables were decorated with scores of pitcher plants, a bold switch from the usual orchids. Sensing that the needle was about to go off the trend meter, I decided to investigate.

We usually associate these plants with glass terrariums—and small boys who delight in dropping bits of hamburger onto the pads of a Venus's-flytrap, for the thrill of watching its prickly embrace. But these vegetable carnivores are outdoor plants by nature. Growing up in New Jersey, I remember seeing pitcher plants and sundews along streams and admiring their bronze-tinged foliage.

Peter D'Amato grew up in Jersey too, in the bogs and swamps of the southern Pine Barrens. He started collecting insect-eating plants when still a boy, showing them at county fairs. Today D'Amato has one of the world's largest private collections, and with Marilee Maertz, runs California Carnivores, a specialty nursery in Forestville.

Maertz opened the greenhouse for a quick tour. A television news crew from CNN had already come and gone, so the needle was definitely off on the trend meter.

"We've been getting a lot of catalog requests from Germany and Japan," Maertz said. The new interest in water gardening and habitat landscapes is having an impact. "Lots of people now come in looking for plants that can be grown outdoors."

Many plants offered here come from Australia, Asia, and South African, and in the Bay Area can be grown outside because the climate conditions are similar. Cold-hardy kinds, the easiest for a beginner to grow, include the American pitcher plant *Sarracenia,* and cobra plant, *Darlingtonia,* of which some are native to the California coast. Their long green tubes, massed along the greenhouse shelves, gave some idea of how they might look if colonized in a garden. Maertz was growing a few pots of *Disa uniflora,* a red orchid, among the cobras and the effect was stunning and sensible—the disa is a summer bloomer that doesn't seem to mind wet feet.

But it's the ability to lure, kill, and eat animal prey that is the weird attraction of carnivorous plants. Nepenthes, bigger cousins to the pitcher plant, hung like evil green balloons from the greenhouse ceilings, their swollen bucketlike sacs filled with water and enzymes—the better to drown and digest struggling insects. Maertz showed me a football-sized nepenthe armed with fanglike thorns that snap down and impale a victim. "This will trap small animals too, such as mice," she explained. "And if a monkey were to stick his hand in, it would get stabbed pretty hard." No plants are big enough to eat people, but even the tiniest can be deadly. Maertz pointed out a miniature species, with pinhead flowers on stiff wire stems less than one inch high: This grows in mossy colonies, the stems bending to gang up on any bug that falls in their midst. "They tear it apart, just like a piranha," she said.

She also showed off some gorgeous butterworts, Central American species with extremely showy flowers in purple and hot pink. Each blossom resembled a large violet, rising on an airy stem from a rosette of limp, transparently yellow leaves. The leaves are covered with sticky soft hairs, which is how this plant catches its prey.

Some butterworts are desert succulents, but most carnivorous plants need constant moisture. Outdoors in California, any undrained container can make a "bog garden." Plastic tubs with removable plugs or children's wading pools are popular with collectors. I liked Maertz's collection of 1950s pottery knickknacks that she uses as table-top planters—low vases, china shoes, souvenir toothpick holders—each holding a miniature specimen.

For two dollars, the nursery sells a book by Peter D'Amato about growing requirements, indoors and outdoors, and in greenhouses and terrariums. If you can't make it to the nursery, they'll assemble a collection for you or you may choose from a mail-order list. Maertz likes to include in all indoor terrariums a little bladderwort, *Utricularia,* because it blooms often and is programmed to attract and eat fungus gnats, those pesky brown flies that sometimes show up when there is standing water around houseplants.

The nursery sits on the grounds of the Mark Crest winery, where they've begun experimenting with using carnivorous plants to keep flies and other insects out of the tasting rooms. "During the crush, there's always a lot of little bugs in the air," Maertz explained. "So we once put out a lot of big sundews in the tasting room, and directed lights on the leaves. By the end of the day they were covered with bugs. Now other wineries are getting carnivorous plants from us, to help keep the flies out of people's glasses in their tasting rooms."

### SOURCES:

*California Carnivores, 7020 Trenton-Healdsburg Road, Forestville, CA 95436; (707) 838-1630. Behind Mark Crest Vineyard; open daily.*

# [A Last Word on Lawns: Notes from the Underground]

*It's high tech and*
*ecologically correct to water*
*your lawn from the*
*roots on up.*

If lawns have a future in California landscaping, their survival may rely on an active underground—but probably not a network of turf-lovers battling legions of the environmentally correct. Lawns of the future are more likely to be *irrigated* from underground, by a subterranean grid of plastic hoses that water grass at the roots—with no surface water loss to evaporation, overspray, or runoff.

Peter Ziebelman installed subterranean drip irrigation under his Palo Alto lawn three years ago. Nearly a mile of three-quarter-inch Geoflow black plastic tubing pulsates underneath his beautifully green and healthy turf. "You don't see it, you don't hear it," he pointed out, "and that to me is an exciting concept."

A venture capitalist by profession, Ziebelman says he doesn't mind being an early adapter of a technology still so new that most home gardeners have never heard of it. Professional landscapers have promoted it for ten years as a tool for water conservation; it has been used on ballfields, corporate campuses, and city parks throughout California.

Ziebelman also had a problem to solve. With three very active boys, he'd been trying to envision a lawn system without loose or pop-up sprinkler heads the kids might trip over. "The big selling point to me was this was how to get a lawn that was free from any obstructions," he explained. He and wife Cindy had some concern at first for the method that Geoflow uses to keep grass and tree roots from entering and blocking the drip emitters: time-release Treflan herbicide tablets fused into the plastic near each emitter hole. "It turned out to be a non-issue," said Cindy Ziebelman. "If anything leaked it would go down into the ground, not where it might get into the kids' mouths."

Once ready to re-landscape, the couple contacted The Urban Farmer Store, an irrigation service firm in San Francisco that has been involved in over one hundred installations of subterranean drip systems. With help from the installer, Mike Sleczkowski, they drew up a landscaping plan for several different areas of lawn around the house. The ground was prepped for turf and graded smoothly, to a depth of about six inches.

Sleczkowski said that each section of lawn was given its own master valve, which controls water flow at the rate of eighteen gallons per minute to an underground network of one-inch plastic tubes, called headers. These in turn feed rows of horizontal three-quarter-inch tubing, set four inches beneath the surface of the sodded grass. "Lines are spaced eighteen inches apart, and there is an emitter every eighteen inches in each line," he explained. The irrigation grid is an eighteen-inch square, pretty normal for residential lawns, said Sleczkowski. "But there's pretty close to two thousand feet of tubing down there."

The system includes air vents and flush valves for maintenance, and a master control system in a box on the garage wall. Automatic timers regulate the irrigation, set up for twenty minutes of underground watering every other day—fifteen minutes for shady areas. "The ground feels a bit wet," said Ziebelman, "but you can walk across it. It's like early morning dew."

The family did wake up one day to find one corner of lawn a sodden mass. "For some reason a valve got stuck open," he said. "So we've seen what happens when you overwater from underneath. If the turf is loose, the sod will actually float." Zeibelman also advised a little care with backyard toys: "If you want to stick in stakes for horseshoes or a beach umbrella you have to be careful not to puncture the line," he said. "Football cleats are okay."

They estimate that they are using between 30 and 50 percent less water than a traditional sprinkler irrigation would require. "Even if we get another drought, we'll still be able to have a lawn for the kids to play on," said Cindy Ziebelman. "If anything ever really goes wrong," added Peter Ziebelman, "we could just drag out a portable sprinkler."

### SOURCES:

*Irrigation design and installation services, and irrigation supplies (including Geoflow tubing) for do-it-yourselfers and landscape pros are available from The Urban Farmer Store, 2833 Vicente Street, San Francisco, CA 94116; (415) 661-2204.*

# [Dazzling Orchids for Outdoors]

*Nothing in*

*your experience can*

*prepare you for a walk in*

*Pui Chin's garden.*

Nothing in your experience can prepare you for a walk through Pui Chin's backyard. Row upon row of dazzling color, the deep vermilions and rich pinks of disa stand at attention, their helmet-shaped flowers as plentiful as geraniums. *Disa uniflora* are rare orchids from South Africa, so rare and reputedly so hard to grow that most orchid books don't even list them. But Pui Chin has solved the puzzle, giving gardeners in California a new, hardy outdoor orchid for pots and perhaps even flower beds in shady places. "In the late 1970s, I was able to have a friend bring me some from South Africa," said Chin. "From a tiny bottle of baby plants came all these that you see here."

Much of disa's reputation as a "difficult" orchid came from experts in temperate-zone or tropical climates, where orchid fanciers from England to Hawaii had pretty much given up on them. But nature was on Chin's side from the start. The disa orchid's native habitat in the

Cape Province is remarkably and happily close to what gardeners can find in the outer reaches of San Francisco's Marina district. Chin's backyard, surrounded on three sides by two-story houses, is a warm pocket that usually evades the fog that drifts from the nearby Presidio.

Chin grows all of his disa outdoors, under shade cloth. "Fifty percent shade makes the healthiest plants," he noted, although more sunshine makes the lipstick-colored flowers bigger. The plants are at least as cold hardy as cymbidiums are, and maybe more so. "During a big freeze, the temperature was in the low twenties for about ten days and every pot I had froze solid to ice," said Chin. "But they all survived."

Disa orchids bloom from March through July in San Francisco. The plants grow vigorously; Chin slipped one out of its pot to show a thick net of roots and fleshy white tubers. "Each of these tubers will produce a new plant," Chin said. "From a single pot, it's not unusual to get five new plants when you divide them in the fall."

A single plant may cost between twenty and forty dollars, but a prudent gardener might soon have enough to replace an entire bed of mundane impatiens with these bright, hardy orchids. "Orchids used to be a hobby just for the rich, but not anymore," said Chin. "From a single plant, you get more, and can exchange them for other kinds with other hobby growers. It doesn't have to be expensive."

A printer by trade, Chin said his orchid-growing hobby "is starting to become a business" because the disa have multiplied so rapidly. Recently he was honored with a First Class Certificate from the American Orchid Society for his named hybrid, 'Foam', a cross of *Disa uniflora* that has a neon-bright vermilion bloom. These flowers are still so new, however, that you can find them only through local hobby groups such as the San Francisco Orchid Society. And if you find a blooming disa, odds are good it was raised by Pui Chin. For their care, he recommends repotting each fall in fresh New Zealand sphagnum moss, watering carefully, and fertilizing weakly—in effect, replicating the natural habitat of this streamside, terrestrial species.

"The general public needs to be more educated about orchids, which are outdoor plants in nature," he said. "I had a friend who tried disa and failed; I gave her one of mine to try again and from one pot she now has eight pots."

# [Gardening on Mars]

*A chat with a NASA scientist on the possible*

*native vegetation and agricultural possibilities of*

*a Mars colony (and why it helps to visualize*

*Arnold Schwarzenegger's role in* Total Recall).

Assuming that we did colonize Mars, could we garden there? Based on scientific data revealed by Pathfinder's rover robot and other space missions, the answer turns out to be a qualified yes. Farming a tomato plant on Mars would be the equivalent of raising a redwood grove on a raft in the Pacific: It's theoretically possible and technically achievable—just not practical, perhaps.

NASA scientists don't discount the possibility that a form of primitive life—perhaps plant life—may already exist on Mars. Or perhaps existed at one time and is now extinct. One of the researchers exploring this angle is Dr. Jack Farmer, who works in the exobiology branch of NASA's Ames Research Center in Mountainview.

"It wouldn't be like a plant you would grow in your garden," says Farmer. "It would probably be a microbial organism, something tiny and single-celled and maybe photosynthetic." Farmer is an exopaleontologist, following up tantalizing leads such as the meteorite thought to be from Mars that appears to have chemical signatures indicative of life forms. "We're going to be getting a piece of that meteorite here at Ames," he says.

One of the reasons that Pathfinder's roving robot was looking at rocks was to see if they might be the type to hold a fossil record of ancient microorganisms that may have once lived. Its more important role, says Farmer, was to lay the groundwork for a mineral analysis of Martian soil. If there is life on Mars, Farmer suggests, it's deep down, below a layer of ice that appears to cover the surface of Mars like a frozen tundra. "If we were going to look for living organisms, we'd need to go deep below the surface, several kilometers down just to get through the ground ice," he notes. "It's a job that would probably require humans, with big drilling rigs."

On the next few missions, roving robots with tiny scoops will take what samples they can, and an orbiting surveyor will tune up a thermal emission spectrometer to discover minerals below the ice. Farmer hopes that the missions will pinpoint areas where the ice is thinner, where thermal gas vents with a concentration of water vapor indicate liquid water below the surface—a likely spot in which living organisms, or their ancient fossils, might be found.

There is plenty of water ice on Mars—so much that it can easily be seen by amateur astronomers in the form of polar ice caps, similar to those on Earth—so it seems at first that agriculture might be possible in some distant era. Air temperatures on the red planet average minus sixty-five degrees below zero (kind of like Minnesota in the wintertime); but there are some spots near the equator that warm up to a balmy sixty-three degrees, just like Marin County in the summer. The Mars atmosphere is full of carbon dioxide (95 percent) and nitrogen (3 percent) and there are some traces of oxygen in the atmosphere as well. So a warm spot near the equator near a gas vent near a thinner layer of ground ice might be the best place to homestead. But Earth pioneers would still have to wear space suits to survive, and crops would have to be grown indoors.

"If you grew any Earth plant on Mars it would have to be in a greenhouse," explained Farmer. "Outside, things would just explode like Arnold Schwarzenegger's head in that movie *Total Recall.* The plant would blow into a million pieces." The problem is atmospheric pressure. Mars is a smaller planet, so its atmosphere has less than 1 percent of the air pressure normal to Earth. "This means, for example, that liquid water vaporizes instantly," Farmer points out. "If you put water in a watering can it would come boiling out into vapor before you could do anything with it."

Because plants (and people) are full of water, the depressurized atmosphere of Mars would rupture our water-filled cells. But science, of course, has an answer. "It's called terraforming," says Farmer. "You go to Mars and then create an atmosphere there, artificially, and progressively introduce elements that would recreate an earthlike environment." Science fiction writers have long dreamed of this, but one of Farmer's colleagues at NASA is actually exploring the options for terraforming. "It's a legitimate idea," says Farmer, "though the process would probably take hundreds of years."

### SOURCES:

*NASA provides several Internet sites for discussion and description of the current Mars missions. Web sites include mpfwww.arc.nasa.gov/.*

# [Spring Bulbs to Fit a Droughtscape]

*Pier 39's Tulipmania maven*
*Denise Dirickson offers tips on*
*managing your tulips through a*
*dry winter season.*

Spring bulbs—those planted in fall to bloom in the spring—are available by September, and that's the time to buy them. Drought-conscious gardeners should focus on the daffodil, which will multiply happily in the landscape without the need for summer water, fertilizers, or pest controls. If the 'King Alfred' yellow trumpet is your only daffodil experience, a look through mail-order bulb catalogs will surprise you. Check out the stately, pure white trumpets ('Stainless' and 'Mount Hood') as well as a garish line of "fancy" hybrid daffodils with ruffled corollas, split cups, double cups, and bicolor petals in mixtures of chrome yellow, hot orange, and salmon pink.

Two of the more successful variations in my garden are 'Ice Follies', a strong-blooming daffodil with a yellow cup and white petals, and 'Salome', a delicate white daffodil with a small pink cup. The tulips I grow vary from year to year, with varying degrees of success. Both daffodils and tulips have the advantage of requiring water during a time of year that California has natural rainfall—from January to May. During a drought year, a deep watering once every week it doesn't rain is necessary for maximum bloom but needn't be a strain on a water allotment, especially if the bulbs are planted in a single area or in a container.

San Francisco's most expert tulip grower may be Denise Dirickson. As the landscape director for Pier 39, a tourist magnet, she's in charge of the annual Tulipmania Festival at the pier, which runs every March. She orders her tulips from commercial catalogs in June, to be shipped in September and planted in November. "That's the right time to plant, when the soil is cool," she said. "But people shouldn't wait until November to buy tulips, because they are in the stores by the end of summer. We usually have warm autumns, and those bulbs are going to be sitting out there, drying out, using up the stored carbohydrates in the flowers. Because tulips are expensive, you should buy them early and put them in a cool spot right away."

Should tulips be refrigerated before planting? Yes, said Dirickson. Gardeners who are originally from the East Coast and accustomed to tulips lying dormant beneath winter snows may believe that cold is necessary for the plants to bloom, but that is not the case. "You just want to keep them cool enough so they remain dormant until planting," Dirickson explained. "The refrigerator's a good place. Never in the freezer."

Dirickson also explained why tulips planted in the Bay Area do not bloom well in the second year. "It's our climate," she said. "Our spring warms up quickly, so tulip foliage dies down early. There just isn't time for leaves to provide the bulb with enough stored food for a good bloom the next year. In Holland, they have very long, very cool, very wet springs, so the foliage stays on for a good long time."

This year, for the Pier 39 deck plantings, Dirickson has ordered more lily-flowered tulips, which have a spiky shape and very tall stems. "I had some last year and people went wild over them," she said. "The one I'm really going to be watching is called 'Ballerina'. It's a lily-shaped tulip that's supposed to be a marigold orange in color. I'll be mixing it with other lily-flowered tulips, 'White Triumphator', and 'William & Mary', a salmon pink. I'll probably use blue nemesia for edging on the containers."

Dirickson likes to mix vegetables, especially lettuces and parsley, into her tulip plantings. It's a smart idea for the gardener restricted to containers or a small space. As an onion-family relative, tulips will not harm any food plants seeded over them. Tulips are also edible enough to be attractive to gophers and mice, so many local gardeners recommend planting the bulbs within a cage of one-quarter-inch wire mesh. Wire baskets for this purpose may be found at garden centers.

Expect to pay about a dollar each for good quality Dutch bulbs. Daffodils are a good investment for the homeowner, as they multiply effortlessly and are well adapted to our droughty summers. Because tulips do not give as good a show the second year, consider pooling a mail order with other gardening friends to take advantage of quantity discounts.

## [Tulip and Daffodil Calendar]

SEPTEMBER Purchase bulbs now for best selection and freshness. Store in a cool place or, bagged and labeled, in your refrigerator.

NOVEMBER Plant tulips and daffodils wide-side down, between four and twelve inches apart and five or six inches deep in well-drained, good soil. A light dusting of bonemeal on loose soil beneath the bulb will be beneficial.

JANUARY Begin watering deeply once a week if there is no rain. When tops begin to show, fertilize with 0-10-10–type fertilizer.

FEBRUARY–APRIL If snails eat blooms, surround plants with a circlet of copper stripping, wood ashes, diatomaceous earth, or a thin band of agricultural lime. Use snail bait if damage is severe.

MAY–JUNE Allow foliage on daffodils to dry completely before removing. Daffodils will multiply if left in place; if you want to move them, lift them now, dust bulbs with sulfur, and store in a paper bag in a cool place until next fall.

# [Trouble in Paradise]

*What's eating your palm tree?*
*Could it be the "mother of all borers," the*
*deadly grub that escaped from Palm Springs?*
*An Arizona entomologist answers all.*

Any gardener who vacations in California is usually enthralled by our palm trees, the more so when they see them thriving so well in the chilly, clammy climate of the Bay Area's decidedly less-than-tropical summer. The matched sets of *Phoenix canariensis* on upper Market Street and along the Embarcadero medians (running all the way, now, to the Caltrain station) have added unimagined elegance to San Francisco's thoroughfares. Small wonder that the palm is once again becoming an enticing option as a garden tree.

Small palms are easy to find in nurseries that carry a good selection of trees in containers. Larger palms are usually brokered or sold wholesale through landscapers, dug up from old homesteads around the Southwest, then shipped and replanted with their tidy small rootball. That palms are easily transplanted is obvious from the City's street trees: Of the hundreds planted in the past four years, few have had to be replaced.

But all this moving of palms appears to have a price. The fly in the ointment, the worm in this apple of apparent paradise, is actually the white, wormy grub of a flying insect pest known as the giant palm borer. Biologists at the University of Arizona know the most about this pest, although it is native to desert California. According to Dr. David Langston, an entomologist at the university's Maricopa campus, the borer is a ticking time bomb for palms. "It's the mother of all borers," says Langston. "And you never know you've got it, until a strong wind comes up to snap the tree right in half."

As the larval stage of a two-inch beetle, the giant palm borer is about the size of your thumb, and will spend anywhere from *three to nine years* hidden within the trunk of a palm tree, chewing miles of tunnel from the woody inside. "Since it doesn't eat the green growing parts, you have absolutely no clue that it's inside," Langston says, "but over time it ruins the structural integrity of the trunk." Slimmer palms such as the California fan palm *(Washingtonia filifera)* suffer the most and are most likely to snap when stressed in a winter windstorm. But the borer has also been found in phoenix palms and Mexican fan palms *(W. robusta)*. Dr. Langston says that landscapers in Arizona are still piqued that this California insect crossed state lines in the late 1980s to become a serious pest there. Once thought to be nearly extinct in its native habitat—the area around Palm Springs—the giant palm borer was hemmed in by colder mountain regions and escaped only as a passenger on palms that had been dug up and transplanted to other parts of the Southwest.

There is no way to tell if your new palm has the grub, unless you find a bit of sawdustlike frass at the point where new fronds start as buds. The only other clue is a three-quarter-inch exit hole, made by the adult beetle. "We tell people who work on cleaning palms that, if they see such a hole, they should stop working and get down from the tree immediately," Langston says, "because it just isn't safe." Insecticides are useless once the tree is infected, but Langston thinks there may be some hope in controlling the adult beetle, which flies at night. "What we're advising now is to apply an insecticide during May or June," he says, "when the beetles are emerging and the females are laying eggs in the green portion of the tree."

Other than that, keeping palms healthy can mitigate borer damage if there are not too many grubs involved. Warm weather boosts palm growth, so the palmier weather of early fall is a good time to fertilize and irrigate landscape trees in California. Until winter rains arrive, hosing down the fronds of palms helps remove dust and small insects such as spider mites and mealybugs that can weaken new foliage growth.

## SOURCES:

*Entomologists at the University of Arizona are very interested in tracking the spread of the giant palm borer, which mainly infests native California stands of the palm* Washingtonia filifera. *If you encounter this grub in your palm tree, please contact Dr. Carl Olson, Department of Entomology, University of Arizona, Tucson, AZ 85721.*

## [Common Problems with Palms]

Hardy as palms are, there are a few other pests that trouble them. Scale insects and mealybugs make an ugly mess when they appear in hordes, as a grey or brown powdery encrustation on the fronds. By sucking plant juices, they make foliage weak and yellowish; whole fronds may die back. Their insect wastes also become a breeding ground for a sticky, black fungus known as sooty mold. Usually, these two pests can be kept down by natural predators, such as a tiny parasitic wasp that unfortunately is easily killed if you attempt to spray the tree with insecticide. Once in the hard-shell stage, scale insects are impervious to chemical sprays, but scraping their crusty bodies off the leaves may bring some relief. The sooty mold can be washed off with a mild soap-and-water rinse.

If you notice palm fronds gradually yellowing and dying back, look for these insects first. If the fronds are clean but the foliage still looks sickly, the problem is most likely poor irrigation or bad soil. The use of herbicides to kill weeds in other parts of the garden can also affect palms, if the herbicide is applied upwind or uphill from the tree.

Though long lived, palms do die of old age, and a venerable specimen may simply stop producing new fronds at its crown. If a landscape palm is in decline, you might wish to install its replacement—a younger, less expensive tree some feet away from the trunk of the first. Smaller plants from nursery containers can be a bargain, and you'll have the added pleasure of watching them grow into stately and valuable property trees.

# IV. Autumn's Ends and Beginnings

## [ Wind at the Weathercock ]

# [Tropical Harvest on the Hill]

*Autumn's bounty includes*
*a papaya-type fruit, grown to*
*perfection on Potrero Hill's*
*"Banana Belt."*

September is the month in which gardeners truly reap the bounty of their labors. By then you know if you will have enough tomatoes, and have begun tucking in new basil starts and scallions to serve with them through the harvest months. In my garden the riches of our warmest and most pleasant season include broccoli, blackberries, shiny gold shallots, and a first crop of tiny and sweet Seckel pears. In your garden you may be enjoying crisp apples and eggplants. It's a time for bragging, and no one feels shy.

One of my favorite harvest stories comes from San Francisco artist and gardener Joni Eisen, who wowed a meeting of the Potrero Hill Garden Club by serving juicy slices of her freshly harvested babaco, a tropical fruit related to the papaya. Eisen picked the fruits from a rangy specimen growing in a protected site, next to the side of a house wall. This sunny pocket suited this tropical oddity well enough for it to fruit, and what fruits they are: each one approximately twelve inches long, deeply ribbed, and taxi yellow when ripe. Sliced crosswise, the fruits have the shape of a star; the edible white flesh and rind have a tart-sweet flavor that's something like banana, something like casaba melon. "To me, the taste and especially the smell, is just like Bazooka bubblegum," said Eisen.

The babaco was a long-term project for Eisen, whose late-summer garden is lavish with apples, tomatoes, peppers, and sweet corn. A native of Ecuador, the babaco arrived as a two-foot potted plant two years ago, a pass-along from a meeting of the Golden Gate Chapter of California Rare Fruit Growers (CRFG).

"It was labeled babaco, but when the fruits started to grow, we thought it was a star fruit (carambola)," Eisen explained. She brought one of the green fruits to a CRFG meeting last autumn and got it positively identified, and was told it would take as long as a year for the rest of the fruit to ripen. "And that was just about right," she said. "There are smaller fruits on the tree right now, and those will be ones that will be ripe next year."

Babaco, *Carica heilbronii,* makes its fruits in clusters, just like a papaya. Kurt Peacock, an expert on rare fruit and the manager of Pacific Tree Farms, a tropical plant nursery in Chula Vista, said he wasn't surprised that one would fruit in San Francisco. "Babaco comes from high land elevations in the Andes," Peacock explained by phone. That's the same kind of cloud forest conditions—mild winters, cool summers, and lots of damp fog—that suit mountain tropicals such as fuchsias, which do so well here. And, just like fuchsias, babacos prefer a dryer winter soil, ideally about half our normal rainfall. Eisen's specimen, he mused, probably benefited from the protection of the house wall, and the excellent drainage of her raised beds. He said that the fruit is grown commercially in New Zealand and Australia, which have a similar Mediterranean climate to the Bay Area.

The plants are cold hardy to 27°F, which makes them far easier to grow than the frost-tender tropical papaya C. *papaya.* Pacific Tree Farms sells both, but Peacock says that most home gardeners in California score better with babaco.

Bill Grimes, who edits the newsletter for the local chapter of CRFG, said that he was surprised Eisen had gotten fruit, though many members have tried to grow it around the Bay. Among its virtues, he said, babaco has "three times the amount of papain," a digestive enzyme also found in papaya, and higher levels of vitamins A and C.

Katherine Pyle, a CRFG member in Berkeley, said she's rarely had a taste of hers. "I had thirty-five pounds of fruit lost overnight in two bad freezes we had."

All three fruit experts say that the secret to growing the sweet tropical babaco is a warm and sheltered space, with rich, well-draining soil. In Eisen's Potrero Hill garden, it lives behind the woodpile. "I just stuck in here next to this old rosebush," said Eisen. "Obviously it's very happy here."

### SOURCES:

*Babaco plants are available through Copacabana Gardens, Orinda, CA; (925) 254-2302. This is also a contact for California Rare Fruit Growers (CRFG) Golden Gate Chapter.*

*Pacific Tree Farms, 4301 Lynnwood Drive, Chula Vista, CA 91910 is a wholesale/retail nursery near San Diego; (619) 422-2400.*

# [Buckwheat Is a Showstopper]

*St. Catherine's lace*
*and other native buckwheats*
*emerge to take a starring role in*
*drought-tolerant borders.*

Once again giant buckwheat is the star of my late-season garden. Everyone who sees the backyard wants to know what THAT PLANT is. "It looks like baby's breath, but it's so huge," they say. Admired by moonlight from the back deck, the white blossoms were mistaken for an elderberry bush by one person; another thought it a giant poison hemlock.

THAT PLANT is *Eriogonum giganteum,* also called St. Catherine's lace. Native only to California's Catalina Island (the blissful car-free isle off the coast of Los Angeles), it has long been my Exhibit A in arguments for growing more California native plants in our gardens. The flower umbels reach a foot and a half across; they start out white and gradually deepen to a rusty, rosy brown. Massed on the plant, which is shrubby and low, they give the appearance of a tea-dyed lace shawl spread out across a bush.

Our local botanist, Glenn Keator, has identified twenty-four *Eriogonum* species suitable for garden use, all described in his book *The Complete Guide to Native Perennials of California*. In his newer companion book on native shrubs, he adds one more that he considers a stellar performer for extreme deserts, *E. heemanii*. All are in the same family as the edible buckwheat you buy as kasha in the grocery store.

As garden subjects buckwheats are compact, rounded plants, forming perfect, rotund cushions when given the space. You can often see wild buckwheats growing on roadside slopes; I think it is the coast buckwheat, *E. latifolium*, by its netting of brownish-pink flowers. If so, this two-foot-high variety would be fine in a formal garden, alternating with similar low, bushy perennials, such as spring-blooming lavenders or santolinas, or set into a perennial flower border near the cushion chrysanthemums. The spoon-shaped leaves are gray, often with a tint of pale greenish gold.

My St. Catherine's lace has a similar leaf, but would be the size of a Buick if I didn't trim it back each winter after local birds have had their share of the ripened seeds. It has its own corner of the garden, once a waste place where nothing would grow because it is an outcropping of serpentine rock, which makes a soil poisonous to many other perennials. One of the graces of buckwheats is that they tolerate serpentine, which is a common garden problem on Potrero Hill, other parts of the city, and parts of the East Bay.

This is also the "no water" part of my garden, which receives no irrigation at all and fertilizer only every other year. But a big buckwheat needs a big frame, so its backdrop is another hardy native, Matilija poppy, *Romneya coulteri*. This is also known as fried-egg plant because the big white summer flowers have a blob of yolk-yellow stamens. If I watered the poppy, its invasive roots would take over my entire yard.

Fortunately, the buckwheats are better behaved. The branches are brittle and easily pruned. Once established, they are very drought tolerant. The smaller kinds, which include yellow-flowered buckwheat *(E. umbellatum)* have stiffer-looking flowers that hold up well in arid, baking-hot spots such as a parking strip or streetside tree pit.

Frilly St. Catherine's lace is more graceful when in bloom, and it always looks good with companions that have spiky flowers. Other tall, drought-tolerant perennials in my patch include lion's tail *(Leonotis leonurus)* and a continuing parade of salvias and penstemons I keep switching just to see how the colors look against the creamy veil of the buckwheat flowers. Grasses also pair excellently with all the decorative buckwheats. My foreground planting includes a fluffy blue fescue, although you could substitute native blue oat grass *(Helictotrichon sempervirens)* for an all-native grouping.

As a bonus, the buckwheats attract all sorts of honeybees and butterflies. They're a guaranteed stopping point for monarch butterflies as they migrate in groups down their coastal flyways. And indoors, St. Catherine's lace makes a great everlasting cut flower. I have found that if the stems are cut while the flowers are still white, they will dry in this stage and not drop pollen or seeds on the tablecloth.

The time to plant native buckwheats in your garden is September, before the rains begin. A good place to find them is at local plant sales by the California Native Plant Society. The East Bay Chapter's annual autumn sale at Merritt College in Oakland generally has a wide selection of wild plants, well grown in nursery containers. These sales are an excellent place to buy and learn about unusual border flowers that do well with us and give an excellent return in exchange for a minimum of water and care.

*SOURCES:*
*California Native Plant Society; for local chapters call the headquarters in Sacramento; (916) 447-2677.*

# [It's Time to Plan Your Deck Garden]

*Balcony*
*and firescape gardening*
*with containers and*
*other pots.*

Attention, apartment dwellers. This one's for you. If you meant to put in a garden on your terrace or balcony this spring but never got around to it, congratulate yourself. Autumn's a far, far better time to plan a deck or balcony garden because it's still warm, dry, and pleasant to work outside, which is not often the case in early spring. When cold weather comes, instead of looking through a sliding glass door to a hodgepodge of wimpy potted plants, you could be gazing into an elegant garden, a four-season patch of paradise, if you start right now.

A first step is to note by the clock how many hours the balcony has sun. Under six hours is not cause for despair: Many potted plants thrive in dim light, including edibles such as mint and onions, flowers such as daffodils, and shrubby bamboo and yew. A deck or balcony where the sun beats down relentlessly, abetted by dry afternoon winds, is actually a worse problem. Plants identified as drought-tolerant will have the best chance to survive.

Deciding where the water will come from is the next step. A plastic gallon milk jug placed near the kitchen sink can collect enough waste water to supply container plants. Whenever you run the tap to get the water hot or cold, fill the jug with water that would otherwise go down the drain. However, hauling buckets to a roof or terrace is a chore that will lose charm fast. A better alternative: Install wall brackets on the inside and outside of a kitchen or bathroom window to hold a standard garden hose that can be attached to a faucet when required.

Depending on space, plan on installing at least one large planter that is two feet deep. Raise all planters with bricks an inch or two for good drainage or attach them securely to a railing. Drip pans may be required for all containers.

Next, no matter how small the balcony, add art or furniture. Do it now, don't wait for the plants. A tiny bistro table and chair, a small stone lantern, an urn, or small bench are the items that will miraculously transform any outdoor space into a real garden.

With containers and furnishings in place, add soil mix. I use equal quantities of potting soil, shredded fir bark, and puffy lightener, such as polystyrene (Styrofoam) packing pellets, vermiculite, or expanded shale. Now you're ready to plant.

What to plant? For real drama, have at least one real tree. A rangy pine (for sun) or dark yew (for shade) can also serve as a windbreak. If the deck gets a lot of wind, avoid tender deciduous trees such as Japanese maple, for their leaves get crispy in autumn's dry winds. Choose a sculptural evergreen, such as cypress or weeping blue Atlas cedar instead.

Container-grown trees, shrubs, and perennials can be planted well into early winter in our region: Azalea and camellia will add color to a shady garden, rosemary and New Zealand flax will provide textural interest in hot sun. Consider also vines to wrap around the balcony rails or climb up a wall: bougainvillea and jasmine for sun, Boston ivy or potato vine for shade.

Don't forget the spring bulbs. Daffodils go first, planted five inches below the soil surface. On top of these press the little corms of anemone and the smaller bulbs of crocus. On top of these, gently set out shallow-rooted annuals for winter color the first year: Shirley poppies, pansies, and calendulas. A few potted chrysanthemums would be the final touch.

Thus with a few simple elements—containers, furniture, a tree, some reliable shrubs, bulbs, and annuals—the balcony garden is born. And the gardener has all winter to research and reflect on a more ambitious and even more elegant landscape plan for spring.

# [Rearranging Fall Borders]

*Lacy's Law on*
*transplanting late bloomers,*
*and other mysteries of*
*musical borders.*

October's a fine month to rearrange the garden, to plant new trees, and add seasonal color, from colorful chrysanthemums in pots to trees that provide fall foliage: maples, beeches, pistache, liquidambars, and spindletrees. Some new items you will see at the nursery are lily turf (a bolder cousin of mondo grass) and Japanese toad lily, *Tricyrtis formosana,* which has orchidlike flowers and makes a great pot plant.

As a general rule, think about dividing and transplanting spring-blooming perennials in fall and summer flowers in late winter. I call this Lacy's Law, because I came across it first in Allen Lacy's book, *The Garden in Autumn.* He makes the point especially that members of the daisy family seem to dislike being moved in autumn. Perhaps this is why the hybrid asters and Michaelmas daisies that we buy in garden centers now often fail to be truly perennial for us. It's certainly true if you want to keep chrysanthemums, for these are best divided and replanted in January, when the new leaves begin to show among last year's blackened stems.

Local wisdom says that California natives, including trees and shrubs, thrive best if planted just before the rainy season. We have few true late bloomers among our natives, the exception being California fuchsia, which is not a fuchsia at all and still confounds botanists (*Zauchneria? Epilobium?*) while it delights the hummingbirds who rummage in its dusty red flowers in fall. But California fuchsia, like our native salvias, may have been in flower for months, although the turn of the year seems to perk them both up. Still, I've had best luck planting salvias in the early spring, and the lone aster in my garden is a native one, frothy white and frail. I have to water it religiously in summer or else it disappears.

Like many gardeners, I find many favorites confounding. Like Lacy, I'm fond of the chocolate cosmos, *Cosmos atrosanguineus*. This plant has small flowers in a lovely dark maroon, and they actually smell a lot like chocolate, especially when the warm sun has been on them for a while. For two years in a row, the transplants disappeared on me— except, this one July, I happened to notice the distinctive purplish green leaves poking up out of a three-inch layer of chipped bark mulch. What revived them? Probably the mulch, with its slightly acid pH and ability to keep soil surfaces moist and cool. Chocolate cosmos grow from little tubers, and mine were just waiting for conditions to suit them. But they flowered disappointingly, and this fall I will transplant them again—in a bed near other acid-loving plants. I've even had trouble with *Sedum* 'Autumn Joy', probably one of the easiest perennials to grow. My succulent sulked for a year until I stuck its limp and blackened stems into the drought border, which has good drainage and gets minimal summer water. You should see the flowers now. If a plant isn't doing its best, moving it to another spot can effect quite a transformation.

Sometimes it just takes time for certain flowers to hit their stride. Japanese anemones—one of our finest fall flowers—and the winter hellebores will both bloom abundantly in dry shade, but both need a few years to get established before they will put out their first nice crop of flowers. And it's really true what they say about ivy: "First it sleeps, then it creeps, then it leaps." Give any vine or ground cover two or three years before you make a judgment.

And don't be afraid to yank anything that clearly isn't working. This month I'm invoking the nonperformance clause on two disappointing tea roses, retiring them to a community garden after a two-year trial run. When you are shopping for new plants, it helps to learn as much as you can about a plant's preferences—and your own soil conditions, such as wet or dry, acid or alkaline, shade or sun. It may also help, on that next trip out to the garden center, to get one of those little kits for testing soil pH. Soil conditions can usually be adjusted, but it's far easier to adjust plants to the site—even if it means playing musical borders for a few seasons.

# [Sage Advice]

*A side trip that sorts*
*through some salvias and other plants*
*often called sage, and which are*
*best in dry borders.*

When I was growing up, it seemed that there were only three kinds of salvia: the cooking sage, the spiky red type beloved as a bedding annual, and *Salvia farinacea,* also known as mealy-cup sage, a perennial that takes its time to produce a tall, powder blue flower in mid-autumn. The culinary sage, *S. officinalis,* is a fine, drought-tolerant herb with a pretty gray leaf for the landscape; the other two salvias usually show up as container plants in California. They need a lot of water to bloom well. Fortunately, we are blessed with dozens of other species in the salvia or sage family, many of them drought tolerant, most with spectacular, late-season flowers. Some other garden plants also get tagged as sage, simply because of a similar fragrance in the leaf; these are fine, too, and get by with similar requirements.

October is a good time for rethinking perennial borders. Here are some sages—true salvias and others called sage—to consider, which can be planted in the garden between now and next spring.

Mexican bush sage, *S. leucantha,* is common here as a drought-tolerant ground cover. The woolly purple flowers are beautiful and long lasting. A slightly rangy habit is offset by this plant's usefulness as an indicator flower—if you're not giving your sunny flower border enough water, the leaves of Mexican bush sage are the first to droop.

*S. guarantica* doesn't seem to have a common name, at least in English. It comes from Paraguay. A lush subshrub, it reaches five-foot heights in the Bay Area and has large flower spikes of intense color that can only be described as French blue. I first ran into this plant at Saso Herb Gardens in Saratoga, where it had a starring role in an all-salvia bed. Large bushes can also be found in San Francisco's Golden Gate Park, for example, off the patio behind the County Fair Building. One caution: Snails love to eat the young growth on this one. Place a circlet of fresh copper stripping around each plant to protect it until the stems grow woodier.

Butterflies and hummingbirds flock to the bright red flowers of pineapple sage, *S. elegans.* In my yard, I watched one grow from four inches to three feet over three months of benign neglect, although I've since found that regular watering over the first year improves flowering. The medium green leaves of pineapple sage have a scent that is slightly citrusy. It's such an easy plant and so attractive to our native hummingbirds that it deserves to be grown more widely.

Jerusalem sage isn't a salvia, though it has a sage smell to its gray green leaf. *Phlomis fruticosa* comes from the Mediterranean and is very drought tolerant. From early summer, the four-foot plants are covered with yellow flowers blooming in doughnut-shaped rings up and down each terminal spike. It's a nice plant for the back of the border. *P. lacianata,* properly *Eremostachys lacianata,* is also sold as Jerusalem sage. This has gray leaves, paler yellow flowers, and grows lower—about two feet.

Russian sage is *Perovskia,* a genus with delicate, waving wands of pale blue or blue purple flowers. From Asia Minor, it too looks best when regularly watered. Plant height for the garden hybrids usually sold is about three feet, but it is airy enough in its spikes to take a place at the front of a border. Deer seem to avoid it.

*Hortus Third* lists seventy-five species of salvia, all of them perennial in mild-winter climates. Sages are plants worth knowing and they are easy to find in local nurseries year-round. When they get rangy and sad looking in February and March, all salvias are quickly renewed by cutting the woody stalks back to six inches.

*SOURCES:*
*Saso Herb Gardens, 14625 Fruitvale Avenue,*
*Saratoga, CA 95070; (408) 867-0307.*

## [Serendipity Pumpkins]

*A streetside patch*
*of bright orange pumpkins*
*brings a Berkeley neighborhood*
*together.*

It's like a little bit of New England, a fine crop of pumpkins seemingly sprouting out of the sidewalk in a quiet Berkeley neighborhood. Crayon orange, the pie-sized pumpkins look as if they were set here just for effect in the weeks before Halloween. But the front-yard pumpkin patch grown by Marilyn and Paul Felber has been nearly a year-long project, although a serendipitous one. "They're just volunteer seedlings that came from the compost pile," says Marilyn. "Usually I just pull them all out, but we kept some in just to see what would happen." When you consider all the effort some gardeners make for food crops, or to make their front yards enviable, it seems a bit unfair that fame and picture-perfect pumpkins have come so easily here. "We went away for three weeks in the summer and nobody even watered them," she notes. "I thought they would be gone, but they survived."

Maybe the Felbers just have good pumpkin karma. They always

decorate their house for Halloween, using the wide brick arms of their front stoop to display an array of intricately carved jack-o'-lanterns. "My husband Paul likes to carve pumpkins, so every year we buy four or five of them," says Felber. She's the gardener in the family, so after the holidays, the discarded pumpkin shells and their seedy pulp go into one of her two black plastic compost bins. In her shaded backyard the compost doesn't cook much, so the seeds often stay viable.

The compost she spread around her front-yard rosebushes this past spring sprouted a number of obviously pumpkin volunteers, and Felber decided to thin them out to four robust seedlings. "This is a corner of the yard where the lawn and other plants have not done very well, so I thought I would give it a try," she says. She only watered the pumpkin plants, but even bereft of fertilizer, they were off and running quickly, vines stretching thirty and forty feet.

Felber may be a casual gardener, but she's a good one, as evidenced by the tidy front garden with the antique rosebushes she rescued with pruning care. A peek in the backyard reveals a small apple tree dotted with ripening red 'McIntosh' apples. Working as a fabric artist (her latest work is a wall quilt commissioned by the El Segundo Library), she is at home a lot, so what she does give her garden is time. Time to pull out weeds, to pluck the snails that often ravage cucurbits, to lay boards beneath the ripening pumpkins so the rinds won't rot.

As the pumpkin vines grew, next-door neighbors who are redoing their own front yard let her annex some frontage. "They have two little ones who are helping us take care of the pumpkin patch," she says. "I do have to do regular clipping, to keep the vines from getting onto the sidewalk. With all the people walking by, we don't want anybody to trip." By midsummer, with its bright orange flowers and burgeoning fruits, the pumpkin patch became a regular stopover for pram-pushing nannies, schoolkids, dogwalkers, and strollers. The vines produced about eight mature pumpkins, much admired.

"What's wonderful is that we have met so many people in our neighborhood," says Felber. The block has a Neighborhood Watch program, but the friendly orange globes on this front lawn have helped put names to faces, and, says Felber, tightened bonds. "Everybody in our neighborhood, all the kids, are helping us keep watch on the pumpkins now," she says, yanking a weed away from the largest one, its classic shape and forty-inch circumference nestled prettily in a stand of white alyssum. "We've only lost one so far, and just made another one into a pumpkin pie."

She doesn't want to think about vandalism. But sometime before Halloween, the Felbers will harvest their crop. "We plan to give a few to the neighborhood kids to carve, and make our own jack-o'-lanterns." The street usually gets a crowd of trick-or-treaters, and neighbors are looking forward to seeing homegrown pumpkins lighting the way for costumed children. The Felbers are hoping their pumpkin karma lasts long enough to provide that very special glow.

# [Rare Violet Makes Its Bay-Area Debut]

*A tantalizing tale*

*of the rare yellow African violet and*

*a glimpse of plant mania—*

*houseplant division.*

Few things are more frustrating to the gardener than the exciting flower you've read about, heard about, but can't get your hands on. For months, local fanciers of African violets were tantalized with tales of a yellow-flowered hybrid few had seen but many coveted. This rare plant was the main draw for California's state African Violet Convention some years back, and word spread fast.

"They had one flown in from Arizona," said Ed Gergosian, who passed on the news to me in his role as publicity director for the African Violet Society of San Francisco.

The yellow African violet made its official debut at the convention of the African Violet Society of America, held in Columbus, Ohio, concurrent with the Ameriflora exhibition. Gergosian said that his club had tried to get some yellow-flowered plants for its Golden Gate Park show at that time. Some local members flew to Columbus for

Ameriflora's opening day to buy some. Asking price was fifty dollars per plant. "But when they got there, there was nothing left to buy," Gergosian said.

Word went round the plant community that "Japanese business-men" had snapped up all the blooming plants before the show opened to the public. Nolan Blansit, a hobbyist from the Midwest who developed the hybrids, said that's not quite true. "We did have some spectacular sales to Japanese buyers, but they didn't buy up all the material," he said. "We had a supply to last till the end of the show, but everything did sell out quickly."

Blansit has worked on perfecting the yellow flowers since 1978. "I previewed the plant at a convention three years ago, to show what was in the works," he said. New varieties are grown out for three generations, about three years, before they are sold. Blansit and his wife used the time to build up stock plants, then turned sales over to Violet Express, a mail-order operation based in Eagle River, Wisconsin.

While being feted at Ameriflora "was a neat experience," Blansit said he didn't make a fortune selling the coveted cultivars. It did, however, land him a job as a full-time African violet hybridizer for a large nursery in Ohio. "I had a goal, and I feel I accomplished something," he said.

The Case of the Vanished Violets had a happy ending in Santa Rosa, too, because a "friend of a friend" of Marie Beeman, one of the Convention organizers, had managed to buy one of the fifty-dollar specimens in Columbus. "A lot of us hung back," said Beeman, a member of the Fancy Bloomers Club, which meets in Santa Rosa. "What was available were teeny plants, with no blooms on them. Ninety-nine percent of the time plants will bloom true, but at that price, it was hard to take a chance."

The Arizona enthusiast who did buy one found that her plant did bloom. "I hadn't seen it," Beeman said, "but it was described to me as a lemon yellow, very soft, but definitely yellow."

The Violet Express, which sold out its first catalog offering of Blansit's three yellow varieties at fifty dollars, will probably sell them for far less in coming years, according to a company saleswoman.

With African violets, availability rises and prices fall quite quickly, because new, identical plants can be created simply by rooting a leaf. That is why most African violet plants sell for five dollars or less, said Beeman. "Unfortunately, it's also a problem for people who show African violets; people who visit shows try to pull off leaves to take them home." The yellow one at the state convention was "well guarded," she added.

"Every hybridizer in the country is excited about this plant," said Beeman, who also breeds and sells African violets under the name Marie's Adoptable Violets. Her specialty: plants with variegated leaves. "Even when they're not in bloom, they're pretty."

African violets are among the easiest houseplants to grow. Beeman said those that won't bloom need more sunlight and frequent fertilizing. Her own regimen is a quarter-strength solution of houseplant food applied every time she waters—once a week.

"Many people kill the plants by overwatering," she noted. "The soil should be moist, but never soggy." Soil should be well draining. Most commercial potting mixes are too heavy, she said: She recommends only the Volkmann brand.

It's a myth, she added, that African violet leaves should never get wet. "You can give them a shower, they really love it," Beeman said. "After all, these are rain forest plants. You just need to let them dry off before you put them in the sun again, or you'll get those ugly brown spots on the leaves."

*SOURCES:*
*The African Violet Society of San Francisco*
*may be contacted through Gary Beck, (415) 771-2342.*

# [Plant a Poppy, Go to Jail]

*The war on drugs has gardeners*
*worried if they'll be arrested if they sow*
*or grow* P. somniferum. *Our man at the*
*DEA sets the record straight.*

One bright election day, when golden ginkgo trees and ruby-toned liquidambars gave San Francisco sidewalks a long-awaited touch of fall color, the people of California entered polling booths to pull a lever to vote, yea or nay, on a plant. It's not often that botanical topics rouse political interest, but one of the most watched ballot measures in our state was the one that attempted to legalize *Cannabis sativa* for medical purposes.

Marijuana is a banned plant in the United States. It is illegal to grow it, but some people do. When they get caught, the penalties are quite stiff. In the weeks around the election, San Francisco saw more than its share of well-publicized arrests of people caught with cannabis—usually in the form of dried leaves, sometimes as homegrown plants.

The publicity has been making some gardeners nervous about another banned plant that we commonly grow: *Papaver somniferum,* the opium poppy. This is also called the breadseed poppy because it is the same species used to produce the little black poppy seeds we find on bagels and in poppy seed cake. Gardeners grow it for the seeds as well as for the flowers, which appear in dreamy shades of pink and mauve. An easy flower to grow, it is an annual that may be seeded directly into the ground in November. In normal rainy seasons, breadseed poppy blooms reliably and bountifully all the way through spring.

It is perfectly legal to buy, sell, or own poppy seeds. If you go to a garden store this month, you can probably find them in the seed packet racks, packaged for the garden by reputable U.S. seed companies. If you sprout the seed and grow the plants, though, you are breaking the law.

That paradox was merely a matter of gardeners' chatter until recently. Now it has become a serious question. What would happen if someone looked over your garden fence, spotted the poppies, and called the police? Would you get arrested? Would you go to jail? Is there a real risk?

For the straight answer, I called Stan Vegar, the public information man at our local office of the Drug Enforcement Agency. He answered the phone cheerily, and after he gave me his own views about "medical marijuana," we drifted into the question of poppies. Vegar, who claims his office is stuffed with thriving houseplants, said he can vaguely recall his mother sowing and growing the pink poppies—"or something very like it"—in her own garden. Like marijuana, once grown only for its hemp fibers used in clothing and rope making, the opium poppy was perfectly legal until the middle of this century. "Opium poppies were widely grown as an ornamental and for their seeds until [Congress] passed the Opium Poppy Control Act in 1942," Vegar said. "The law still exists, and it is absolutely true that it is illegal to grow this species of poppy in your garden."

Vegar said that poppy seeds sold for cooking or sold by U.S. flower seed companies in the United States come from countries where there is no ban. In some of these countries, of course, the milky juice from the unripe seedpods of *P. somniferum* is turned into opium or heroin. There is no poppy seed farming in the United States because no one is allowed to grow the plants to produce the seeds. If you have poppy seeds, Vegar would rather see you putting them "into a cake or cookie" than into the garden. "There are other types of poppies to grow," he pointed out.

Certainly there are. Safe and pretty alternatives include the annual Shirley poppy *(P. rhoeas)* and the golden California poppy *(Eschscholzia californica),* both of which can be seeded into bare garden spots in late fall. You can also find Shirley poppies in six-pack starts at garden centers, along with wildflower seed mixes that include California poppy.

But if you sow *P. somniferum* and it comes up, you do risk arrest, Vegar said, if someone calls the cops. Just how far you would be prosecuted for violating the Opium Poppy Control Act is something he declined to speculate about. "Heroin production in this country has never been a big problem," he admitted. "But please don't give your readers the impression that we won't do anything because we don't have time or we don't care."

# [Grow Garlic, Confuse the Aphids]

*Garlic bulbs should*
*be planted in November; how*
*about putting some in the*
*rose garden?*

It's not just vampires who are repelled by garlic—it's aphids too. The old idea about planting garlic around your rosebushes to repel aphids gained new respect recently, when a study sponsored by Clemson University in South Carolina revealed that aphids are attracted to flowers by smell. This suggests that by confusing plant odors, a gardener could steer these obnoxious little insects away from roses and other fragrant flowers.

The report came to our attention through UC Berkeley plant pathologist Bob Raabe, who kindly supplied an abstract in the quarterly reports he publishes in *Pacific Horticulture*. The Clemson study was done by monitoring smell signals that pass through an aphid's antennae. "The antennae are so sensitive that experiments could not be run while grass was [being] mowed outside the laboratory," Raabe noted.

The scent of new-mown grass is a pleasant one, but the gamy tang of garlic has its fans as well. Many organic gardeners are already planting flowers among their vegetables to attract beneficial (that is, aphid-eating) insects. So why not plant vegetables among the flowers?

November is the best time to plant garlic in the Bay Area, and nurseries sell mother bulbs for you to plant. These are bigger than store-bought garlic and haven't been treated to prevent sprouting. Garlic likes a rich, fluffy, and well-drained soil, so you'll have success if you plant it in a raised bed. A well-made flower bed or deep flower box will do, too. Separate the mother bulb into its cloves, but don't peel the cloves. Plant each clove an inch deep in heavy soil (two inches in sandy soil) and about eight inches apart. After planting, soak the ground deeply.

My own attempts at garlic growing have always been more successful when winter rains helped me with the watering chores. Garlic needs abundant water to turn each clove into a full-sized head of garlic, a process that takes about six months. If rains are scant, water your garlic bed deeply once a week.

The long lead time required for garlic to mature means that it does take up space in your vegetable bed. You might plant the green tops in rows to make a decorative edging that lasts six months, or you can certainly plant them in circles around your rosebushes. I'm thinking about planting garlic around some artichoke plants next year, to see if they will keep the black winter aphids from attacking the artichokes. Both garlic and artichoke can be planted together in November, and will end their active growing season at the same time, in late June.

When garlic is ripe, the green tops start to brown and die back. You can hasten this process by knocking over the tops with a trowel or hoe. This will signal the bulb to harden off its papery clove coverings. After the surface leaves have become withered and quite brown, you can gently lift the bulbs out of the ground with a spading fork. Hang the garlic to air dry and it will keep for four to six months.

Many garlic varieties thrive here. If you want a long-keeping garlic, choose 'California Late White', a smooth-skinned bulb with pinkish cloves. A variety with rougher skin and tan cloves is 'California Early White'. This is the variety most often sold in grocery stores; it's easy for a beginner but can't be stored as long as 'Late White' can. You might also look for red-skinned garlics, popular with Italian and Spanish cooks. These have stiff, thick stems, are very pungent, and are easy to peel. For the mildest flavor, try elephant garlic. This one makes big cloves, in big bulbs that often weigh a pound apiece.

I'd be remiss if I didn't mention a false garlic that's right at home in flower beds. *Tulbaghia fragrans* is called society garlic and it is grown for its purple winter flowers, which rise like pom-poms above a cluster of evergreen stems. The garlic scent is faint, but it's there: The flowers are edible and can be used in winter salads. A larger and more odorous relative, *T. violacea,* is the one that flowers in spring and summer.

Will any of these keep aphids off your flowers? Perhaps. In rose-growing circles, strongly scented herbs such as lavender, catmint, and thyme have traditionally been planted at the foot of rosebushes to ward off pests. With crawling insects that target flowers by smell, any pungent odor at ground level—not nose level—may be enough to confuse or mask an aphid's scent signal.

# ["It's a Jungle Out There"]

*A lush tropical*

*garden on a small scale*

*produces an urban*

*rainforest environment.*

By five o'clock in the evening, the fog is rolling over Sonny Garcia's house and garden in the western part of San Francisco. The thickly planted grass and low-maintenance plants in his front yard wave in the rising wind, offering just a hint of Garcia's tropical, lush garden at the rear. It's a jungle out there.

"This area's very cold, windy, and foggy, and many would be surprised to see subtropicals growing here," Garcia says. "On the other hand, the wind gives good air circulation, and the fog keeps them moist."

If the mist is natural, the rain forest effect is intentional, starting with a lath house built on an existing concrete patio. True jungle plants growing in the dim, filtered light include an assortment of bromeliads, orchids, rare flowering vines, and ferns; the air is kept moist by a mossy rock fish-pond and an automatic fogging system that drips a fine mist for twenty minutes every other day. "Having grown up in the Philippines, I always wanted to have a garden with the kinds of plants that would remind me of my childhood," says Garcia. "To sit in here is very comfortable."

Garcia's backyard, at first glance, seems to contain very few plants the average San Francisco gardener might recognize. The thick winding trunk of an aged tree at the rear is "an escallonia in tree form," Garcia explains. "Usually you see them only as hedges." The tree is so old, he adds, that the branches have started to die and fall down. He's planted an acacia behind it as a replacement, but in the meantime the branches hold an array of bromeliads and epiphytic plants. Bromeliads of all sizes are in the garden, and add much to the jungle effect. "People know them only as houseplants, and never think to use them as landscape plants," Garcia notes. "They are very low maintenance, and many are very hardy here."

He points to a fan palm whose scaly trunk is brightened with the scarlet rosettes of a *Neoregelia* cultivar called 'Rio Red'. He says that all palms can be natural hosts to bromeliads. "You just pull out a trunk section and stick one in there; they don't even need soil," he says. "They're epiphytes, that's why some people call them air plants." Other bromeliads such as spidery *Tillandsia* hang in moss-lined baskets; terrestrial *Puya* grow in beefy whorls in the ground. Most send up long flower shoots in spring, with long-lasting blooms of metallic blue, turquoise, or coral red.

Vines add to the lush look: A double redwood deck is heavy with jasmine and honeysuckle, the lath house and a wall are hung with blue and pink wisteria. Small trees enhance the privacy of the boundary fence. Incredibly, the garden is only thirty feet wide and fifty-six feet deep, but it is packed with hundreds of unusual specimens.

Traditional plants are here too, looking at home in this tropical mix. The red fruits of two espaliered apple trees are spots of color on the lath house wall. Blue-tinged succulents *Monarda* and *Heuchera* 'Palace Purple' are tucked at the feet of a bee balm 'Croftway Pink', and fountains of ornamental grass take on a jungly look when planted next to a small-flowered fuchsia.

"I get my plants from every mail-order catalog I can get my hands on—North Carolina, Oregon, Seattle," Garcia says, "and of course I visit growers all over the Bay Area." As a member of the Bromeliad Society and the California Horticultural Society, he often has the opportunity to buy and trade rare species.

"I keep a lot of plants in pots, because I like to move them around, according to the season and what looks best," he says. "Also, I'm running out of space. It's hard for me to pass up an unusual plant, but what happens now is I often dig something up to make room for something new."

Garcia is quick to point out that the structural elements, not the plants, make the garden more than a mere collection of species. There are three areas for sitting: a paved area holding two lawn chairs, a two-tiered deck for entertaining that is detached and at the rear of the property, and a balcony on the rear of the house that provides an overall garden view. The balcony itself is a small wonder, crowned with a mauve-and-blue painted Victorian trim of turned finials and gingerbread, and topped with a brass weather vane.

"The challenge here was that when you walk into a small garden you immediately see everything. I designed this so you can't see it all at once, so there are surprises in every corner and when you turn around," he explained. An architect by profession, Garcia and a partner, Tom Valva, are branching out into landscape design in their spare time.

"I designed, installed, and maintain this garden myself," Garcia points out. "There's nothing that was done here the average person couldn't do. The decks are regular redwood decks; the paving is sixteen-inch-square pebbled concrete tile, laid down on sand." The turned wood and Victorian molding came ready-made from a lumber store. Garcia's latest project is the pergola, topped with more mauve-and-blue trim. It contains a stone and metal fountain he designed, and a mirror behind an array of plants that have striped or mottled yellow and green foliage.

"They say don't combine too many variegated plants together, but as you can see it really brightens up this shady corner," he says. "I've got *Acoris*, different forms of *Carex*, variegated ivy, *Houttuynia*, variegated hydrangea. It's packed with plants. The mirror in the rear is to reflect the sun, and give the space a little depth; this being a small garden I try every trick to make it look bigger."

# V. What We Call Winter

[ Long Shadows and Mist ]

# [Sasanqua: A Camellia for November]

*Smaller-flowered*

*sasanquas have a fleeting*

*beauty but offer lasting value*

*for the landscape.*

I picked sasanquas until Christmas Day. The last one was 'Pink Snow', only slightly yellowed like old silk. After Christmas Dawn it was still blooming. A low of nineteen [degrees] did little more than turn the petals to ivory.

—Elizabeth Lawrence,
*Through the Garden Gate*

The late Elizabeth Lawrence, one of the great garden writers of the United States, always used to go on about sasanquas, one of her favorite plants. This species of camellia is so early blooming that it's sometimes designated as late blooming, as the blossom season starts and peaks in November and December.

Camellias are treasured by California gardeners as well as by those in the Deep South (Lawrence lived in North Carolina) because in both regions they bloom in winter. Just when you think the yard has no surprises left in the waning year, their bright red and pink flowers lure you back into the garden.

In the landscape, camellias can be trimmed as hedges, espaliered against a wall, grown as a single shrub in a mixed border, or miniaturized as a potted plant. The most common type of yard camellia, *Camellia japonica,* is the one with formal, rose-shaped blossoms that keep well as a cut flower. Japonicas typically bloom from late December until well into April or May.

The beauty of November-flowering sasanquas *(C. sasanqua)* is a fleeting one. The blossoms are more perishable and of thinner substance; Lawrence's comparison with the fragility of old silk rings true. If you hurried yourself indoors during the short, dampish days of November and December, you might easily miss their show altogether. But the many single-flowered types are quite charming, with their antique hues accented by a bright gold center.

"Japonicas are the most popular, the show flowers," agrees Gordon Goff, an engineering consultant and past president of the Camellia Society in Concord. "Sasanquas have much smaller flowers, but masses of them," he said. "And for several reasons they make a great landscape plant." Most camellias prefer shade, but sasanquas don't mind the sun, which, Goff said, makes them valuable for hot zones. Sasanquas will even tolerate very hot sun without leaf scorch, provided they are watered regularly in summer. In mild winter areas, they bloom prolifically.

"Sasanquas are practically free of diseases, compared to other camellias," Goff said. "They don't get dieback, they're resistant to root rot." Sasanquas are also untroubled by petal blight, the disease that makes the flowers on a camellia bush turn mushy brown and fall off. Goff says that's because petal blight is triggered by extended periods of wet weather; sasanquas bloom only in the beginning of our rainy season, he explained, and so do not fall prey to this disease.

Lack of bloom is the big complaint about sasanquas and it's usually caused by two things. The first is lack of heat. These plants start to form flower buds in July and August; warm nights are required. A chilly, foggy July and August mean that many sasanquas won't bloom well. The second but fixable mistake is pruning at the wrong time. For all camellias, the best time to prune is when the bloom is all over. As a rule of thumb, you might think of pruning japonicas when you trim citrus (May or June) and prune sasanquas along with your roses (February or March). Goff said it won't hurt the plants to trim off a flowering branch or two in the dead of winter if you'd like some for indoor arrangements. The best place to site a sasanqua bush may be near a window, where it will cheer you up on a fog-ridden day. Along with other camellias, sasanquas in bloom start showing up in Bay Area garden centers in late fall: One you might look for is 'Yuletide', an old favorite with red flowers that looks quite nice when planted near a stand of foundation evergreens. This and other sasanquas can also be pruned small and kept in a container. For years I kept a 'Yuletide' in a bonsai pot, moving it indoors when frost threatened. It always reliably bloomed for me at Christmas.

# [Winter-Sown Wildflowers, Naturally]

*A wildflower expert,*

*via Texas, rustles up some good advice*

*about planting wildflowers from seed, as*

*a fun winter project for the family.*

Late fall in California is the "natural" time to sow and transplant wild-flowers. If you are in the mood to seed a low-maintenance swathe of color in a parking strip or the hotter side of a house wall, or should you want a garden project for the winter, try an experiment with wildflow-ers. The greater availability of native flowers at retail outlets and pack-aging methods such as the "garden in a can" have made it easier than ever to rediscover the delicate shades and forms of our indigenous flora.

"A wildflower garden is a way of preserving the natural history of your region," avers Beth Blair, who works at the Lady Bird Johnson (for-merly National) Wildflower Center in Austin, Texas. "Even if you don't remember growing up with wildflowers, a small wildflower garden can help teach children a lot about the nature that was here before we came."

Blair lived in the Bay Area for about two years, when work brought her engineer husband to Silicon Valley. During that period she worked as a Master Gardener in Alameda County, where we met. She soon made a specialty of wildflower research in the canyons and parks of the East Bay, introducing many fellow Master Gardeners to such delights as the golden California violets that bloom along Berkeley's Strawberry Creek in the early spring. Now she does research at the Austin Center, which was founded in 1982 by Lady Bird Johnson, the former first lady. The center exists as a clearinghouse for information and research on native plants in all states, says Blair. "No matter where you live, it can supply a list of wildflowers native to your area, and a list of where to buy the appropriate plants and seeds."

The quickest way to start a wildflower patch is to establish a small area with container plants. Many local nurseries carry perennial wildflowers in containers, usually costing between five and ten dollars a plant. But if your wildflower garden will be larger than a hundred square feet, Blair recommends using seeds. One local source to try is Larner Seeds of Bolinas. This firm offers bagged wildflower mixes along with customized, authentic blends of native seed for various habitats in Northern California.

"A big concern among environmentalists is where people get their seeds and plants," Blair says. The amateur's habit of collecting wild seeds in autumn is now frowned upon, for if everybody did it there would be nothing left to self-sow or feed birds in winter. "Fortunately," adds Blair, "there are many companies now that grow and harvest their own seeds and propagate natives, without taking anything away from the wild."

Complete instructions come on the back of the package if you get bagged or canned seeds. Here are Beth Blair's own tips for planting a wildflower garden:

• Sow seeds in the fall, not in spring. Many species sprout in warm fall temperatures but need cold weather or winter rains to snap them into blooming. Before sowing the seeds, till the ground and rake the planting area smooth, as you would for any flower bed.

• Mix the seed with a bit of sand so as to be able to tell if you're spreading it evenly. The most important thing is to press the seed firmly into the ground, with the end of your hoe or your feet. Good soil contact is what you want.

• The planted area should be watered deeply and kept moist for several weeks until the seeds sprout.

• Be patient with nature. Sometimes it takes two years before a seeded wildflower bed looks like anything other than a vacant lot. By then, perennial flowers will begin to bloom. It's okay to "cheat" that first year by transplanting some perennials from containers or sowing annual flowers, such as cosmos or Shirley poppy.

• For neatness, you may want to mow the patch down at the end of the first year, after you are sure that all the seeds have dropped from the dry brown stalks.

If you'd like wildflowers but want a more controlled effect, Blair suggests simply planting some perennial wildflowers in a flower bed. Species that would look right at home in a cottage-style garden include coneflower, which looks like a droopy, pink-petaled black-eyed Susan, wild columbine, *Aquilegia formosa,* a native of serpentine rock climes, or Douglas iris, a native iris suited to dryish sites.

### SOURCES:
*Larner Seeds, PO Box 407, Bolinas, CA 94924;*
*(415) 868-9407. Catalog: $2.50.*

*Lady Bird Johnson Wildflower Center, 4801 La Cross Avenue,*
*Austin, TX 78739; (512) 292-4200. Send a self-addressed envelope to receive*
*information about ordering plant lists for any state in the United States.*

# [Tree Dahlia, a Tender Beauty]

*The world's largest herbaceous perennial*

*blooms in time for Thanksgiving, with pink and*

*purple flowers six to eight inches across. So why*

*does* Sunset *call it a turkey?*

A flower that blooms at the tail end of the year, the tree dahlia is a magnificent addition to mild-winter gardens, but still a little-known one. Shooting up to twenty feet in a single season, the tree dahlia bursts forth with an array of pink or purple daisy flowers, each six to eight inches across. This canopy of flowers peaks in late November—just in time for Thanksgiving—but the first glancing frost will collapse the whole plant, so horticulturists consider this plant a turkey.

Most garden books don't even bother to list this tall, tender perennial, a species related to the common garden dahlia. My old edition of the *Sunset Western Garden Book* disparages *Dahlia imperialis* as a mere novelty: "If it bloomed longer or remained evergreen, it would be a valuable landscape plant." The flower has been neglected largely because it's impossible to get it to bloom in the temperate United States. That's no reason to not grow it here. Gardeners who do grow tree dahlias say the flowers are easily cared for and well adapted to Bay Area backyards.

Emil Miland's garden in San Francisco's Mission District has several tree dahlias in full bloom every November, their arching branches of pink and purple blossoms stretched nearly to the third story of his house. Each eight-petaled flower is bigger than your hand, with a bright yellow center. "Tree dahlia could be used a lot more," says Miland, a musician and principal cellist for the New Century Chamber Orchestra. "It's not just for that late-season surprise of having all these flowers. While it's growing, it's like an instant shade tree. It leafs out the most in the hottest part of our year. And because it dies back in winter, you can plant all kinds of spring flowers under it."

Miland says he values the tree dahlias mostly because their bamboo-like stems take only a few square inches of garden ground space; this makes them ideal perennials to plant against a house wall or fence, or at the rear of a tight mixed border. Like other dahlias, tree dahlias take average summer water and like sunshine.

To give his plants a head start in spring, Miland cuts the woody stems back to six feet when the top growth wilts in late winter. "I also take off the lower side branches, as they grow, to force the growth up and make it more like a tree." The stems can be cut lower, but Miland keeps them high to prevent snails from climbing up to munch the new growth. (Bands of copper stripping wrapped around the stems also work.) In cooler microclimates, stems die back to the ground and should be protected from freezing by a thick mulch. "This would be a great tree for kids to grow, because it grows so quickly," Miland points out. "You can see the progress, sometimes a foot per week. And then the flowers are spectacular."

No, the tree dahlia is not a turkey, although getting one can be as hard as catching the wily wild gobbler. Out of favor means out of commercial propagation. Most gardeners receive it as a pass-along plant, because all it takes is a segment of the bamboolike stem to start a new plant. Set halfway down in damp soil, the stem piece roots quickly. "In nature, that's how the plant spreads," says Miland. "When it gets too big, it falls down from the weight onto the forest floor. All the little nodes have babies, rooting all along the fallen stems."

Miland got his tree dahlias from a friend, Michael Barclay, the owner of Really Special Plants and Gardens, a design firm in Kensington, California. Barclay got his from Western Hills Nursery in Occidental, California, one of the few retail outlets that offers tree dahlias.

In late November, one can see tree dahlias in bloom at Strybing Arboretum in Golden Gate Park in San Francisco, and the University of California's Botanical Garden in Berkeley (look for them in the Cloud Forest sections). Both public gardens occasionally offer tree dahlia starts at their fund-raising plant sales. It remains to be seen whether interest in *D. imperialis* will ever prompt more commercial nurseries to carry this flowering perennial, which has potential as a quick summer shade plant and for late late-season color in the border.

# [Strategies for Late Bloomers]

*Suddenly, everyone's looking*

*for wintersweet. Before you buy one,*

*consider your space, and winter shrub*

*options that may be better choices.*

Suddenly, everyone's looking for wintersweet. *Chimonanthus praecox* is a collector's oddity, prized for its spicy midwinter blooms in climates where the snow falls. In line with the current vogue for viburnums and the huzzahs for winter hazels, wintersweet is trendy, but in California, of course, winter-flowering plants are not so hard to find. What's problematic about most deciduous winter-flowering shrubs is the brevity of their performance. If you have limited garden space, does it make sense to make room for a plant that blooms for just a week or two?

If there is room to tuck in a few seasonal surprises, make sure to put them where you are likely to see them. Your daily walk to replenish the bird feeder should pass by the arching sprays of witch hazel—otherwise, you might miss the show of pale, ragged flowers and their faint scent. To find a good spot for wintersweet, it helps to know that the flowers are not flashy and the plant will eventually grow into a large, water-thirsty bush. The kitchen garden, perhaps? Keep in mind that the bloom time is mid-December into January and that it may take some years for a small plant to flower. Some gardeners might instead prefer to sow sweet peas or set out a few six-packs of sweet stock in their vegetable beds to get winter-fragrant flowers for cutting.

A winter specimen shrub with a bit more visual appeal is contorted filbert, *Corylus avellana* 'Contorta'. This shrub is known to British gardeners as Harry Lauder's walking stick; the name refers to the signature cane used by the late vaudeville actor. It has no scent although a fine texture and form in the way winter's pale green catkins hang off the twisty stems, and it always looks best against a wall or other plain backdrop. But put contorted filbert where you won't mind how it looks the other ten months of the year, with its array of wrinkled, droopy leaves that look vaguely diseased. Or treat contorted filbert as I do—as a patio pot plant. It lives well in containers and can then be rotated out of the limelight during its ugly season.

Some scented small trees are on-again, off-again bloomers during our winter months. Nurseries promote dwarf magnolias and michelias, which bloom dutifully but can be hard to place in a small garden because of their large tropical leaves and vaselike spread of limbs. Star magnolia can be kept very dwarf but it blooms at best for a week or two. If you want a broad-leaved evergreen that is fragrant, citrus is a better choice, for the orange-blossom scent of the small flowers and the bright colors of the fruit.

If I could have but one flowering tree for wintertime, it would be the weeping autumn cherry, *Prunus subhirtella* 'Pendula'. My specimen starts throwing out a few pink flowers in late October, even before its yellowing autumn leaves fall. This sweetly melancholy performance doesn't seem to affect its ability to produce cheerful clouds of pink flowers the following March. The weeping form makes a sculptural tree that is easy to place in a small mixed border. If you want an upright vase-shaped tree, get *P. s.* 'Autumnalis'. Unfortunately, any autumn cherry is hard to find locally.

Also hard to find are winter-blooming mahonias. *Mahonia japonica* and *M. bealei* both have the same spiny leaves as our native mahonia has but the Asian species grow more erect. Sweetly fragrant chrome yellow sprays appear through midwinter, followed by summer clusters of blue berries. A single plant will thrive in a damp or shady corner; a grouping might be a finer alternative to traffic-stopping yellow acacias, which also bloom freely in winter but have developed reputations as hay-fever plants.

The most reliable bloomers for winter's long haul are camellias, starting with the dainty-blossomed sasanquas, which open in November, and going on to the blowsy, doubled pom-poms of japonicas that last through March. If you find the doubled flowers of modern camellias too blobby, look for singles or semidoubles, which have a lighter effect. You have your choice of pink, coral, red, or white flowers. Camellias give good value because their glossy evergreen leaves make a good backdrop during the rest of the year. These shrubs prefer some shade from summer heat, but can't take freezing weather. Plant them in a sheltered position against a fence or house wall where you can see the flowers through a window on a rainy day.

## SOURCES:

*If you can't find the shrubs you want locally, try mail-order: Forestfarm, 990 Tetherow Road, Williams, OR 97544-9599; (541)846-7269. Catalog $4.*

*Greer Gardens, 1280 Goodpasture Island Road, Eugene, OR 97401-1794 (541) 686-8266. Catalog $3.*

*Woodlanders, 1128 Colleton Avenue, Aiken, SC 29801; (803) 648-7522. Catalog $2.*

# [Holiday Lighting Adds Drama]

*Outdoor lighting*
*ideas to add magic or*
*solve practical problems in*
*winter-dark gardens.*

Winter guests from out of town frequently ask about the lights outlining the buildings of the Embarcadero Center in San Francisco. They always want to know if this illumination, which transforms the skyline as seen from my street, runs year-round or only during the holiday shopping season. Sadly, it disappears with the turn of the year, so we must enjoy the elegant outline—as if the waterfront were stacked with giant Christmas boxes—when we can.

I confess to a childish fondness for outdoor lighting, whether it is the "official Christmas tree" in a downtown park or the ropes of colored bulbs swagged around rooflines and house windows in the quieter neighborhoods. Outdoors in the night, those sparkly lights add magic and festivity, whether you are celebrating Christmas, Hanukkah, Kwanza, or the winter solstice—all in their way festivals of light.

A string of twinkly fairy lights entwined in the bare branches of a tree and glimpsed through a window on a cold winter's night is the kind of special effect a garden could have year round. Fancy restaurants like Tavern on the Green, a fixture in New York's Central Park, have always used outdoor tree lights this way. There's no reason that they can't be used tastefully in a small garden. A potted tree strung with lights on a balcony suggests a romantic possibility; lights run up a trellis or around the top of a wall could give architectural interest to a night garden, à la Embarcadero Center.

Strands of so-called Christmas lights for garden illumination should be clearly marked as UL-approved for outdoor use. (All white, all clear, or a single color may be preferred to multicolored bulbs.) They can be plugged into an outdoor outlet. If an extension cord is needed, make sure that it, too, is a heavy-duty, waterproof model approved for outdoor use. A bit of PVC plastic tubing or a piece of old garden hose might be used to further insure that the junction between the two cords is waterproof.

Directional lights, even simple spotlights, can add dramatic effects to highlight a particular plant. Chris Clos, of the landscape firm Westbrook Clos in Sausalito, will often use a directional spotlight to good effect to backlight a deciduous tree, such a valley oak, in order to show off its winter silhouette.

Directional lights can also be functional. Say you've got an herb garden: You like to gather fresh herbs for dinner, but in winter it's too dark out there to tell the cilantro and parsley apart. A good solution might be to retrofit a back porch light with a directional spotlight that sends its beams into that particular part of the yard.

Walkway lights are important functional elements, particularly near the front walk and garden steps. Most of the electric kind available in garden centers have a low-voltage draw, are made of plastic, and plug into outdoor sockets, with the wires buried. Further up the spending scale are lamps with custom metal shades in the shape of a flower or bell, and walkway lights fitted with electric eyes, so that they turn on and turn off only when someone walks on the path. A kind of lamp that needs no external wiring is a solar lamp, powered by a solar cell and built-in, rechargeable batteries. No drain on the utility bill, solar lamps are getting cheaper—and, fortunately, better looking—as the years go by.

If you think your garden might benefit from footlights of some sort, try the concept out inexpensively by borrowing from the Southwestern Christmas custom of *luminaria*. Traditionally, these were paper bags, weighted with sand and holding a candle, used to line streets and sidewalks to mark the way for the house-to-house Christmas Eve procession known as *Posada*. You can find paper *luminarias* at housewares stores and Hispanic gift shops. A dozen usually cost less than ten dollars; you add your own sand or soil (about two inches on the bottom) and your own votive-sized candle. Some *luminaria* have cutouts to let the candlelight sparkle through them. Try placing them at strategic points around the garden or patio when you entertain. There's nothing like seeing your garden in a new light.

# [Wassail, Wassail, All Over the Town]

*East Bay gardeners share*

*their tradition of wassailing fruit trees.*

*Some hints: Buy the ale at the Safeway and point*

*your stereo speakers out the window.*

Lots of people talk to their plants. Some threaten them: One friend says this worked extremely well with a tangerine that he loudly threatened to remove; he returned from vacation to find the tree fruiting at last. This holiday season you might try singing to your fruit trees. The tradition is an old one, and it's called wassailing. The season starts on the winter solstice, although sometimes the festivities are held on Twelfth Night, January 6. A tradition that predates Christmas, it was absorbed into the later holiday. "Here we come a-wassailing, among the leaves so green," is a Christmas carol many know.

Wassailing your backyard orchard is a pretty simple process—you sing a few songs and actually share a holiday toast with your apple or plum trees. The traditional libation is hard cider, spiced and hot; you take a sip of your drink and pour the rest upon the ground, near the tree roots. Modern wassailers use mulled wine, nonalcoholic ciders, beer, or apple juice.

Petra MacDonnell, who describes herself as "a student of folk song" has been wassailing and gardening for years. "When we lived in Tuolumne County, I had a big orchard and did the whole wassail bit," she recalls. "I'd make genuine wassail, with good ale in it, egg whites, and spices. But now I live in Berkeley and have only one old apple tree, a 'McIntosh'."

But still she wassails, having collected many songs over the years, some from the *Oxford Book of Carols,* which she recommends. She sings quietly, to avoid disturbing the neighbors or embarrassing her family: "They know this is just Mom's little thing that she does every winter solstice."

These days, her wassail may come from the Safeway. "If you look in the beer section of a supermarket, you can find a lot of special Christmas ales and seasonal dark brews," MacDonnell notes. She just adds spices, such as ginger, cinnamon, and cloves. "Heat it up if you like it that way, and that's a fine wassail."

The word *wassail,* she explains, comes from a Celtic toast that may be translated as "Good health." The more social aspects of wassailing—when farm workers caroused from house to house, offering songs of good wishes in exchange for food or wine—came later, she says. One carol of this later period, "Wassail, wassail, all over the town," wishes the master the good health of his cattle as well. "Originally it was a blessing of the fruit trees, which is something that gardeners can understand," says MacDonnell. "I have a friend in New York City who grows sweet corn in a barrel on her roof. She wassails her cornstalks, because that's all she has."

Elizabeth Lloyd Mayer, the artistic director for the San Francisco Revels, is helping to get wassailing back into style. There was wassailing on stage in the "Christmas Revels," an annual holiday program of pageantry and early music held at the Scottish Rite Auditorium in Oakland. The performance included the "Apple Tree Wassail," an ancient tune that may be traced from Gloucestershire in England:

*Old apple tree we wassail thee,*
*And hoping thou wilt bear,*
*The Lord does know where we shall be*
*To be merry another year.*
*To blow well and to bear well,*
*And so merry let us be,*
*Let every man drink up his cup,*
*Here's to the old apple tree.*

The song ends with chants: "Caps full! Hats full! Bushels full, barrels full!"—a holiday wish and exhortation for a good harvest next year. In gardening terms, to blow well means to blossom well, and apple tree owners all know that many flowers mean more fruit.

Mayer knows that too, so she also wassails at home, and sometimes makes a party of it with her musical friends. "I did it last year and it was quite wonderful," she says. There are many old fruit trees in her East Bay garden, "and we get fabulous crops every year. I can't say we have a better crop because we sang to the trees, but we sure have a good time."

For those who want to wassail at home, both MacDonnell and Mayer recommend *The Oxford Book of Carols* and especially *The Christmas Revels Songbook,* which includes sheet music for several wassail songs. I was able to find the songbook at Tupper Reed, a sheet-music store in Berkeley.

In this modern era, you might even serenade your backyard fruit trees electronically. Just point your stereo speakers out of the window and turn on the Revels recordings of wassail songs on compact disc and cassette. The *Christmas Revels* disc includes the "Apple Tree Wassail." Another recording, *Wassail, Wassail,* has later American carols, such as the "Cherry Tree Carol," and "Kentucky Wassail."

### SOURCES:

*Musical Offerings, a record store in Berkeley that specializes in unusual music, keeps both recordings in stock; call (510) 849-0211.*

The Christmas Revels Songbook, *cassettes, and CDs may be ordered by telephone through Revels, Inc.; call (617) 621-0505.*

# [Parma Violets Make a Comeback]

*There is only one place in
America where you can buy a bunch
of scented Parma violets to pin to your coat
in the French style: Union Square.*

Real rain will be arriving soon, but meanwhile it's raining violets in San Francisco. Petite flurries of these scented purple flowers are indeed seasonal: The bloom period of Parma violets lasts only a few weeks, from late November through January. You might spot them at a florist shop or displayed on a flower stand in Union Square, those old-fashioned, scented Parmas tied in a nosegay with a collar of green leaves.

That we have them at all is something of a miracle. There is only one commercial grower of Parma violets left in the United States, and that's Don Garibaldi of Año Nuevo Nursery in Pescadero. A few times a week Garibaldi and his family bring the violets up to a stall at the San Francisco Flower Mart, much as his grandfather did, for the Victorian ladies who prized the Parma violet for their Christmas corsages. Each bunch is hand picked and hand tied, then gently wrapped in newspaper to survive the trip to florists throughout Northern California.

The scent of Parma violets is elusive. A tiny bouquet will fill a room with a candylike scent, but if you sniff the bunch straight on, you won't smell anything. Their beauty, too, is fleeting, like summer's white peaches or a springtime rainbow. Even in water, these violets hardly last three days.

Most gardeners do not know the Parma violets, their rich purple blossoms so evocative of a gentler time. Nearly lost to cultivation, the scented Parma violet *(Viola odorata)* is poised for a big comeback, perhaps as a "new" border perennial for California gardeners. The little violet has some big supporters, among them Tovah Martin, the author and scented-plant specialist, and John Whittlesey, who owns Canyon Creek Gardens in Oroville. They helped found the International Violet Association (IVA) in 1993, linking home gardeners to a network that hopes to return a few of what once were hundreds of scented violet cultivars to the trade.

"There's a strong California connection to the whole violet movement," said Norma Beredjiklian, a gardener in Virginia who edits the association's newsletter. "About half of our members come from California, including people who are interested in getting violets into the food industry, as part of the edible flower market."

When the IVA held its annual meeting in San Francisco, a small group toured the Año Nuevo Nursery growing grounds. More importantly, the Whittlesey and Garibaldi families got together to exchange information—and later, plants.

"It turns out that California is the ideal climate to grow scented violets," said John Whittlesey, who lists more than a dozen in his mail-order catalog. According to Beredjiklian, some old Parma strains were rediscovered in Australia; Whittlesey has in turned passed on some stock plants to Año Nuevo, part of a joint effort to revive the market for cut violets.

Because of their fragility, a bunch of Parmas costs only a few dollars, a memorable adornment for hat or lapel at a holiday lunch or trip to the *Nutcracker.* When violets are in season, I always get a bunch from the gentlemen who sell them outside Macy's, to pin on my coat while running errands downtown. Other cities may get snow, or our hoped-for rain, but the winter violet is uniquely a San Francisco treat.

## [Parma Violets]

Frost tender, Parma violets *(Viola odorata)* are Mediterranean-climate plants but their propagation is somewhat like that of a strawberry. Divisions are set out in April or May, in a site that offers summer shade and winter sun.

Any stolons, or runners, that form from spring to summer should be trimmed away to give strength to the plants so that they will produce the biggest flowers in winter and early spring.

A reliable cultivar to try is 'Royal Robe', a large, dark purple flower. Pink, white, mauve, and blue flowers, some doubled or striped, are also becoming available.

The work of the International Violet Association in recent years has clarified both the nomenclature and horticultural practice for scented Parma violets, which in old books and catalogs have also been called sweet violets or czar violets or mislabeled as *V. alba*. At the beginning of this century more than 200 named varieties were available to florists and home gardeners, with some of the best work in hybridizing done by Edith Pawla, a pioneering nursey-woman who farmed violets at Soquel, near Santa Cruz. 'Royal Robe', a Pawla introduction, is one of a few dozen cultivars that survived the violet's fall from fashion in the 1920s, when hothouse orchids replaced violets as a winter corsage flower.

*SOURCES:*

*International Violet Association, c/o Geyer,*
*2285 Country Club Drive, Altadena, CA 91001.*

*Canyon Creek Nursery, 3527 Dry Creek Road, Oroville, CA 95965;*
*(530) 533-2166. Call before you visit; mail-order catalog $2.*

# [Trimmings and Clippings]

*Pruning wood for pleasure;*
*a gentle introduction to tool care,*
*and the sensual side of late winter's*
*cleanup chores.*

Somewhere under the second compost pile are my gray-handled pruning shears. I'm pretty sure they are rusting gently where I was doing a sheet-compost experiment over the old strawberry bed, smothering the weeds with a rising pile of clippings. The bed should have been dug under before the rains started; now it's too late to do anything in the drizzle but root around for the metal shears.

I guess I'll retrieve my pruners once I'm sure the mice have left their nest under the mulch. Not that I've seen many mice lately, not since the day I was poking around the late broccoli and a big, red hawk came to rest on the top of the chain-link fence. It was not a surprise; I thought I'd seen it once or twice, a few backyards away, and once a swooping shadow briefly blocked the light from a window one morning, while I sat at the computer. So it was gratifying to see the hawk, after so many signs of its existence. Even at the eastern edge of a tense city the natural world is all around us, and the great gift of gardening is learning to see grace in small things, in odd corners, in off moments defined by the fall of a petal or the flap of a wing.

Next month it will be time to start pruning roses and dormant fruit trees. Sharpening shears and pruners is a job that can be done indoors, at the kitchen table, if you have got a sharpening stone. Some folks really enjoy this—whetting tools gives them a warm feeling, like having a well-stocked woodpile or a hoard of home-canned summer peaches.

Even Gertrude Jekyll found something primal in woodsmen's tools. In her first book, *Wood and Garden*, she describes with great awe and in great detail how a single man with one ax can reduce a great tree to assorted sizes of firewood. Forestry is a skill gardeners don't need much these days; during Jekyll's era, even hedges were harvested on a five- or six-year cycle to provide garden gear—you couldn't simply buy bamboo poles at the garden center, back in 1895.

"Throughout the copse are stools of Spanish chestnut," she wrote, "From this we get good straight stakes for Dahlias and Hollyhocks, also beanpoles." The very best birch tops, she wrote, were "cut into peasticks" and brushy twigs were saved for daisies and "special lengths" cut for peonies and lilies.

"To provide all this in winter, when other work is slack or impossible, is an important matter in the economy of a garden," she wrote, "for all gardeners know how distressing and harassing it is to find themselves without the right sort of sticks or stakes in summer, and what a long job it then seems to have to look them up and cut them."

If you're the self-sufficient sort of gardener, you can plan to trim your prunings for next spring's plant supports, and you'll find sharpening stones at hardware stores. There's a great selection at the Berkeley shop of the Hida Tool Company. They even carry sharpening stones for bonsai tools, traditionally kept razor-sharp. (Masakuni, one manufacturer, reputedly got its start selling samurai swords.)

For a few dollars you can buy what is called a bonsai eraser, a very handy bit of gear for all gardeners. You rub it against your shears and it removes the gunk and old pine sap and most of the rust. Then you use the sharpening stone, wetting it first with water or oil, gently pressing the edge of each blade (as if you were rowing it toward you) along the stone until the blade is sharp again. This can put you in a zenlike trance, but if you don't have the inclination, just send out your tools to be sharpened. Look in your phone book under "Sharpening Services." In San Francisco, Jivano's and the Overnite Saw & Tool Service, both located in the Mission, accept garden tools for sharpening.

But back to Jekyll. *Wood and Garden* and its sequels were reprinted in 1994 by the Antique Collectors' Club Ltd., of Surrey, England, and can now be found in U.S. bookstores. These facsimile editions are not pretty, but they are a good read because so much of what's new in gardening was old hat a hundred years ago. Stooling, for example, is a technique used by some gardeners to multiply flowering shrubs.

It's not a far leap, if you already view all weedy debris as potential compost, to begin appreciating trees and shrubs not just for their beauty, but for how they can be integrated into the entire garden's overall health. *Wood and Garden* starts with a walk through the woods in January, Gertrude pointing out why the peeling skin of a birch reminds her of a German ball gown. Yet she's just as happy pillaging a nut tree for dahlia stakes: "When summer side-twigs have grown and leafed, it will be fairly well clothed—and meanwhile the Hellebores will be the better for the thinner shade."

If you walk through your own garden, you might notice long, straight canes of rosebushes that could find a second life as dahlia or lily stakes—especially if you cut off the sharp tip of each thorn with your newly sharpened pruning shears.

# [A Christmas Bunch]

*An old custom of*
*gathering flowers on Christmas Day*
*provides some private time between*
*the day's festivities.*

An old custom among gardeners is the Christmas bunch, a bouquet freshly picked on Christmas Day, gathered only from the flowers you find blooming in the yard on December 25. It's partly a game to see how many flowers you can find in the darkest days of the year. Coincidentally you get a nice walk in the fresh air and a little private time during the day's festivities.

Naturally the game is best played where winters are generally mild: in Britain, Gertrude Jekyll and Rosemary Verey, and in the American South, Elizabeth Lawrence, are just a few garden writers who logged for posterity their tender harvest. Writing the list in your garden diary or noting it in a letter to a friend is part of the tradition, and men play as well as women. Lawrence quotes a gentleman whose December bouquet included: "one snowdrop; three blooms of purple stock; a dandelion; two violets" and so on.

You could probably do better in your own yard. To play properly, dress for the weather and for walking on sodden grass. A mad dash with no sweater is no fun: Aim for a leisurely stroll, to poke around the bulb beds, observe a luminous mushroom on the tangly lawn, pay homage to that manzanita you planted only as a background shrub, which is now madly blooming with pinky-white flowers.

Between winter-blooming natives and exotics, Californians can count on quite an array of garden flowers in December. Here a Christmas bunch is a reminder of the reasons that people come to live here. We have camellias bursting with bloom, and roses if we care to let them troop on through the winter rains; callas are unfurling, cymbidiums are spiking, and our flower boxes can be exuberant with primroses, violas, pansies, and stocks. The best surprises will be winter bloomers just now coming into their own, such as snowdrops, paperwhite narcissus, arums, callas, and different hellebores. *Helleborus foetidus* is always a reliable bloomer for Christmas, and its bright green flowers look freshest now. Strawberry trees, *Arbutus unedo,* are another delight: Rains have revived them, and the branches are a pretty holiday mix of white bell flowers, apple green leaves, and round red fruits.

My own Christmas bunch will probably include these, arranged with a leafy collar of purplish green Russian kale, the final salute from the vegetable patch. I may have some purple violas, which have just been set out to fill the bare spaces in a flower bed designed to be mostly green and white for wintertime—I like cool colors in a cool season. This bed has two rounded pads of evergreen candytuft, and these usually open a few flat white flowers well ahead of springtime. If I squint a bit, I like to imagine it looks like snow.

# [What Will We Bring?]

*Ikebana icon Fay Kramer's
recipe for Volcano Salad is a reminder
to conserve both plants and plant lore
into the next millennium.*

A year ends and, as I write this, we edge closer to another century. What will we bring with us? As gardeners perhaps it not too early to think about what we'll be packing as we cross the great divide from one millennium to the next, what we might carry—in the way that the pioneers carried in their western wagon trains the withered ends of iris and cuttings of rosebushes and lilacs. It is precious to bring a bit of one's old life into the new.

What would you bring? What garden memory would you save? What plant or skill would you like to pass on to a future generation?

I've decided I'd like to bring Fay Kramer's recipe for Volcano Salad, which is served packed into a ceramic tube: When the tube is lifted, the ingredients fall onto the plate into a designed pattern of string carrots, cellophane noodles, chicken, and shredded lettuce. I certainly will carry the memory of the luncheon at which she served it, to the most

diverse group of women I have ever partied with—all ages, all ethnici-
ties—all brought together by a mutual love of flowers. For dessert we
each received a peeled persimmon intricately hand-carved by Fay, a
grand master of five schools of flower arranging.

Why keep this? Because I also remember the Anchor Steam folks
once brewing up a Sumerian beer from a recipe that had been decoded
from another millennium's stone tablets. It tasted a lot like the sweet,
thick, and fruity beers you can find on your supermarket shelf today.
Someone in the future will want to recreate Fay's luncheon menu, in its
way as evocative and emblematic of midcentury, midcoast California
living as a redwood deck or a landscape by Thomas Church.

What I would really like to carry into the next century is something
of Fay's ability to bring people together, as she continues to do, most
recently by helping to design the Internet web site for Ikebana
International. (Fay said she'll send the salad recipe along by e-mail.
She's not sure if she can write out the directions for carving the persimmons: "Most of the Japanese ladies I'm working with now never
learned how to do it.")

Connections mean something. Garden clubs and horticultural societies pass on not only plants but also useful lore. San Francisco has
already lost its Carnation Society, which had dwindled to ten members
before disbanding. If in the next century there is a mania for cottage
pinks, we gardeners will have to scramble to relearn all the techniques
that were lost.

Flowers, too, can get lost. January's flood of seed and plant catalogs
will bring you an array of heirloom vegetables, vintage roses, and historic fruit trees. But it's worth remembering that only a decade ago it
was nearly impossible to find or buy a striped moss rose. We came so
close, in this century, to losing many centuries' worth of heritage plants,
which were dwindling as seed stock or dying abandoned in hedgerows.
Their beauty—not to mention their DNA—might have been lost forever, had it not been for people who dedicated themselves to saving seed
or passing on the skills of grafting and propagating. Some things have
been irretrievably lost: Of the hundred-odd varieties of scented violet
popular in 1897, fewer than two dozen can now be found.

Look around in your own garden. What would you save? It is certainly likely that some modern hybrid roses will disappear from the trade. It's already pretty hard to find 'Helmut Schmidt', arguably the best large-flowered yellow rose for foggy California gardens. In the next century perhaps the hot pink 'Sexy Rexy' floribunda will be as avidly sought and as joyfully rediscovered as the cooler pink 'Betty Prior' rose is today.

Around San Francisco small groups of gardeners have begun this dialogue, to preserve what may be precious or useful. One friend on Potrero Hill is distributing her own seed for a perennializing green pepper that survives our warm winters and fruits in our foggy summer nights; another neighbor is enlarging her Spanish vocabulary to be able to discuss subtropical flowers with recent immigrants who can shed some light on plant requirements of climate and tilth.

Perhaps the flower or fruit you will be looking for twenty or thirty years from now is already growing in your neighbor's yard; the knowledge of how to grow that flower or fruit to garden perfection may be embedded in the mind of your neighbor's elderly grandfather, or obtained from the aunt just arrived from Guam or Quito or Kennebec.

Sometimes it is hard to reach across the garden gate, when backyard fences are high or a language is different. But these are false barriers: Gardeners speak their own language, and a love for beauty and flavorsome food is universal. Crammed in our neighborhoods like the ingredients of a Volcano Salad, we have to fall together to let the pattern of textures, flavors, and colors unfold.

The most dynamic gardening groups are those that skip across boundaries of race, age, and status. This will be critical as we pack our virtual wagon trains for Roadtrip 2000. To garden globally we must be democratic; to preserve our own gardening heritage, we have to lose the notion that we are unrelated strangers. As we near a new century, we all need to reach out, and reach back, before we can build any Eden of the future.

# BIBLIOGRAPHY

Amato, Mia. *The Garden Explored.* New York: Henry Holt, 1997.

Hale, Hudson D. *The Old Farmer's Almanac.* New York: Random House, 1992.

Jekyll, Gertrude. *Wood and Garden.* 1896. Reprint. Woodbridge, Suffolk, England: Antique Collectors' Club, 1981.

Keator, Glenn. *The Complete Garden Guide to the Native Perennials of California.* San Francisco: Chronicle Books, 1991.

————. *The Complete Garden Guide to the Native Shrubs of California.* San Francisco: Chronicle Books, 1994.

Lacy, Allen. *The Garden in Autumn.* New York: Atlantic Monthly Press, 1990.

Lawrence, Elizabeth. *Through the Garden Gate.* Chapel Hill, NC: University of North Carolina Press, 1990.

Peirce, Pam. *Golden Gate Gardening.* Rev. edition. Seattle, WA: Sasquatch Books, 1998.

Rheinhardt, Thomas and Martina, and Mark Moscowitz. *Ornamental Grass Growing.* New York: Friedman Group, 1994.

Staff of the Liberty Hyde Bailey Hortorium, Cornell University.

*Hortus Third.* New York: Macmillan, 1976.

Stevens, Barbara, and Nancy Conner. *Where on Earth: A Guide to Specialty Nurseries and Other Resources for California Gardeners.* 3d edition. Berkeley, CA: Heyday Books, 1997.

*Sunset Western Garden Book.* Menlo Park, CA: Sunset Publishing, 1995.

Yang, Linda. *The City and Town Gardener.* New York: Random House, 1990.

# INDEX